21

THE TWO TYCOONS

A Personal Memoir of
Jack Cotton and Charles Clore

by

Charles Gordon

Hamish Hamilton London

First published in Great Britain 1984
by Hamish Hamilton Ltd
Garden House 57-59 Long Acre London WC2E 9JZ

British Library Cataloguing in Publication Data

Gordon, Charles
  The two tycoons.
  1. Clore, Charles   2. Cotton, Jack
  I. Title
  338.7'092'   HC252.5.C/

ISBN 0-241-11256-7

Typeset by Pioneer
Printed in Great Britain by
St Edmundsbury Press, Suffolk

To the memory of Harold Wincott, Charles Anderson and Margot Naylor, outstanding financial journalists, who made a lasting contribution to their profession.

Contents

List of Illustrations

1. The Dorchester Hotel (courtesy Donald Southern)
2. 22 Park Street, Mayfair (courtesy Donald Southern)
3. Jack Cotton (Keystone Press)
4. Charles Clore (Keystone Press)
5. Cotton at his daughter Jill's wedding
6. Clore on holiday with his wife Francine
7. Clore and Cotton with Douglas Tovey
8. The honeymoon toast
9. Cartoon by Cummings
10. The tycoons in white tie
11. Piccadilly (courtesy Donald Southern)
12. The Pan-American building (Camera Press/Dick Hanley)
13. 40 Wall Street
14. The Zeckendorfs
15. Walter Flack (Camera Press/Desmond O'Neill)
16. Edward Plumridge (Elliott & Fry)
17. The Pearl Assurance building
18. Eric Young
19. Felix Fenston (courtesy Marcus Harrison)
20. Isadore Kerman
21. Jocelyn Hambro (Camera Press/Freddie Mansfield)
22. Aubrey Orchard-Lisle
23. Lord Bearsted (Camera Press/John Bulmer)
24. Lord Rayne (Camera Press/Tom Hustler)
25. Leonard Sainer (Camera Press/Tom Hustler)
26. Lord Samuel
27. Thames Lawn at Marlow
28. Cotton's house in Nassau
29. Cotton and the author
30. On holiday with Clore in Mustique

Acknowledgements

The idea for this book took shape in the two or three years before Charles Clore died. He spent much of that time in Paris where we lived. We would dine out at the old and new, and in his now mellow mood he would regale my wife Nadia and myself with countless stories and anecdotes frequently ending one with the demand, 'put it in the book'.

The book, from any point of view, could never have been commenced nor completed without Nadia's constant encouragement and inspiration. My first and deepest thanks to her.

Next I wish to thank above all Aubrey Orchard-Lisle and Douglas Tovey, the two staunch friends and property advisers to Jack Cotton and Charles Clore. They were each of immense help and they provided many hours of their time and many insights into their relationships with the two tycoons.

I received invaluable assistance from Freddie Lindgren who for a long time was Jack Cotton's closest business associate; and to Leonard Sainer, who for an even longer time was Charles Clore's closest business associate, I also extend my thanks.

Eddie Footring, Isadore Kerman and William Zeckendorf Jnr were of special help and I am most grateful to them. Eric Young, before he died, went to tremendous trouble to provide me with essential information and I shall always be extremely grateful to him.

I am especially indebted to John Plender, Oliver Marriott and Michael Brett who read the typescript and made vital suggestions and criticisms. I also wish to thank two more *alumni* of the *Investors' Chronicle*, John Roberts who helped considerably with the early research and Gary Arnott for answering a large number of questions.

I am also most grateful to Arnold Lee, a most perceptive and intelligent property pundit who put me right on a large number of points, and to Sidney Mason, a most far-sighted international property strategist, who aided me immeasurably.

I also wish to express my gratitude to Lord Bearsted, Edward Erdman, Louis Freedman, Peter Hardy, Freddie Garner, George Ross Goobey, Rupert Hambro, (Freddie) Kay, Raphe Langham, Govi Mallinckrodt, Cob Stenham, Harry Sporborg and Lord Zuckerman for their important help in various ways and on diverse aspects.

I owe a special thanks to Miss Lucy Dew of Sothebys, to Mr Hooper of the Pearl Assurance, to Miss Pratt of the Legal and General.

The children of Jack Cotton were most helpful and my very grateful thanks to them, especially to Jill whose affinity with her father is remarkable and refreshing. Charles Clore's brother David, a kindly and tenacious person who stands very much on his own feet, provided much valuable background. Charles' son Alan and I discussed various aspects of the book in its very early stages.

I also wish to thank many friends and acquaintances in the property and institutional world in London and New York and in the City who have provided much information and help and who have simply asked that I do not mention them by name.

Finally, it has been a distinct pleasure to be represented by Felicity Bryan, to be edited by Julian Evans, and to be published by Christopher Sinclair-Stevenson. My warmest appreciation and thanks to them.

Charles Gordon
April 1984

Prologue

In the 1950s Jack Cotton was the pioneer of a completely new form of corporate association between property developers and financial institutions. In the late sixties, through an investment bank I founded called Spey Investments, I helped extend this form of association into venture capital and financial services, having pursued a route as a financial journalist analysing property companies and writing about the men behind them, then as financial consultant to Jack Cotton and Charles Clore during the great property boom of the early sixties, then to becoming a merchant banker at Hambros Bank.

Corporate associations between entrepreneurs and institutions are now a normal channel of business activity, but when Jack Cotton first formed a joint development company with the Legal & General insurance group in the mid-fifties, it was unprecedented.

As a creative catalyst, the entrepreneur cannot succeed without financial and management support. The larger his enterprise, the greater his need for finance and the greater his need for organisation; the bigger the amounts involved, the more crucial is his dependence upon the financial institutions and upon his own team. The need for financial follow-through is essential, but no more than the need for management follow-through. I learnt this lesson to my cost when Spey fell apart at the seams in the early seventies.

The entrepreneur is a driving force, who in very rare cases may even alter the commercial culture of his country, but he is mortal; whereas the faceless financial institutions which supported him remain extant and still faceless. After the entrepreneur has gone, one or more of his colleagues will endeavour, with varying results, to carry on the burden of continuity. But some entrepreneurs, by virtue of their innovative achievements, are historic figures and deserve recognition as such.

Two of these are Jack Cotton and Charles Clore: Cotton a driving force in revolutionising the property industry by forging equity links with the institutions and thus opening the way for similar associations in other sectors of business; Clore a driving force in initiating as the controlling shareholder the concept and practice of the contested takeover bid which helped considerably to improve Britain's competitiveness in the latter part of this century. This book is a personal memoir of these two great tycoons, whose business partnership started as a sensational marriage and ended three years later as a disastrous divorce.

Part I

The Marriage

Chapter One

Early Days

In this portrait of an extraordinary business partnership, I have tried to paint the scene as an impression of the atmosphere and mood of the times, conveying the notion and the sense of what Jack Cotton's partnership with Charles Clore was like during its month-by-month existence. I have also tried to keep to the minimum the forensic aspects of property development and finance, explaining only those technical aspects which are essential to the narrative. Although this is a very personal account of the merger of the two great entrepreneurs and their subsequent bitter battle it also, I hope, provides an illuminating picture of their particular milieu.

This was a business milieu where being indecisive or hesitant or weak could quite literally be fatal. It was also a business milieu where I first learnt that in almost every case the leading characters were prompted not by greed, nor by a lust for power, but were motivated by a profound psychological and social need for acceptance. I found to my surprise that, pervading every relationship, there was a peculiar aroma of insecurity. An entrepreneur's sudden course of action was almost never inspired by logic but almost always by an emotion brought to the surface erupting from a feeling of anxiety, from a sense of insecurity, from a desire to 'show them' — them being a member of the establishment, or a partner or a competitor or a family relation. If there is one common trait in every entrepreneur it is that he is a thoroughly insecure animal whose main drive is vanity and whose main passion is a worship for prestige. His need for money is a need for protection. His headlong quest for creating wealth in all its manifestations, implementing deals, transactions, mergers, takeovers is really a quest for approbation, not for money and possessions *per se*, not for power *per se*, but for approbation from people mostly as insecure as he is himself, but who with the timely accoutrements of wealth and with a tincture of taste and culture have managed over decades to overlay their own and their descendants' anxieties with a seemingly imperturbable façade.

The Cotton-Clore business environment was where I also discovered that an entrepreneur's strength of will was more vital to his survival than his talent for moneymaking. The sharpest moral lesson I learnt was that, with very rare exceptions, loyalty even between the closest of friends vanished like a puff of smoke, when put under the slightest strain.

Of the two tycoons, Cotton was the specialist *par excellence*. When he died, the large banner heading in *The Times* was 'Jack Cotton, A Great Property Entrepreneur'. This could not have been more apt, for he was the most flamboyant property Daddy of them all, the king of real estate who lost his throne, the twentieth-century Lear who divided his huge fortune into several family trusts and who died in 1964 ranting in despair on his private beach in Nassau, not against his family but against some of his closest colleagues.

Charles Clore, on the other hand, was the generalist tycoon, the true initiator of the takeover as we know it today, the first begetter of the conglomerate, the entrepreneur with a finger in every pie. He was an alchemist who with concentrated ruthlessness and immense strength of character made a colossal fortune out of nothing. He was a man respected and admired by all, feared by many, hated by some and loved by very few.

Cotton and Clore were business partners for less than three years, from the autumn of 1960 when they merged their enormous property interests to the summer of 1963 when Cotton resigned as Chairman. For Cotton property was his all; he had no business interests outside property, nor did he want any. For Clore property represented only part of his holdings; it did not include his holdings in such diverse interests as shops, ships, shares and shoes and so on.

Their partnership, except for a short honeymoon period, was a personal disaster from beginning to end. It destroyed Jack Cotton, and it destroyed Charles Clore's fiercest ambition to be a major property force. The demise of their partnership also destroyed dozens of old and new friendships and relationships and associations. It was, I believe, an extraordinary personal confrontation in the annals of business during an extraordinary business era of this century — the great property boom of the fifties and sixties.

My involvement started whilst I was a financial journalist at the *Investors' Chronicle*, part of the Financial Times Group, during

1959 and 1960, and more directly in February 1961 when I became the financial consultant to their merged property group, known as City Centre Properties Ltd or, variously, as CCP, Cotton-Clore Properties, or 'the two C's'. I was the only person who was an ardent supporter of Jack Cotton in his fight against Clore, who subsequently became one of Charles Clore's most intimate friends.

The early years of my own career had gone much as I had hoped. I had no fixed ideas except that after coming down from Cambridge I felt like going on to the Sorbonne, then perhaps to Florence and later to Harvard. I had read English and worked under Dr Leavis at his creative best during the late forties, his prickly genius blossoming and flowering from his small pokey rooms at Downing College. (As I was at Christ's I was given special dispensation to go to Leavis by my tutor Sidney Grose, the exquisitely described hero of his colleague C. P. Snow's best novel *The Masters*.) I had also read Law, stayed an additional fourth year for no better reason than indulgence, and come down with a couple of degrees, BA and LLB, which subsequently proved worthless from any point of view.

At Cambridge one evening in May I met my wife Nadia. We met at a party I gave for the Sadlers Wells, later to become the Royal Ballet, after their opening night at the Arts Theatre. Nadia was its gem, from South Africa, wrapped in sunshine and poetry, utterly delightful and just at the beginning of the artistic journey which led to her becoming one of the world's great ballerinas.

When I came down my father had strong views about my career, typical of the successful patriarchal Baltic Jew. He was the sole owner of a large engineering company located in Wembley with sales and service offices in Zurich, New York and South Africa; He and I agreed when I came down from Cambridge, that I would go round the world working in his offices; a modern 'grand tour'. When I returned to London I trained as an accountant but was quickly disillusioned by the inflexible curriculum of an accountant's life.

Many of my friends were already in the City in merchant banks and with brokers and they had developed various skills with apparent ease. I was an avid reader of the *Investors' Chronicle* and was in awe of its eclectic and well-written company analyses. I sought out Johnny Speyer, a banker friend in the City who as an intellectual hobby was also their foreign bonds correspondent, to ask him what he thought of my working for the *Chronicle* pending the accountancy exams and pending joining a City Bank.

7

Johnny Speyer was a City sage, a refugee from the Nazis, an expert in foreign bonds, that esoteric world of half-submerged governments and countries, of railway stocks in Central America, of pre-war Balkan promises, of old, forgotten (by all except Johnny Speyer) colonial guarantees. The foreign bond specialist is a linguist, a market trader, an economist, a gossiper, a traveller, an historian, a philosopher, a cynic. Johnny was full of wisdom; with his longish nose and dark, gentle, apprehensive German-Jewish eyes he looked not merely as if he had read it all, but as if he had also written it all.

He was not very encouraging about my joining the *Investors' Chronicle*, though he offered to write to his old friend, Harold Wincott, the illustrious editor-in-chief of the paper. Wincott, who was writing his celebrated 'Dad and Son' column in the *Financial Times* had already passed on the weekly editing to Charles Anderson, whose own sense of integrity matched that of his friend and colleague. It was Anderson who interviewed me. He immediately told me that there was no possibility whatsoever of him taking me on but indicated that, of course, if I wanted to become a financial journalist, especially with his paper, he had to grant, reluctantly, that I showed a glimmer of intelligence. It was strange listening to this dry, grey, utterly nice man in his office up a scruffy City lane by the Midland Bank headquarters. With a wave of his hand, Anderson indicated the mass of proofs, papers, letters, photographs, journals, books, scattered around him and said that I was probably too pampered, like that graduate lot up the road at the *FT*, to work in crowded, windowless surroundings. He concluded the interview by inviting me to come again, but apologised for his negative response.

I wrote to Anderson for another interview. I saw him on Thursday; he was infinitely more relaxed. It is the rhythm of a newspaper, that innate rhythm in journalism, whether daily, weekly or monthly, which is the drug that makes a journalist an addict with little or no power to withdraw. The *Chronicle* went to press on Wednesdays; Mondays were frenetic, plenty of writing; Tuesdays were near hysterical, especially if there were lots of press releases or conferences or last-minute company reports; Thursdays were quiet, the storm was over. The paper was being printed, nothing more could be done.

Fortunately I saw Charles Anderson this second occasion on the best possible day — Thursday. He decided to take me on. What got his quick agreement was my suggestion that I would receive no salary and that I would stay for at least a year. He insisted, however, on paying me a nominal sum — £5 per week as expenses.

*   *   *

The City, in my first days in the latter part of 1958, was a very different place from today. It was six years after the end of meat rationing and six years before the introduction of Capital Gains Tax, two of the more disparate but cataclysmic events of post-war Britain. The City was then a genuine village; the veritable square mile. Most people knew each other or knew of each other. Physically too it was much smaller, with the bank messengers doing their rounds in a fifth of the time it takes today. Brokers seeking offices in New London Wall, past Moorgate towards Aldersgate, were thought to be considering commercial suicide. The new Bank of England building by St Paul's was the first dramatic enlargement of the City; Charles Clore's Moor House in Moorgate was the second. The centre of gravity for banking, insurance, broking and commodities had traditionally been between Bishopsgate, Lime Street, the Bank of England and the Stock Exchange. It was the leapfrog location of the new Bank of England building which dramatically shifted the City to St Paul's and to the Guildhall. When the Wiggins Teape building, now the HQ of the Bank of America, was built, it was considered way-out, as was the new pastiche *Financial Times* building opposite in Queen Victoria Street. Today, way-out is in Fleet Street going west, Islington going north, Whitechapel going east and Hays Wharf going south.

Apart from the swollen size and loss of intimacy, the character of the City has also changed considerably. Now, because there are many more people in responsible positions who hardly know each other, there is far less, if any, reliance on somebody's word. Today suspicions are as rampant and profuse as documents and agreements. My Parkinson rider is that distrust between parties increases in direct proportion to the increase in paperwork. The lawyers' great boom period had not yet started; their pious credo that the other party to a contract is dishonest is one of the cleverest and most successful marketing ploys of all time, creating one of the greatest growth industries of all time. The City was still Victorian in the way it thought management should treat its staff and the way it thought staff should treat their jobs. There was no legislation on office conditions and little thought was given to it. Luncheon vouchers were then an innovation and regarded as a great concession; staff asking for increases were considered impudent, the traditional system

9

being to wait for a possible, by no means certain, annual review; giving notice or leaving a job was definitely lower-class in the ranks and bad form at the top; dress was still formal, bowlers were black, shirts were white and suits were dark. Many still wore detachable collars and cuffs; I doubt if you can buy a back collar stud in the City today. If a coloured shirt was worn, the wearer's job was in jeopardy. An extraordinary innovation, strange as it now seems, was that the brokers, stock and insurance and the merchant banks were beginning to open their doors to people judged solely on merit, with no connections or capital. The foreign banks were only just reappearing, paying higher salaries and providing better conditions, and women too, to the disgust of many people in the City, were beginning to be taken on for jobs other than as seretaries.

I think, however, the biggest change of all was in the attitude to the press. Two major events, the Bank Rate Tribunal of 1957 and the British Aluminium takeover battle of 1958, accelerated an important underlying shift of opinion, mood and policy. By being made aware of the increasing power of the financial press, the City houses had to alter their fundamental attitude to commercial life hitherto based on confidentiality, secrecy and a definite feeling of 'mind your own business'. They had to face up to political and public interest and they had to realise that in the new burgeoning corporate finance and portfolio investment businesses, good relations with the press were not merely advisable, but essential. This open and necessary approach to the press more than anything else blew out generations of cobwebs in the City.

Industrial companies too, though deeply committed to the business of marketing their products, gave scant regard to marketing their corporate results and merely printed their Chairman's annual statement in the manner of a black-bordered funeral announcement. Interim statements were a novelty. The financial press agents, few as they were, were only just beginning to urge their clients to hold press conferences, to invite financial journalists for discussions and interviews, to make more information available, and they exhorted their clients to learn to come to terms with the growing power and the growing responsibility of the financial press. The merchant banks too were learning to appreciate that their image, reflected in press reports and press comments, was an integral part of their business. Some of them understood this far earlier than others, and one or two, like Sigmund Warburg, later himself a respected city mandarin but then considered an upstart, certainly appreciated that one could win or lose a customer or a takeover battle on the skilful use or otherwise of the press. Curiously the newspapers themselves were rather slow to appreciate their own power, and it was only the impetus of more financial advertising which caused them eventually to increase staff and coverage. Financial matters, particularly takeover battles written up as fights between personalities, became national news and were beginning to appear on the front pages. Share prices increasingly reflected press comment and the acknowledgement that this was so made press comment even more influential. The *Financial Times* was now being read outside the square mile, outside the old cosy compartment of the City, in factories and offices in Birmingham and Manchester, by industrialists, economists and bankers throughout the country and abroad, and it was getting fatter, as was its sister paper, the *Investors' Chronicle.*

We at the *Chronicle* were still housed in what Anderson called our crummy offices by the Midland Bank headquarters. Journalists of all ages, shapes and sizes sat in every corner. There were rickety desks, proofs, newspapers, company reports and slide rules all over the place. No calculating machines, no typewriters. We did our own calculations and we wrote our articles in long-hand. The *Chronicle* team was not large, about twenty-five in all, and though we got on pretty well our backgrounds could not have been more different. Outstanding amongst us all was Margot Naylor.

I met her on my second day. She was already into her middle years, brimming with intelligence and charm, not good-looking but exceptionally attractive, always seeming to be slightly larger than her clothes and usually bearing down resolutely on the object of her scorn or interest, blinking behind her large glasses and bobbing her coiffure. Almost her first words to me were, 'You must not suppose I am the usual Girton girl'. She knew full well that there was absolutely no danger of me or anyone else supposing that.

Although it was Harold Wincott who inspired all of us at the *Chronicle* and who set the high standards now accepted as the normal level in the profession, and although it was Charles Anderson who led the team and supported his journalists, never letting any of them down even when there was pressure from the 'bosses', it was nevertheless Margot Naylor who brought to the *Chronicle* its particular fame and reputation as a crusading journal for stamping out iniquitous financial practices. She, like the other two, loathed any form of chicanery. At the first whiff of impropriety or the slightest possibility that the rights of shareholders were being abused or neglected, these three stalwart, upright commercial missionaries were not only morally and profoundly outraged, but were prepared to do something about it. In Margot Naylor we had a colleague who converted outrage into disciplined and controlled action, who invented a new form of journalism, based on a penetrating and unremitting look at all the facts — burrowing unstintingly, searching files, researching with painstaking detail, interrogating and inter-viewing and re-interviewing. She was utterly relentless and fearless in her pursuit of financial villainy and trickery, armed with an unnerving talent for discerning lies and falsehoods. She used her formidable intelligence like a pile-driver, hitting her targets with immense force and impact; little escaped her attention. On the track of the improper she pulverised anyone standing in her way. In making it her crusade to examine any company or fund which looked as if it was trying to bend the law or mislead its shareholders or its depositors, she led the fight for full disclosure. She urged the most severe legal sanctions against wrongdoers; the public in her view was totally gullible, it always would be gullible and it had to be protected by more realistic legislation. She was particularly angered by advertisements soliciting money which were clearly misleading but not outside the law; her nostrils flared on the subject of switch selling (the notorious practice of ostensibly selling one thing, while actually selling another); her eyes blazed with fury at the mention of false prospectuses. Her sense of justice was based on a powerful pragmatic sense of fair play. Finally, when she felt she had the facts, she would swoop on her target and expose whatever crookedness there was in a series of blistering articles. Her attack, her approach, her thoroughness, started a new genre. It spawned numerous journalists who learned how to engage in what is now called investigative journalism, and who are probably entirely oblivious of the fact that its progenitor was the most unexpected person ever to come into the financial press.

Chapter Two

The Property Jackpot

After the early weeks at the *Chronicle*, in order to thank Johnny Speyer directly for his introduction, I had lunch with him in the famous Long Room of Joe Lyons Café in Throgmorton Avenue opposite the Stock Exchange. When the room was stuffed with brokers and jobbers it meant that it was very quiet on the Floor and they moaned about the lack of business; when the room was empty they moaned about being too busy to eat or drink. There is no way of satisfying brokers unless they can buy and sell and eat and drink at the same time, which fortunately for them and the investing public they will soon be able to do when the computers take over and make a better job of it.

The Long Room in those days was mostly empty and deserted and for good reason. The City was at the beginning of a bull market which roared through '59, '60 and '61 to end on 29 May 1962 — Black Tuesday — when Wall Street fell a full 60 points in one day, the sharpest fall since October 1929. It was the long glorious bull market of the early sixties, remembered like an Edwardian summer. It was the last market when investors could buy at 11.00 a.m., sell at 11.30 a.m. and keep all the profits tax-free; not even Edwardian summers were as cloudless and as satisfying. In the previous bull market the favourite sector, and a very hectic one at that, had been oils; now oils were neglected. Which sector was going to be the favourite of this new bull market? The question was on everyone's mind.

One of the reasons why we at the *Chronicle* were able to fulfil a role at all, was that investment analysis and research was at that time a very new science, by no means today's calling based on precise data and precise principles. In evaluating shares, brokers had been brought up on the old English principles of rule of thumb, hunch, instinct,

13

gut feeling, osmosis, grapevine acoustics, intuition. Some of these principles and methods can certainly work if they are honestly admitted and honestly directed. But brokers are inherently schizophrenic; while one of their psyches comprises a concern for the rise and fall of the markets, another comprises an equally strong but not always compatible concern for the rise and fall of their own profits. The investment managers of the unit trusts, of the investment trusts, of the insurance companies and of the pension funds were in general slightly more wide-awake and more conscious of the need for research, but this is not saying much in the context of this era. The press, led by the *Financial Times* (particularly in its 'Lex' column written by Arthur Winspear, William Rees-Mogg, Nigel Lawson) and the *Investors' Chronicle*, were more pragmatic, feeling their way towards new, more scientific methods of analysis. Gradually this seeped through and investment analysis and research started becoming an accepted way of investment life with specialist staff being taken on by the City brokers (a disproportionate number of them from the *Chronicle*). Research departments were formed from scratch by the pioneering brokers and funds, with the merchant banks (normally in the forefront) only following suit. It is incredible to think that as recently as twenty years ago, you could count on one hand those brokers who had any research staff of any kind. When Phillips and Drew took on an actuary years before anyone else to head up and organise their new research department, the decision was greeted with bewilderment and derision by their fellow brokers. Though some institutions took on their own researchers, most of them still relied to a large extent on verbal and written advice from the brokers. Circulars, as the name still denotes, had the smell of soliciting, of share-pushing: it was infra dig, it was bucket shop.

In general, the investment and stockbroking world seemed incredibly slapdash and amateurish, the advice generally given being arbitrary and *ad hoc*. There seemed to be a lack of definition, a lack of discipline and no professionalism. There were no formal examinations for brokers, no basic training, no qualifications — yet here they were blithely telling their clients, from widows to institutions, what to buy and what to sell. There was the flimsiest of evidence that the Stock Exchange was beginning to appreciate that we were approaching the final quarter of the twentieth century, and possibly the best sign of this was in the growth of investment research. But I still find it astonishing that the first full-time chief executive of the Stock Exchange was not appointed until 1972. In

14

its small way however, the *Chronicle*, under the leadership of Wincott, tried to make the fee- and commission-earning investment advisers more professional.

Soon afterwards, I analysed my first balance sheet of a property company. Sitting at my table in the general office of the *Chronicle* with its dirty windows clouding the back of the Midland, the effect on me was not that of Chapman's Homer nor the Peaks of Darien, but I did have a somewhat similar personal illumination. From the moment that I studied that first property company annual report I felt on familiar ground, completely at home. I asked Charles Anderson if I could concentrate on property by starting a special section in the paper devoted solely to that sector. To convince and urge him, I had to promise that I would make it my business to become the leading City expert on property shares. Thus began the property section of the paper, and thus I became its first property editor. The seeds were sown of my later friendship with the two tycoons. Today there is no serious financial journal in the UK or elsewhere without its property section, the *Chronicle* having the credit of being the first. My successor was Gary Arnott, and he in turn was succeeded by Oliver Marriott. Between us the property section of the *Investors' Chronicle* became a powerful force in the City. Indeed, it was the most respected and informative voice on the property sector and in its heyday in the sixties it has an important influence, not only in England, but also in Europe.

My own permanent contribution, specifically in terms of property share analysis was, I think, to formulate a more scientific method of evaluating the shares. I also went behind the figures and balance sheets to the buildings and to the property men who built and owned them.

The *Chronicle*, through its property section, slowly became a definite factor in persuading the major institutions to invest in *the* real estate, and to convince those institutions which needed convincing — far too many of them — that property was not only a prime investment outlet, but also a vital part of the country's financial and industrial structure. In this way we played a meaningful role in the great property boom.

From a practical point of view, however, my tenure was remembered for the strong, almost lone bullish view I took on property shares. After nearly two years as property editor I was to write in autumn 1960: 'In a sense it is extraordinary when looking back that, apart from the *Chronicle* and isolated brokers, the general investment view until recently has continually been rather doubtful of the investment status of property shares. . . . The *Investors' Chronicle* has been an almost lone protagonist for two years. . . .' Looking back now, I still think it was extraordinary.

What had happened in real investment and money-making terms was that, with the removal of the wartime building restrictions in the mid-fifties, the floodgates were opened and new buildings shot up everywhere. The new legislation was predictably too complex to be effective, so almost anyone with a modicum of brain could get round it. Its main restriction, plot ratio — the ratio of the size of a new building to the size of the plot — was a commercial joke and a commercial jackpot.

We were then in the midst of the Macmillan era, the notorious 'never had it so good' times, the era of commercial television, of advertisements depicting the good life, prodding the consumer to spend more with less guilt, with advertisers becoming the new bishops of society sanctimoniously telling the public what was good or bad for them. It was the era of the motor car and it was the era of the biggest retail boom of all time. Multiple shops multiplied; grocery shops became supermarkets, rearing their super-efficient heads; England was no longer a nation of shopkeepers, but a nation of retailers. It was also an era when it apparently didn't matter that savings were no longer a virtue, that industry was not re-investing, that the housing shortage was, like the weather, becoming a permanent blight on British life, and that rising inflation was beginning to rot the economic structure.

Amidst all this, property development provided a money-making investment opportunity which was quite simply fantastic. Planning consents were oozing out from the planning committees of the local authorities for office buildings, shop developments and town centre schemes and a profusion of tenants with major covenants were eagerly looking for space and taking up leases. In particular, finance was freely available on fabulous terms to the borrower. Long-term rates were around 5% to 6%, the borrower not having to part with any equity, inflation was still only at 3% to 4% and the return on cost of new properties was not usually less than 10%. From the point of view of investing in property itself, or in property companies, or in property shares, the money-making possibilities arising from these simple figures could not have been more startling. It was crystal clear that the shares of property companies, and in particular the property development companies, were grossly undervalued. I couldn't fathom why the market, usually discounting new opportunities with smooth clairvoyance, hadn't realised it, nor could some of the property developers themselves. Virtually all the investment experts were ignoring one of the greatest buying opportunities for decades.

As simply as possible I will try to describe the truly marvellous money-making possibilities arising from the figures above. Assume that the all-in cost of a building of that period is £1 million and that it consists of offices with 40,000 sq. ft. of net lettable space. The all-in cost includes the cost of the land, the cost of building, the cost of professional fees and the cost of money. Assume that the building is leased to a tenant at £2.50 per sq. ft. Forty thousand square feet times £2.50 equals £100,000. This yields a return of 10% on the cost of £1 million. We now come to the crucial value of the building based on the tenant paying this rent of £100,000 per annum, for in terms of the valuation of the buildings you ignore the cost of the building. The sole principle, ridiculous as it may sound to a layman, but the kernel of money-making in property, is the actuarial value of that £100,000 of rent paid per year which has nothing to do with the cost of the building. In valuing this £100,000, the lease having been signed at current market value, several factors are taken into account: one, the financial strength of the tenant — this is called the strength of the covenant; two, the terms of the lease — how long? are there rent reviews? are there restrictive clauses?; three, the state of the investment market — on what basis will the insurance companies and pension funds buy that property for investment, will they expect a 5% immediate return on their money or 4.5% or 6%? This return or yield depends upon demand and supply, upon competing outlets for investment monies, upon gilt-edged rates, upon inflation, upon expected growth in rents. Let us assume the investment yield which a purchaser would require is 5%. We then come to the magic multiplier, which quantifies the significance of that 5%. The valuer calls this multiplier the number of 'Years Purchase', so many 'YP' times the rent. It is a simple calculation. You divide 5 into 100 and you get a multiplier of 20, the 5% yield is worth twenty years' purchase. This multiplier of 20 is then multiplied against the rent of £100,000 and you arrive at a figure of £2 million. If the institution buys that building for £2 million it will receive a rent of £100,000 per annum which is an immediate 5% return on its money, which is twenty years' purchase of the rent.

The multiplier, the number of years' purchase, the YP, is the key to the entire process of property financing. The lower the yield, the greater the YP, the higher the value of the building. One cannot begin to understand property financing unless one understands this simple fact. If the investment market is strong, institutions will expect a lower return, let us say 4%. This divided into a hundred is 25; 25 times £100,000 taking our example, provides a valuation figure of £2.5 million. If the market is very weak, the institution will expect a return of 7.5% then the multiplier, the YP, is 13.3; 13.3 times £100,000 gives you a figure of approximately £1,330,000. The slightest difference in yield up or down makes a tremendous difference in value. There are of course several other important aspects concerning the investment yield required by property investors, some of which are discussed later, but for the purpose of describing the enormity of money-making possibilities in the Clore and Cotton era, I am deliberately over-simplifying.

The building which has cost as little as £1 million providing an initial investment yield of 5% has now been valued at £2 million, throwing up a surplus of £1 million over cost. We now come to the interest rate on borrowing. We can assume that the developer has borrowed £1 million for a period of twenty years at a fixed interest rate of, say, 5%. When inflation is low this interest rate might be in balance with the investment yield. When inflation is high, interest rates are high and the higher the interest rate the more disparity between the rate of interest and the yield. Many people find it difficult to understand how a pension fund can buy a building showing a return of, say, only 4% when interest rates are 12%, three times the return. The main reason is that interest rates are essentially short-term and investment yields based on increasing yields from increasing rents are essentially long-term. Now, coming back to our example, the developer will have leased the building with rent reviews. This means that the tenant who starts off paying £100,000 has agreed to a rent review say in three, five, seven or fourteen or twenty-one years' time, this review being based on the then current rental value of the space. In 1960 rent reviews were an innovation (see Chapter 5) and the reviews, if there were any, were usually every fourteen or twenty-one years; by 1965 their incidence was pitched more frequently over every seven or fourteen years. Assume our example took place in 1958 with a rent review every fourteen years. By 1972, fourteen years later, the rent starting at £100,000 would probably have trebled to £300,000. The value (taking the same investment yield of 5% and the same multiplier of 20 which originally made the development worth £2 million) is now £6 million, and the developer's original capital surplus of £1 million has risen to £5 million. This is a classic example of gearing, of leverage. But the arithmetical jackpot does not end here.

We have assumed a return of 10% on cost. But what happens when the yield is, say, 15% on cost? — a more likely return in those heady days. The rent at 15% on a cost of £1 million is £150,000 per year. Taking the same YP of 20, the immediate value is £3 million. The net surplus over cost to the developer is £2 million. The profit is more staggering when you relate that to the rent review fourteen years later in 1972. The rent of £150,000 has trebled to £450,000 and on the same multiplier of 20 this shows a value of £9 million. If you deduct the original cost of £1 million the surplus is now £8 million. It should of course be appreciated that the annual rent has risen partly because demand has pushed up property rents, but partly also because of inflation. If one adjusts for inflation, the 1972 value (in 1958 pound values) would be about £3 million if the original rent was £100,000 and £4.5 million if the original rent had been £150,000. Still a staggering surplus.

The reader may well consider that I am exaggerating, and that there must have been very onerous tax implications. Not at all. If a company made a practice of selling properties frequently it would be taxed as a dealing company. But why sell? For the jackpot continues its merry way. You, the developer, can float your company on the Stock Exchange, and on a very favourable basis, yet the property valuations would have had the full approval of the Institute of Chartered Accountants, the Stock Exchange and the Institution of Chartered Surveyors. Returning to the original example, the property developer has a building which has cost him £1 million. He has a loan of £1 million against it, and the building has been valued by a leading firm of chartered surveyors at £2 million, showing a net surplus of £1 million. This surplus will not necessarily be written into the accounts. If the building is owned by a £100 company and is floated on the Stock Exchange just on this net asset value of £1 million, the developer selling 25% to the public and retaining 75% will receive £250,000 in cash and will have £750,000 worth of quoted shares. He has transformed his balance sheet valuation surplus into cash and into valuable quoted shares which may well have shot up in price, without selling the building. And he still has not invested more than £100 of his own money.

Does this unique Midas story end here? Once again, no. Why

should the developer wait fourteen years for part of the great jackpot if he can cash in now, instead of waiting? The final wonderful twist of gold lay with these flotation aspects. We have seen that the developer could retain the 75% profit on his completed building through his shares in his new floated company and realise a cash profit on the 25% sold to the public. If he wanted to he could buy more properties or better still obtain empty sites by issuing more of his quoted shares. If the valuers were prepared to value empty sites on the basis that the buildings had been erected, and had also been fully let, then why not bring in a lot of empty sites with planning permission, or bring in half-finished buildings from other independent developers. He wouldn't even have to pay these sellers in cash. He could offer as consideration his own newly quoted shares at, say, half or three-quarters of the professional valuation of the completed building after all costs. He could do a quick assembly of sites of this nature and bring the whole caboodle to the Stock Exchange as a 'serious' package. An increasing number of buyers were prepared to buy shares on this basis, and the shares would jump up on each announcement of a new development project or new acquisition. Once the company was floated, it was the easiest thing in the world to issue more quoted shares for more properties or more companies owning properties. And as very few people knew the true value of the shares being issued they took the Stock Exchange values at face value. The prospectus of Clore's company City and Central stated the following in respect of valuation: 'In the valuation of Messrs Healey and Baker set out below, the properties owned by the Company and its subsidiaries (*including those in the course of construction at their value when completed and let*) have been valued . . .' (my italics).

The extraordinary thing is that the Stock Exchange and the Institute of Chartered Accountants and the Royal Institution of Chartered Surveyors permitted this basis of valuation. I sought explanations from all three bodies: the Stock Exchange people were polite but ignorant; the surveyors were polite but unforthcoming; the accountants were impolite, ignorant and unforthcoming.

Like all jackpots it seemed never-ending. Property development provided a sensational way of making money, and the amounts of money are even more staggering if you add a nought to the example above and realise that not one or two but literally dozens of developers were in this amazing big league.

As I have said, the shares of property companies were grossly undervalued in 1959 and 1960, and yet it is the irony of economic moods and investment trends that notwithstanding these hope-values, whoever bought property shares in this period could and did make considerable profits.

The big institutional buyers were out of the market for a variety of reasons, but mainly because they were still rigidly fixed-interest minded, just learning about a new-fangled thing called equity shares. Equity, the dirty word of the post-war decade, was no longer considered unsavoury; it was now to be the turn of property. Furthermore, the important buyers couldn't understand property company balance sheets. Who could? They were obscure, complicated, difficult to unravel; the shares seemed impossible to evaluate. How was one to work out the true value of a property share? Particularly the value of the shares of the new-fangled property development companies?

What I tried to achieve was a consistent method of evaluation. Gary Arnott and I formulated certain principles and invented the term 'capital conversion factor' which calculated precisely the effect a new development, or acquisition or reversion, would have on the value of the company's shares. I think we succeeded in cutting through what was previously an investment jungle. Certainly when Oliver Marriott after us refined and strengthened the analytical principles, it was far easier for the institutions, brokers and investment trusts to evaluate property shares themselves with some precision.

With great enthusiasm week after week I wrote about the value of property shares, about property financing methods, about the developers and about the institutions. The general reaction from readers was immensely encouraging and as a result of those weekly articles I not only kept my promise to Anderson but I also made numerous long-term grateful friends in the City, from small investors to large institutions. During 1959 and 1960, as the property section hammered home its bullish weekly paean, the prices of many of the property company shares quadrupled and quintupled and several went up 30 or 40 or 100, even 200 times.

There were around fifty quoted companies with a genuine market in 1958, most of which had been listed pre-war. In 1960, only two years later, there were nearly two hundred. Some of the original companies had their beginnings as landed estates or as family-owned urban property, or they arose out of a gradual association, later formalised, between the landlord and his insurance company. Western Ground Rents now owned by the BP Pension Fund was a hive-off from the Marquess of Bute's estates in the city of Cardiff, the New River Company, the earliest incorporated entity in London, was formed out of riverside rights given to worthy aldermen over the New River at Islington; Rowton Houses was the result of a Victorian attempt to provide low-cost rented housing and services; the history of many of these pre-war quoted companies provides an intriguing kaleidoscope of the social history of England during the early decades of the century.

However, the one hundred and fifty odd new property companies which started coming to the Stock Exchange for their public quotation at the end of the fifties and the beginning of the sixties were a different breed altogether. They arose from the emergence of a unique entrepreneur — the British property developer. This modern post-war property man altered the skyline of every city in England within a single decade and in doing so was probably responsible for the most monumental amount of undistinguished architecture in history. He was born out of the commercial and statutory conditions of the early and mid-fifties, grasping every opportunity he could and making as much money as he could. He was favoured by the banks, in spite of frequent Bank of England restraints on property lending; he was fawned over by the local authorities anxious to rebuild their city centres and to raise their revenues; he was cosseted by institutions which were beginning to realise that property was not an investment evil but a possible investment blessing. He was born a hero, and twenty years later died a villain, for in the early seventies the Heath Tory government, ambivalent about capitalism and emotional about property entrepreneurs, enacted more vicious anti-capitalist legislation than any previous socialist administration.

Certainly many of this later generation of developers were wildly irresponsible and personally disagreeable. But the government decided that capitalism had another face and it stupidly ignored the fact that whatever the face, property was a main artery, and justifiably so, of the whole financial corpus. It became determined to exterminate the property developer, and for a time it virtually did. It also in the process very nearly destroyed the entire banking system.

In his short life, this strident, creative, opportunist post-war property developer made more money for himself and his family trusts than the nabobs of Kimberley or the Greek shipowners of

Liberia. But in so doing, he also made hundreds of millions of pounds for pensioners and policy holders who, as the true owners of investment property, became the beneficiaries of much of the wealth created. Gradually the property developer, without being fully aware of the changing nature of his trade, became in effect the catalyst, performing that essential entrepreneurial function for the institutions who have now learnt the ground rules themselves.

In the course of looking into the ingredients of this wonderful honey-pot and as part of my job I visited the local authorities, the LCC (now GLC) planning and architectural departments, Ministers and spokesmen in the House of Commons, professional bodies, surveyors, architects, taxation experts, brokers and jobbers, actuaries, investment advisors, portfolio managers. I got to know a large number of real estate agents and a larger number of bankers — clearing bankers, merchant bankers and investment bankers. I visited dozens of insurance companies and met and talked to their directors, investment managers and property managers. I visited numerous pension funds and discussed their investment policies with their investment managers, investment committees and trustees. I visited building sites, talked with builders, quantity surveyors and engineers. I learned a great deal from all these people, but I learned most of all then and later from the property men themselves. From Jack Cotton of City Centre; Sidney Mason of Hammersons; Claude Leigh of Metropolitan Estates (now MEPC); Donald Nixon of City of London Real Property; Felix Fenston of Metropolitan & Provincial Properties; Louis Freedman of Land Securities; Max Rayne of London Merchant Securities; Barry East of Town & City; Jack Andrews of St Martins; Archie Sherman of City & Central; Peter McKay of McKay Securities.

These were men of character and experience. They could address full meetings of local authorities, senior managers of clearing banks, trustees of pension funds, investment committees of insurance companies. They were men of substance not only in a financial sense, but in the sense of their own personal authority arising from their ability and knowledge. A decade or two later, alas, many of the property developers were fly-by-night characters, superficial surveyors, asset strippers, a pale imitation of their forbears, some just out of their teens intellectually if not literally. In the early sixties the property developer could speak for himself; in the early seventies his retained surveyor or accountant had to speak for him. In the early sixties the property developer knew his rental values, his property values and his share values, and he was ready to take a long-term view; in the early seventies the property developer was more concerned with his banker's values and quick money.

By the early sixties the one property developer who towered above all the others in charisma and achievement was Jack Cotton.

Chapter Three

Enter the Bow Tie

Jack Cotton always made a good impression. Of middle height with thick jet-black hair and a stocky build, wearing lightweight shiny dark-blue suits, bow-tie and matching handkerchief, with a red rose in his buttonhole specially brought to London that morning by his chauffeur from his Marlow garden, he could easily have been mistaken for a genial intelligent impresario; there was certainly a strong element of the showman about him. Because his fundamental nature was compounded of kindness and gentleness he had an immediate pleasing effect on anyone he met. He had a habit of saying 'Bless You' and somehow one felt he meant it. His sense of humour was always on the surface and was imbued with a natural wit and bonhomie which not many could resist. He was not, however, easy with everyone he came across and could sometimes be petulant and prickly, particularly with his own family.

But behind his easily furrowed, well-formed brow, was a marvellous property brain superior to any other real estate man I encountered, except Bill Zeckendorf Sr in America. When he was at the top of his form Jack Cotton, like Big Bill, was able to analyse and to sum up correctly the answer to any property transaction, no matter how complex. During his peak he unhesitatingly made the right judgment, and always with boundless self-confidence. Though I had more to do with him during his decline, I was in constant admiration of his immense talent. Time after time I was fortunate enough to be present at meetings when he would be listening to a major project or a proposal for the first time, with rarely if ever any need to refer to documentation. He would ask several questions, make a seemingly idle note or doodle. After several minutes, slightly jovial on the surface but extremely serious underneath, drawing on his Monte Cristo he would declare with that peculiarly pungent and deliberately unctuous voice of his, that the only — he would elongate 'only' — way a transaction could possibly be made was this only way, and he would expound and explain this only way based on difficult arithmetic involving complicated ownerships and assumptions. Even Felix Fenston, a property man who was vehemently competitive, frequently expressed his admiration for Cotton's masterful ability to get to the core, altering and amending and refining the transaction in his head and able to come up with the only way. When Cotton said 'only way', what he meant of course was his way — the Cotton way.

His memory, like that of many outstanding entrepreneurs, was prodigious. He knew every rent, lease, sale price,, interest rate, repayment term of every transaction that he had ever been involved in from the very first day he had started in business. He knew the name of every tenant and every landlord with whom he had signed a lease. He remembered the exact words of every conversation he had conducted in his business negotiations throughout his career. (He also claimed to be able to recall every bridge hand of every game he had played.) Despite the occasions when he was over-drinking, his memory was never clouded or affected by alcohol. Anyone who had spent an evening with him stretching into the small hours, whether in the Dorchester suite or in his home at Marlow or elsewhere, liberally laced with whisky, wine, champagne, liqueurs — and there were many who had — would know that next morning, despite his slurring conversation of the night before, Cotton had remembered every word spoken by himself and anyone else present and could repeat it all verbatim if asked. Aubrey Orchard-Lisle, one of his closest and longest-standing cohorts, learnt this very early on when, having discussed a complicated real estate transaction late at night with Jack giving every appearance of being tipsy, Jack remembered the entire conversation verbatim next day. Angus Ogilvy, who came into Jack's life through Glamford Finance (a company we co-founded), met Jack on Glamford business in Nassau on his way back from New York. Arriving late, he joined Jack at the Bahamian Club and their discussion continued till near dawn. Next morning Angus, conscientious as always, wanted to go over the details because Jack had seemingly been in an alcoholic daze the night before. To Ogilvy's permanent astonishment Jack remembered their conversation more clearly than he did himself, and indeed declared vociferously that he had given his commitment the night before and that when he gave his word, no matter what the hour or where it was given, it was his bond. And so it always was.

26

Cotton was a brilliant property man, knowing every inch of his trade, able to communicate to others what he knew and what he thought, able to conceive, initiate and implement completely original property thinking, able to grasp someone else's idea and sculpt it, change it, transform it, improve it and execute it to perfection. He became the symbolic figure of success incarnate, the heroic English property tycoon in this vintage period, thoroughly enjoying his many varied friendships extending across the whole spectrum of human activity; and in receiving and welcoming the constant procession of visitors to his Dorchester suite there was always a twinkle and an intelligence and a courtesy which disarmed all who came to see him.

Then, alas, he was devastated by that most fateful of all business diseases. This kindly, affectionate man caught the worst commercial bug of all — the media bug. It attacked him until he succumbed totally, shamefully and abjectly, until he wanted more than anything else to see his name and photograph splashed continuously in the papers. The early symptoms were mild, not really disagreeable; it was social media drinking, the first signs apparent through a gradually increasing habit of adjusting his engagements and his transactions to attract the press, then spreading alarmingly into an addiction, his single abiding objective being the amount of press coverage he could obtain — this becoming the criterion for a transaction rather than its inherent merit. Towards the end of his career he became entirely overwhelmed by the press bug. It reached the point where he was incapable of relaxing from one day to the next without seeing his name in the paper or hearing about himself on the radio or seeing himself on television. He became besotted by press relations, by press conferences, by TV interviews, not even going to bed until he had seen the next day's early morning editions. In his later period, if there was no coverage, he was dejected, irritated, troubled. But during 1960, 1961, 1962 and 1963 there was sufficient exposure to satisfy even his most intense cravings. Not a week, more usually not a day, passed without some mention, headline, story, article, interview or cartoon. Possibly no other businessman has ever received as much publicity over such an extended period. City Centre Properties was making so many deals it was like a never-ending fire-cracker. And if it wasn't business which elicited attention it was a charitable bequest, and if it wasn't philanthropy it was the purchase of another painting.

Yet Jack Cotton had been known for years as a reticent and retiring Birmingham businessman who was not even on the board of the public company he controlled for the first ten years of its quoted existence. He was the unknown Midlands property developer, who took special pride in being firmly in the background, who abhorred being in the public eye. He was the man who remarked, after Harold Samuel as head of Land Securities received considerable publicity in 1955 when his company raised £20 million at a rate lower than gilt-edged government stock, 'Harold Samuel can have all that publicity. I don't want it. It is not for me. The company must come first, not the personality.'

Wry, indeed, coming from the celebrated Jack Cotton known by millions through the media. But was there perhaps a hint of envy, particularly envy of Harold Samuel, a hint also of what was to come? What caused his extraordinary metamorphosis? What made him change from a press recluse to a pressaholic? And when?

Those who knew him longest and those who knew him best disagree on the cause and on the exact timing but they all agree on one thing, that he changed fundamentally. Many friends and acquaintances have since died and though I have spoken to most of those who were close to him during this period it is difficult to pin down the exact processes which caused his psychological transformation. The cause, however, is crucial to a comprehension of his later actions and behaviour and of his attitude to Clore. Was there a clue in his earlier life? I believe there was.

Cotton was born in Edgbaston, Birmingham, on 1 January 1904. His family was conventional middle-class Jewish with some kinsmen settled in South Africa. Through them his father's firm, trading in silver plate, did a flourishing business with South Africa before the Boer War. His Uncle Eph was a fairly rich Birmingham jeweller; his grandfather, Aaron Cotton, was one of the founders of the Jewish congregation. Jack went to Cheltenham — in those days going to public school was a sure sign of middle-class aspiration and affluence — and there he met his lifelong friend Isadore Kerman, who was to become his personal lawyer, trustee to his family trusts and a director of City Centre. Today Kerman is seventy-eight but, looking back to their school days, he still remembers Jack as an alive, clever boy who played the cello in the school orchestra.

When he left school Cotton worked as an articled clerk in a firm of estate agents, and as soon as he passed his auctioneer's examinations he wanted to start his own firm. He was opposed by his father, and it was his mother who lent him the proverbial £50 with which to get going. What then became known as Jack Cotton &

Partners, his start as a property agent, began in 1924. During the twenties he worked on his own, again from the proverbial one room, collecting rents and conducting auctions. Later his original secretary, Ruby Frost, joined him. She was extremely competent and was to become a vital part of his Birmingham set-up until his death. In 1931, aged twenty-seven, Jack married his wife Marjorie. There were four children; all now in their forties or fifties with children and grandchildren of their own. Derek, the eldest boy, qualified as a chartered surveyor and stayed on in Birmingham with Jack Cotton & Partners; Gordon became a chartered secretary and worked for his father's company; Jill, the only daughter, attractive and intelligent, was endowed with much of her father's brain; and Jeremy, the youngest of the sons, became a solicitor, a merchant banker, a stockbroker and a farmer, all with equal success. With young children growing up in Birmingham, their father became more established, taking up responsibilities in the city's civic activities. A close friend, guide and mentor was Sol Joseph, always at hand to provide encouragement and support. He separated from his wife soon after the war. She married again and died in 1980. Jack never remarried, but kept up a full family life with the children's ex-nanny, Betty Beaman, who later acted as his hostess in London and Marlow.

Cotton began to deal on his own account in the thirties, buying farmland and selling it off for new housing development. At that time his bank manager was Norman Iles who later said of him, 'Whenever Jack Cotton found a way of raising money, he raised it. His affairs were always very involved. But for his banker the big point about Jack Cotton was that he was always scrupulously true to his word. When he said a thing would happen, it happened, and within the stated time.'

In 1935 Cotton developed Hartnell Court, a block of flats in Birmingham. This turned out to be a disaster and an historic one in the context of property, because he vowed he would never again engage in residential property and he never did. It was in this year that Freddie Lindgren, a London chartered accountant who was to become Jack's early associate in City Centre, first entered his life.

Freddie Lindgren, with the manner of a kindly schoolmaster, very organised, correct and proper, was the confidant who kept Jack's business affairs tidy. He was also Jack's front man, the man who was chairman of City Centre until Jack's accession in 1958. Lindgren is a meticulous person who reads relevant papers carefully, who is not easily influenced by anyone, who knows his own mind and who makes it up himself. Whenever he disagreed with Jack he made his position clear with courtesy and with firmness, and it was Lindgren's advice which Jack heeded first of all. In many ways they were opposites. Cotton ebullient, dynamic, creative; Lindgren retiring, fastidious and orderly; but they were close business friends who listened to each other carefully with mutual respect and affection. Lindgren as a professional chartered accountant running his own firm was Cotton's right-hand man, holding a somewhat similar position to Leonard Sainer, a professional solicitor, in respect of Clore. Lindgren's heart attack, which meant him giving up some of his business activities, occurred at the height of the battle with Clore, just when Cotton needed him most. Freddie Lindgren's finesse, integrity and total fearlessness of Clore and Sainer would have afforded Cotton just the strength he required to stiffen his resolve against Clore and, though it is idle to speculate what might have been, it is useful and salutary to note that a legal case brought against Lindgren as a Cotton trustee by Clore and Sainer was settled in Lindgren's favour four years after Cotton's death, when Lindgren clearly showed his determination and will.

In property matters, however, Jack Cotton turned almost exclusively to Aubrey Orchard-Lisle, just as Clore turned to Orchard-Lisle's partner, Douglas Tovey. In the annals of UK property lore, not enough generally has been remarked about the role of several great real estate agents who were as significant in the makings of the property boom as the developers themselves.* But Aubrey Orchard-Lisle and Douglas Tovey are in a class apart. Remarkable as they were as the architects of the astonishing growth of their firm Healey & Baker in the shops sector, their greatest achievements lay in the very special role they played as agents to their very special retail clients. It should not be forgotten that the true groundswell of the property boom came from the explosive retail expansion of the fifties, not from the somewhat later boom in office buildings. In this

* There was Edward Erdman, for example, modest and reliable, a born diplomat, almost to the point of invisibility and a born negotiator, he was the calm property professional behind Isaac Wolfson's tremendous retail growth; there was Bob Roberts, the prime force in the establishment of Richard Ellis as a leading offices agency, who gave excellent advice in respect of the early property portfolio of the Electricity Council and Imperial Group pension funds. At Jones Lang Wootton, the largest of all the agencies, there was not one person but four — Noel and Eric Taylor, Norman Bowie and Jack Hughes, the brilliant quartet who helped to establish on a massive scale the property portfolios of numerous developers and institutions.

shops sector the leading specialists Orchard-Lisle and Tovey were concluding transactions in tens of millions of pounds well before the sixties boom, and their famous retail clients would be the first to admit that without the instigation of their agents, they couldn't possibly have attained the success they did. For these two agents did not just react to instructions from their clients, they actively initiated transactions for them. Moreover, in putting up a proposal they not only created an opportunity, they also obtained the tenant and the finance. They literally made their clients' fortunes. As superb agents geared to act for someone else, their outstanding talent lay in seeking the right principal who acted for himself and made his own decisions.

If Jack Cotton said yes to Aubrey Orchard-Lisle or if Charles Clore said yes to Douglas Tovey, they were saying yes to a full package which included acquisition, letting and funding. These titans of their profession, these towering species of an earlier generation of agents never lost their personal touch. The careers of Aubrey Orchard-Lisle entwined with Jack Cotton, and of Douglas Tovey entwined with Charles Clore, were outstanding in the property world. But the unique element of their success in acting for Cotton and Clore lay in their own partnership with each other, each one a foil to the other, interchanging and intermingling when appropriate with the other's special clients, striving always to interpret, to satisfy, and indeed to encourage their clients' needs — which is after all the basic function of a first-class real estate agent, or any agent for that matter. In the property world at large it was of course well known that Orchard-Lisle was Cotton's man and that Tovey was Clore's, and it is an impressive testimonial to the character and ability of both Orchard-Lisle and Tovey that neither tycoon lost his respect and liking for the other's property adviser, not anytime, not even during their fiercest battles.

Orchard-Lisle who is about the same age as Tovey, Cotton and Clore, is a large, tall bespectacled man with well-defined features, wavy hair now going white and with a deliberate, pleasing well-modulated voice. He first met Cotton in 1938, by which time Jack was a successful agent and a wealthy property owner doing a certain amount of business with Healey & Baker. When Orchard-Lisle decided to open an office in Birmingham, he specifically went to see Jack to inform him, because the new venture would reduce the amount of business between them. Characteristically, instead of taking umbrage, Jack immediately offered to find premises for him. Again, on the outbreak of war, when Healey & Baker Birmingham had to be closed down, Jack went out of his way to sort out their lease. First as agent and then as friend, Orchard-Lisle's relationship with Cotton became warmer by the year, especially after the Orchard-Lisles purchased from one of the Cotton trusts a house in Marlow, located across the river from Jack's. In the context of their propinquity Aubrey tells a delightful story about Jack claiming to be able to see him through his binoculars reading the *Financial Times* in his lounge on the other side of the Thames. One Saturday morning, whilst reading his *FT*, Aubrey had a phone call from Jack who said, 'Don't waste your time. Turn to page five and you will see a reference to City Centre Properties.'

In Aubrey's view, Jack was a consummate property man because he was a craftsman who knew his trade intimately and because he had an amazing property instinct. Cotton always knew what he wanted and could give an immediate yes, which surprised people like Erwin Wolfson, his partner on the Pan-Am Building, and indeed occasionally surprised Aubrey; but his property smell or instinct rarely let him down. Location was his secret. Many property men assert their total obeisance to location but they frequently compromise. Cotton never compromised on location. On one occasion Aubrey offered him, for a purchase, a fully documented portfolio. Jack simply asked for the location of the separate properties. When he told him, Cotton said, 'Buy it.' Aubrey was taken aback by this immediate decision, for the portfolio was of a significant size. The transaction was completed and the day after Jack said, 'Come along Aubrey, we are going to look at the properties this afternoon.' As they went around looking at each shop Aubrey realised that Jack, having made up his mind in a split second to purchase the portfolio because of its location, had thereafter studied the documents and knew every detail of each property. His decisions were immediate and unhesitating, though his eagerness sometimes betrayed the typical fear of the entrepreneur not wishing to lose a deal; but after the rapid business decision, Cotton the craftsman did his homework.

The pre-war and immediate post-war period of Cotton's career was spent in organising Jack Cotton & Partners as property agents, in seeing that the architectural firm he had established, Cotton Ballard & Blow, obtained sufficient work and of course in expanding the various companies and trusts comprising his increasingly substantial personal property interests. During this phase Lindgren and Kerman would go up to Birmingham each week for a regular meeting. There, in his own city, Cotton was already emerging as a major property figure; he had developed the site of his pre-Cheltenham school in New Street, he had helped out the Air Ministry when it needed a shadow factory of over seventy-five acres, he had converted the Chamber of Commerce Buildings into shops and ice-cream parlours, and he had started on his enormous Big Top project, central shop and office complex in Birmingham now known as the Bullring. Ironically his first investment in London was not made through Orchard-Lisle, but through Tovey. This was Dorland House, in Lower Regent Street, which housed the popular Hungarian Restaurant amongst other prestigious tenants. As Tovey says, 'It was during the war. I had only enough petrol to go up to Stratford and back. So Jack arranged to meet me at the Welcombe Hotel in Stratford. I brought a photo and schedule with me and told Jack it was a bargain. He instructed me to purchase the property. He knew the location well. He didn't want to come down to inspect it because he said he would take my word for it.'

Then suddenly in Birmingham, Cotton created a scandal; this was the disgraceful skeleton in his otherwise impeccably clean cupboard and explains his almost hermit-like reticence which lasted so many years.

Cotton, the homebody from the City of Birmingham, had been proudly and solidly entrenched there all his life; he was born there, he grew up there, he married there, he built his fortune there. He had led a seemingly blameless life, success had led to success; he was entirely above reproach from any of his friends or business acquaintances for any of his actions. This man of enduring roots, of enduring location, uprooted himself and moved south to the Thames and to London. What had happened?

Very simply, just after the end of the war, Jack Cotton was struck off as an auctioneer.

He had been instructed to act as the agent of a motor distributor who wished to sell his property. Cotton bought the property as a principal. There was ensuing litigation but finally a settlement was made out of court. Cotton's action was entirely reprehensible. From any point of view it was an appalling disgrace to be struck off. So that when it happened Jack's natural instincts were to seek new pastures. He could justify his departure by declaring that he had to look after his growing interests in London. There he could hope that no one would know what had happened. As a man with the proudest of instincts this was a very painful skeleton. It had to be, and was, firmly locked in the cupboard. Few were aware of it. Certainly not his grand financial advisers, Hambros & Schroders, certainly not his new institutional friends at the mighty Legal & General and Pearl insurance companies, and certainly not Charles Clore. In leaving Birmingham he was excessively careful to hide his secret. He steadfastly kept away from the press and he even refused to go on the board of his own public company. He was painstakingly concerned not to do anything which might let the scandal out, which might lead to any knowledge of his stigma. In my view it was this deep anxiety and guilt which explains his later transformation.

For some years he had made regular visits to London for business, always staying at the Dorchester whose owners, the McAlpine building family, he knew well. He took a permanent suite, Number 120, which was gradually enlarged. This was the suite which later became famous throughout the property world. Number 120 on the first floor, a separate entrance on Park Lane, more like entering an apartment house, with its own liftmen and porters, a discreet entrance which suited the deliberately discreet Mr Cotton, the deliberately quiet property man from Birmingham. Also just after the war in 1946 he bought his house in Marlow by the Thames, a cream stately villa sitting amongst thousands of tulips and facing the Edwardian Compleat Angler Hotel on the other side of the river, where its patrons sitting in the restaurant and on the lawns, could stare wistfully at this splendid symbol of Thames Valley affluence, owned by the then quiet and unknown property millionaire.

During the period of his move south, until he became chairman of City Centre in 1958, Cotton laid the solid foundations of his great expansion which was to take him from being the leading developer in the Midlands to the leading developer in the country. In December 1954 when Kerman brought him Central Commercial Properties owned by the Edgson family (whose head, Stanley Edgson, the senior partner of Hillier Parker the leading shops agents, had recently died), he jumped a step ahead; this was one of his best ever buys. Another major acquisition was in March 1957 when he purchased the town section of the Tredegar Estate brought to him this time by Orchard-Lisle. 'We agreed the purchase price,' Aubrey recalls, 'subject to the right to sell between exchange and completion of contract those properties which did not fit into the City Centre portfolio. By the date of completion, money was owed to City Centre by the Tredegar Estate rather than the other way round'. Self-financing and money-making of the most elegant kind.

In working with Cotton both Isadore Kerman and Freddie

Lindgren remember these productive years as being the happiest and most zestful of all. Usually joined by Aubrey Orchard-Lisle, they would meet Cotton most evenings at the Dorchester for a drink and a gregarious discussion until 8.00 or 8.30 p.m. when they each departed for their various dinner engagements. Jack, secure in his masterminding role in the back seat, avoiding any notice outside the real estate world, especially anxious in avoiding the press, was an apparently contented and serene man.

The key to the timing and beginning of his transformation was the wedding of his daughter Jill to a London stockbroker in 1957. The elaborate ceremony and party took place in Birmingham and Jack, wishing to do his only daughter proud, laid on a special train to Birmingham for guests from London. But the *Daily Express* got hold of the story and splashed the headline 'The Mink and Champagne Express' with a graphic account of the great expense incurred by the bride's father. Other papers followed suit, most of them calling him a property millionaire or a property tycoon. He was severely criticised for his ostentation and stung by this unexpected and unintentional glare of publicity; he declared that he would be happy to explain himself to the press at any time if they so wished. They did so wish, and he was inundated with interviews. The journalists discovered a tycoon who was not only natural and without guile, but who treated them as he treated everyone, as genuine equals. They found he had no side. He was wonderful copy, a beaming, benevolent property tycoon ensconced at the Dorchester.

This unsolicited publicity arising from his daughter's wedding had not provoked one reference to his being struck off, not even in Birmingham. To his immense relief he no longer had to be a press recluse. His anxiety and guilt vanished. His ebullience was unbridled. He was free. Released from all restraints, he breathed the heady air of recognition, of increasing fame, and he embraced the publicity with all the enthusiasm of a rekindled early passion. He was Big Daddy now to all and sundry. He would show the world. He was fifty-three, in the prime of life.

Then, sailing with Marcus Brown to South Africa in early 1958, he caught mumps, a very grave illness for a man of Cotton's age with its embarrassing after-effects. In affecting his potency it caused him to become over-assertive and hyper-active. His incessant creativity after his illness, his constant search for new partners, his striving for new associations, new friends, new projects, his accelerating all-consuming obsession with publicity were part of his attempt, I believe, to find a substitute for his temporary loss of virility. From a psychological point of view a great change took place. It is therefore essential to look at the facts carefully. His emotional state from this stage onwards, feeding on an ever increasing need for recognition, was going to lead him to some sort of catastrophe. He not only thoroughly enjoyed the sensation of publicity, he also needed to assert himself, to pit himself against others, to be ever more competitive. He had to be the biggest. He was especially envious of other strong men, men of outstanding achievement like Harold Samuel, like Charles Clore. If moreover they were sexually arrogant, as Clore was, he would suffer additional pangs of envy and insecurity which would make him want to strive that much harder to attain an equal level of power and potency. From now onwards he needed no persuasion to go on to the board of his company, to become its chairman. On the contrary, he wanted all the trappings, his ego needed to be satisfied by bold recognition, he had to be in the forefront. He wanted to be talked about, to be written about, to be photographed, to be acclaimed. Suffering from a profound emotional and sexual vacuum, his needs could only be satisfied by more recognition, more publicity, more business transactions and ever more activity. A partnership, a marriage, with someone like Clore, was inevitable. All his adrenalin, all his needs, all his anxieties were geared for an outcome of this sort. When Douglas Tovey popped the question as the marriage broker, Cotton was more than a willing partner. In fact, applying one of his favourite sayings, he was ready to jump into bed before breakfast.

So, on 29 October 1958, just two years before the merger, Cotton was appointed to the board of City Centre and was made chairman. Freddie Lindgren stepped down to deputy chairman. In his first year as chairman Cotton purchased L & P Estates from the estate of Sir Henry Price, owning Piccadilly House, Piccadilly; Golden Cross House, Strand; Maddox House, Regent Street; and other London and provincial assets. He also completed the first stage of the Big Top, now comprising nearly four acres in the heart of Birmingham, Regina House in the Edgware Road in London, a new office building in Old Broad Street, and the purchase of the site of what is now 45 Park Lane. He went ahead with his other joint development with Louis Freedman — the Notting Hill Gate project. He did a deal on BP House through Barranquilla, another joint company involving the Pearl Assurance, Felix Fenston and Harry Hyams and owning Longbow House in Chiswell Street, London, Beecham House in

Brentford and other City development sites. He acquired the site of what is now Bow Bells House in Cheapside. He also acquired Dunlop House on the site of the old St James's Theatre which had been developed by Felix Fenston, Balfour House on Finsbury Pavement and the Empress State Building in Earl's Court. In Birmingham, apart from the Big Top, several properties were acquired, the most notable being the *Birmingham Post & Mail* building in Cannon Street, equivalent to a stretch of Regent Street. He forged links with Woolworth's, Shell-Mex and BP Ltd, Barclays Bank DCO.

In 1959 there was the crowning transaction, the announcement of his 50% interest in the Pan-Am building. At the time it was claimed to be the largest office building in the world. He also acquired *La Pensée*, one of Renoir's greatest paintings, a masterpiece which even Clore coveted, and still in 1959 the Jack Cotton Chair of Biochemistry was endowed at the Royal College of Surgeons. *Annus mirabilis.*

Jack Cotton's name over the years has become synonymous with Piccadilly Circus. This was because of his Monico development — yet it was his biggest blunder. On his own doorstep Cotton was convinced that he had a ready-made world beater. It could not be more emotive; Piccadilly Circus, Eros, the epicentre of London, the tangible soul of the old Empire, the greatest location in the entire Commonwealth. Everyone would talk about his Monico site. And they did, but for the wrong reason. The way Jack handled the Monico was a fiasco. It was a miscalculation of awe-inspiring ineptitude, for the Monico which certainly could have been one of the most important and significant of projects, was killed by self-generated publicity. It was virtually destroyed by a press conference. The Café Monico, not then known as a site, was owned by the Express Dairy Group, its controlling shareholder being Walter Nell, whose daughter had married Sam Messer, Cotton's partner and the head of Jack Cotton and Partners in London. In 1954 Kerman however initiated and activated the purchase with Jack's enormous enthusiasm. He asked Jack, 'Have you been to see the place?' Jack said, 'No, I don't need to because if I see it I will see the problems and if I see the problems I won't buy it and I want to buy it because of the location.' After the purchase there were oysters and champagne at Scotts, the celebrated fish restaurant then almost next door to the Monico and now flourishing in Mount Street still owned by the Kerman family.

After much work on the project Cotton issued a press announcement in September 1959, stating that his joint company, with the Legal & General Assurance, had obtained outline planning consent for the Monico. The handling of the Monico project signalled Cotton's first big transaction with Legal & General, and it signalled to the outside world his deepening addiction to the press. For despite having made a perfectly proper press announcement, he decided in October, a month later, to have another press encounter to present a model. This wholly unnecessary conference cost him dearly. There was an immediate public and press outcry, referring in many instances to an 'ugly building with an ugly thing on top'. What was on top was the window cleaning crane which on the model was out of all proportion, seeming half the size of the building itself. As a direct result of the outcry, Henry Brooke, the Housing Minister, ordered an enquiry. Lindgren told me, 'We didn't want a conference. We didn't want a model. We already had outline planning. It was unnecessary. But Jack insisted.' When the Housing Inspector, the same Mr Buchanan who subsequently wrote the noted Buchanan Report on 'Traffic in Towns', published his Monico Report, he said, 'The applicants must now greatly regret that they put out the prospective sketch which they did at Mr Cotton's press conference in October 1959. Had this not been issued it is a fair guess that the building would now be in the course of erection.' I was at that press conference, reporting for the *Investors' Chronicle*. It was held in the Criterion Rooms above the Lillywhite's sports shop on the other side of Piccadilly Circus opposite the Monico site. Jack sat at the table glowing with pride, the ugly model and sketches prominently displayed. Lindgren was by his side, together with other factotums including representatives of the Legal & General. One of them, John Crickmay, the joint chief surveyor of the Legal & General and a director of the Monico joint company, told me later that 'it was a little awkward sitting there listening to the questions'.

In May, Brooke announced the rejection of the Monico plan. Lord Zuckerman was with Jack the night he heard the verdict. They were dining alone and Solly Zuckerman recalls that Jack was shattered, rambling on about his dismay and disappointment until 2.30 a.m. when Zuckerman felt he had provided sufficient moral support to help his friend over the initial shock of the news. The Monico project was passionately dear to Cotton's heart; it was his first major current development in London and he identified himself with it as much as he did with the Pan-Am and the Big Top.

He did not give up. In July 1960, in another forlorn attempt to sway public opinion to his favour, Cotton gave a further Monico press conference, this time at the Dorchester, to introduce Gropius as the great international architect who would be looking at the plans for the Monico.*

During 1959 I met Cotton on several occasions. I had written about the progress of City Centre Properties in the *Chronicle* and was particularly fascinated by the pattern of the company's growth, its unique feature being the numerous partnerships forged by Cotton rather than the undertaking of individual property developments. 'I am a true developer, not Cotton,' Fenston said to me on one occasion. 'Jack's just a bloody genius'. The occasion was soon after Fenston, stretched financially which was a habit he made endearing by its frequency, had approached Cotton for the financing of a specific development owned by one of his companies, Eron Investments, and had left the Dorchester, having agreed to sell his entire company outright. 'I didn't go to sell. A bloody genius, that's what he is,' Fenton growled in wonder and admiration.

Felix Fenston was accurate about himself being a true developer, but not about Cotton who was, of course, also a true developer. What Jack was doing in addition, and doing with sublime simplicity time after time, was to accelerate the growth of his own company and his own fortune by buying other property men's developments at low prices.

Partnership and associations were the essence of Cotton's thinking. He was the first important property man to appreciate that sooner or later the institutions would not continue providing finance on a straight loan basis, that they would want a piece of the action and that their piece would become larger and the developer's smaller. He also perceived very early on, long before other property developers, that the method by which the institutions could invest in property could as easily be implemented by a corporate transaction as by a specific property transaction. He engineered the process of linking with institutions, adding a completely new dimension to the structure of the industry.

* Gropius the Maestro also looked at 45 Park Lane, previously the home of Barney Barnato the diamond magnate, and after him the home of Sir Philip Sassoon. All Gropius was able to do in Park Lane was to suggest concrete instead of Portland stone. Thus the only visible manifestation of this great architect in London is the facing of what was the Playboy Club in Park Lane.

1960 too was a year of incessant activity. This was the year when Walter Flack first came into Jack's life through a joint transaction involving the acquisition of Whitehall Court followed by the acquisition of the Boucheron *hôtel particulier* in Avenue Foch. In February the ground lease for the Pan-Am building on Grand Central Station was finally agreed with New York Central. Demolition would start soon. One transaction followed another, noted with amazement in the property world and in the City, and studied closely, also with some amazement, by Mr Charles Clore.

In August of 1960, the property world was quiet. Jack spent most of it at Marlow, looking at the boats chugging peacefully past his river bank, having drinks on the lawn during the long summer evenings, discussing with his friends his plans to become bigger than Harold Samuel, to become the biggest property tycoon in the world. Little did he know that, before the end of that summer, one of the greatest ever property salesmen flying from New York to London would have a brainwave which could make his dream come true — a dream which would later turn into a nightmare.

Chapter Four

Enter the Black Tie

What about Charles Clore, the other half of this astonishing union? Known for decades as Mr Clore, feared, respected, disliked, admired, he seemed as Sir Charles (he got his knighthood in 1970 long after numerous lesser lights, which rankled until his last days) more benign, more amiable, less likely to strike a chord of terror. But the truculent, tough, unyielding character never changed.

Physically too, he never changed. A profusion of grey to silver hair on a strong handsome face, he was short with a wide firm body, looking at his best in an immaculate ivory shirt, black tie and the inevitable and beautifully cut dinner jacket.

Charles Clore was a business genius in the sense that he was always in control or seemed to be in control. He never took undue risks; he either committed or he didn't commit. A business situation was stripped of inessentials and he either went ahead full blast or, with a laconic grunted expletive, threw the proposal out of the window. He was rarely prone to hesitate, to vacillate, even in trivial matters like the choice of restaurant, and in all the years of our friendship I have never ever seen him show a trace of fear — except in June 1979. This was a month before he died, when we were lunching alone together in Beaulieu by the marina, and his eyes the colour of the Mediterranean sky above us flickered as he described the arrangements for his impending operation. He looked at me with naked apprehension and we went through the rest of the lunch in friendly silence. His only generally admitted anxiety was swimming out of his depth, having nearly drowned as a child — so in the water, chest high only in the pool at his country estate at Stype, with water wings naturally. Being out of his depth, in any way, was anathema to him. During his prime, his decision-making was always remarkably direct, ice-cool, clear, sharp, quick as an arrow, right on target; always dead straight. There was no concern whatsoever for anything or anybody standing in his way. Once the decision was made Leonard Sainer, the perfect right-hand man, would be told to get on with the technicalities and the implementation. Clore's sense of a good transaction was intuitive, but for groundwork he relied on direct information and facts. He never actively sought anyone else's advice with the possible exception of Sainer's. Only facts. Only information. Then the shaft of intuition, then the decision, then the thrust at the target. Sainer and others would execute the transaction and work out the details: Clore's commands were simple: stabilise the management, increase the margins, increase the profits.

Undoubtedly Clore's greatest virtue was his utterly ruthless honesty. As our friendship grew deeper over the years, seeing each other frequently during the week, at weekends and on holidays and trips abroad, I found that it was this one quality of downright honesty in his powerful character which was most compelling and attractive. His will had the force of granite; his cobalt eyes made people cringe, people who were big men in their own right. His loathing for exaggeration, for dissembling, for delusion — where he was as strict with himself as with anyone else — was the central feature of his make-up, and it was this feature which earned him the respect, admiration and eventually some affection from people who would normally be repelled by his rudeness, his selfishness and his insularity.

All his business life Clore searched for the truth, and when he found it, no matter what effect his action might have on any person standing in his way he went ahead with quiet ferocity. This explains his decisive act against Cotton; he very simply came to the conclusion that as chairman of their vast group, Cotton would not do. He told Cotton what he thought; it was nothing personal, just the truth as far as Clore was concerned. Essentially Clore had more innate respect for human failings than for human strengths. In the realms of business he regarded weakness as the main driving force and as a profound sceptic he exploited to the full this cynical and melancholic view of life. He expected the worst of people and was rarely surprised. In probing for weakness, he sought to undermine the other person's confidence and in so doing he obtained an abundance of gratuitous facts and information, much of it meaningful. He sifted the salient bits and without hesitation acted upon what he had garnered.

Charles Clore invented the takeover as we know it today. Acquisitions BC were, according to one industrial wag, 'before Clore'. If a company BC merged or associated with another, almost invariably the boards of both companies were in full agreement. Clore was the first entrepreneur who, as the controlling shareholder of his own company, was fully prepared to make an offer for the shares of another company above the heads and against the protests of the directors, and to make his offer without any prior consultation. It appealed to his sense of brutal honesty: it was a natural part of his make-up to adopt the brutal approach. He may not have been the first to seek unexploited assets, but he was the first to do something positive about it by buying asset-rich companies in the teeth of bitter opposition. He was amongst the first to use the sale and leaseback principle as a financial tool in his acquisitions. He was certainly the first man to collect businesses under what is now known as a conglomerate, before these corporate animals were even known in the United States. In a sense one can describe ICI as a conglomerate, but the establishment of a quoted holding company guided and controlled by one man, owning disparate subsidiaries acquired mostly by forced takeovers, was entirely new. As to financing, Clore's approach was tidy, simplistic, exemplary. No commitment was made until the short-term borrowings had been secured nor until the long-term funding had been agreed. As far as the terms of financing were concerned, he was single-minded: borrow money long-term at the lowest rate of interest without giving anything away, particularly not any equity. When his personal property company, City & Central, the very group which later formed the merger with Cotton, was floated on the Stock Exchange, almost the entire capital was owned by Clore and his family trusts.

His financing methods were diametrically opposed to Jack Cotton's. Clore had no objection to having financial partners as long as the partner gave as much as possible and Clore gave as little as possible. Jack, on the other hand, based his entire approach to financing on a genuine partnership; give and take on both sides. This is a principle with which many businessmen profoundly concur, but Clore through sheer weight of personality and authority usually got the terms he wanted and from institutions happy to provide it and happy to be associated with him.

As Charles Clore, he became well known throughout the world. He was a natural star; on entering any room, whether in London, New York, Paris, everyone was immediately conscious of his presence. All his life, he had the feeling of divine right, that he was superior, that he was a special person. Even as a child, according to his brother David, he was always neatly dressed, never ruffled, not taking part in the everyday East End street frolics of his schoolfriends. Later, when he had started on the road to his immense riches, with chauffeurs, chefs, nannies, gardeners, butlers, he would remonstrate with his staff that something was not for Mr Clore, that it was provincial — his most pejorative word — that it was not good enough: for dessert therefore it was grapes of only the very choicest selection, nothing so 'provincial' as pears. Only the best for Mr Clore.

His God however was not divine, but mammon. He worshipped at only one altar: money. He was a zealot for money, his grasping for it was a form of gluttony, an appetite which was voracious, never satisfied though somewhat muted in his later years. Even before his merger with Jack it was said that, whereas Cotton would do anything for publicity, Clore would do anything for money.

Later, he had a second gluttony: women. It is vital to understand this part of Clore's character, because his virility and his appetite for women unnerved many of his social and business acquaintances, leading them to accept a subordinate status in their personal relationships and consequently inferior terms in their business transactions with him. His overbearing virility, as I have already remarked, was very germane to Jack Cotton's own psychological weakness, and from the very beginning of the merger it was curious how Clore's powerful personality even influenced Cotton's terminology, reflecting the nature of their relationship. Jack said he was going to marry Charles. Jack said he was going to wear the trousers. Jack said that he was going to be the dominant partner. Jack said that Charles was going to be his number two.

Charles never even bothered to enter the ring. He was number one whatever the title. He knew he was someone special. He did not need to pit himself against anyone. He was in the class of Niarchos and Getty, the world class. He would always win. He would always get what he wanted. Not only all the money in the world, but all the girls in the world. Girls were for his pleasure, the taller and younger the better and every night if possible, right into his seventies until his final illness. In his prime it was any girl of any social level. All that mattered was availability. In the last years of his life he mellowed, developing friendships when romance occasionally blossomed. But his sexual will was indomitable. Some women were attracted by it, others fought it and succumbed, others were repelled by it. From a social point of view it was tawdry, made worse by some acquaintances, particularly amongst the commercial *demi-mondains* who wished to do business with him, who not only pandered to him but acted as

44

willing procurers. Many hostesses deplored his behaviour. A particular habit which occasionally ruined the evening was groping for the knee of the girl sitting next to him at dinner, someone he had probably met for the first time an hour earlier. He was impatient; he couldn't wait; he had to have it now. He hadn't the slightest concern for the sexual niceties, and genuinely did not care what people thought of his behaviour. Most women ignored his blunt demands, they chided him and received in return the boyish Clore smile of temporary contrition. Others would never invite him again. It was a gluttony of shameful proportions.

During his whole life Charles Clore was only truly fond of one person: his wife Francine. He had fallen deeply in love with her, and it was his outraged sense of pride that she would actually leave him for another man, coupled to a fanatical sense of possession, which unleashed his sexual militancy towards nearly all women thereafter. After Francine left him no other woman affected him emotionally in any way.

His wife departed in 1956 when he was fifty-two years old, and for the next twenty years he went on a determined sexual rampage, never finding companionship, because he never sought it. Francine was the only woman who ever plucked his heart strings. I recall one warm June evening fifteen years after their divorce, on the terrace of the Hôtel de Paris in Monte Carlo when he, Nadia and I were dining together, and Francine came in with her escort and sat at a nearby table. As soon as he saw her his eyes lit up and he spent the rest of the evening quite deliberately entertaining Nadia and myself with stories of his early life so as to capture Francine's interest and to spoil her dinner. Rarely calling her by name, it was too hurtful, she was always his 'ex', he never managed to get her out of his system.

He had little or no affection for his children, he hardly ever spoke to them and when he tried he didn't know what to say. He couldn't understand his son Alan, regretted having made him independently rich and questioned his social habits openly with his friends. He was brought closer to his daughter because of his affection for her children. He was not especially fond of his family, one exception being his brother David, though all relations were well looked after by one or other of his trusts. Although for many years he had been in daily contact with Sainer there was still a formality in their relationship. He had very little real affection for friends like myself, though he was especially fond of my wife Nadia because she was a famous

45

ballerina and because her directness and sincerity gave him a sense of dignity so that he was always on his best behaviour in her company. During the last years of his life, a frequent companion was Lady Milford Haven, a dark flashy-eyed beauty from Bermuda, whose abundant sense of humour and wit appealed strongly to him. He once said to me, disclosing once again his abrupt sense of honesty, that though he was fond of her he wouldn't seek marriage because what he liked most was her title. But even with Janet Milford Haven he grumbled about her inadequacies rather than extolling her virtues. He spoke affectionately of his father, of Leonard Sainer's father, of his brother David's wife; he almost never spoke well of others and when he did it was a special bouquet for the recipient. Only once in twenty years did I ever hear him describe at length his affection and admiration for anyone, and that was for Marcus Sieff, now Lord Sieff, until recently the chairman of Marks & Spencer.

Francine, the sole idol of his affections, was and is a beautiful woman. From a well-known Jewish-French family, she was born in 1920, and in the middle of the War, when twenty-two and already a Croix de Guerre heroine in the Free French forces, she met and married Clore. He was thirty-nine, a man of substance, the Soames Forsyte of the Jewish middle class, but not yet the man of the world; it was Francine who brought to Clore the culture and taste of the well-educated, sophisticated French upper class and, as Clore took some pains to remind those of his acquaintances who were not aware of it, her mother was the sister of Edmond de Rothschild's mother.

But whence came this indomitable money-maker, one of the most talked-about businessmen in the UK, certainly the most glamorous, who made grown men quake at their knees and who made other tycoons jibber like schoolboys? Where else but from the proverbial Jewish East End. To the end of his life his mild cockney accent never changed; he was not ashamed of it as he was not ashamed of anything: 'I'm just a little Jewish boy who has learned one or two things in life,' he would say at a grand dinner party with total unconcern.

He was born in the East End of London on Boxing Day, 1904. This section of the London of his childhood was the repository of thousands of Jewish immigrants arriving from Russia and Poland at the turn of the century, many of whose sons, like Clore and Max Rayne, have since achieved high success in most walks of life. His father was a tailor, there were five children, two brothers and two sisters, but from the beginning it was clear to Clore's family that he was destined for greatness. When he was twenty, the family decided that their special progeny had to have special treatment and they clubbed together to send him to South Africa to seek his fortune. Like Cotton, he had well-to-do connections there, including the famous Rose family of Outshorn which owned the ostrich farms producing the feathers for the fashionable, extravagant Edwardians. It was the African sub-continent which gave Clore the opportunity for his celebrated first deal by obtaining the South African film rights to the Tunney-Dempsey fight. He went to see the man who had the overseas rights and asked him for the South African territory. As he recounted the story to me, he was turned down flat, but as he got to the door to leave he was called back and told, 'I've changed my mind. You'll have the rights because it will enrage Schlesinger.' It did. Schlesinger had amongst other vast interests the monopoly of all the cinemas in South Africa and was forced to do a deal. Back in London at the age of twenty-four, Clore bought the ailing Cricklewood Skating Rink and made it profitable. By 1931, three years later, he was rich enough to purchase the Prince of Wales Theatre in partnership with Alfred Esdaile, a theatrical producer. It was this company which owned the theatre and which, under the name of City & Central Properties, merged with Cotton's City Centre Properties. By the time war broke out Clore was rich by any standards. In 1939, taking one of many examples of shrewd buying, he purchased for 30p per share and retained a large holding in a South African mine recommended to him by his friend and stockbroker Max Rose. By the end of the war the shares had risen to £8 each. A modest profit, he would say without complacency.

Whatever he did, whether buying property or buying and selling companies, or buying shares, he made money. He came into public prominence when he was nominated as Hilton's associate for the purchase of the Grosvenor House Hotel. The bid was unsuccessful. But the real turning point came in 1953 with the bid for Sears, the True-Form Boot Company, the parent of Freeman, Hardy & Willis.

The purchase of Freeman, Hardy & Willis was probably his most significant acquisition in that it provided his group with an enormous equity surplus at an early stage of its growth (in today's values something like £100 million). The origin and inception of that deal is another example of the way chance plays its part in big business. The bid started because Douglas Tovey put it to him out of the blue during one of their drinks together in Clore's house in Park Street.

47

One is prompted to speculate on the vagaries of the good fortune of entrepreneurs, for in effect what was eventually called the British Shoe Corporation, the largest manufacturer and retailer of shoes in Europe, was initiated by Tovey's idea, passed on by him casually to Charles Clore in his house one evening. It supports the view that on the acquisition trail, *ad hoc* opportunities have as much, if not more, credence and respectability than the professional search for a logical acquisition based on elaborate corporate strategies.

Tovey was born in Portishead, Somerset, near Bristol in 1905. He won a scholarship to the choir at Wells Cathedral, remaining there till he was seventeen when his father lost the tiny remnants of the family money. The freemasons came to the rescue and introduced Tovey to a Mr Scarisbrooke, who happened to be the deputy chief surveyor of the Great Western Railway. By 1938 Tovey was earning £300 per annum and Scarisbrooke advised him to join a West End property organisation owned by a man he knew, because the railway wage structure inhibited any further salary increases. The man he knew was Edward Lotery who engaged Tovey at £1,000 per year, putting him in charge of his shop-letting division. Lotery was the pioneer of the outer London growth of shops, constructed as parades with flats above, catering for the needs of the new suburbs built round the London underground system. Well over half of these pre-war London and suburban shopping parades were developed by Lotery. It was the flowering of the High Street multiples with names like Dewhurst, Woolworth's, Sketchley, encompassing the early days of that remarkable businessman, Jack Cohen of Tesco, a prominent Lotery tenant who expressed his later very famous business slogan to the young bustling Tovey: 'Never hide the goods. Stack them high. You must be able to see them and you must be able to pick them up.'

Lotery's agents were Healey & Baker. Tovey soon exhibited his tremendous talents and was obtaining as many tenants directly for Lotery as Healey & Baker. The Monday after war was declared he went into his office to be met by the accountant who told him that Mr Lotery and his family had left the country and had decided to spend the rest of the war in the US. Out of a job, he pondered his next move. A week later he received a letter from Aubrey Orchard-Lisle, inviting him to join the firm, nearly all of whose staff had joined the forces. He agreed and thus started the famous partnership which culminated in Healey & Baker being regarded then and now by most of the property fraternity as the leading shop agents in the country.

Tovey, a voluble gregarious man who looks like a well-preserved US senator with his handsome features and impressive appearance, lives today with his wife Nora in great comfort and style on his farm in Nettlebed, next door to the banking Flemings, and deriving particular pleasure from discussing his farming plans with his bailiff and friend of thirty years' standing. He also derives particular pleasure from his association with some of the most outstanding entrepreneurs of the mid-century. In building up Healey & Baker with Aubrey Orchard-Lisle, Tovey developed quite a clientele, but the three major businessmen whose lives he altered and who altered his life, who stuck to him through thick and thin, were Montague Burton, Hugh Fraser and Charles Clore, all three of whom have their stores emblazoned on every high street in England. The dull, uninspired sameness of these high streets today was due to the rapid Lotery-type expansion of multiple shops during the ribbon development of the thirties and the overwhelming sprawl during the retail boom of the fifties and sixties. Woolworth's and Marks & Spencer were of course early multiples, but the originator and one of the most spectacular successes of any multiple group was the Montague Burton chain with its distinctive art-deco shop fronts, a constant reminder to the young clerk that he couldn't possibly be promoted in his job without the neat made-to-measure Burton suit. Orchard-Lisle and Douglas Tovey were the exclusive agents behind the stupendous build-up of the Burton shops into the largest men's clothing retailers in the world, the great entrepreneur Montague Burton recognising their flair and trusting the two young men completely. He once told Tovey they would always work well together if he kept to one paramount rule, which was to 'keep the zippa on the lippa', to keep every offer, every negotiation, every price, utterly secret. Tovey and Orchard-Lisle became leading experts on the rental value of shops throughout the country and together they developed the series of sale and leasebacks, mostly with George Bridge of the Legal & General, which became the characteristic feature of the Burton, Fraser, Clore expansion and the hallmark of the Legal & General's own early success in property investment.

The relationship between Montague Burton, Orchard-Lisle and Tovey was that of the master with his pupils, of the uncle with his nephews. The relationship however between the master draper, Hugh Fraser and Douglas Tovey, was that of two great friends, of two buddies looking over balance sheets and analyses of companies together, staying at the Hotel de Paris together, cooking up deals together, scrutinising department stores together and gambling in Monte Carlo together.

Hugh Fraser originally sought out Tovey, who remembers the day when his office door opened and a thin man entered still wearing his trilby, a cigarette drooping from his mouth. 'You're only a wee little man,' said Fraser to a surprised Tovey. 'You will have to come to Scotland to meet Katie. If she likes you we'll do business together. Can't do business with anyone unless she likes them.' It was fortunate for Hugh Fraser that Katie liked Douglas Tovey, for the Toveys were not only to become the Frasers' close companions, but directly for the House of Fraser, Douglas organised Derry & Toms, Barker's, D. H. Evans and of course Harrods.* What a cluster: not only did Tovey provide the property expertise and advice, but he arranged most of the financing with the Legal & General, the balance with the Pearl and the Pru and nearly all of it on favourable ninety-nine-year leasebacks.

However, although it was Joe Levy of D. E. & J. Levy who was the first person to act for Clore in property, providing for Clore his earliest guidance in property, it was Clore himself, seeing what Fraser was achieving, who went out of his way to seek out Tovey. One day towards the end of the forties he asked Douglas home to Park Street for a chat. Clore, untypically forthcoming, spoke to Douglas of his dearest ambition which was to assemble the most formidable portfolio of property in the land.

---

* The department store wanted by everyone, but especially by Fraser, was of course Harrods, believed to be well out of everyone's reach, though Tovey frequently and bombastically said that one day he would get it for Fraser — and he did. There is a curious mystique and magnetism about certain businesses, with a particular appeal to the acquisitive entrepreneur, for which he will pay a handsome, sometimes fatal premium. In these cases it is a company best known in its sector, with distinguished international names and run by a board of directors perceptively higher in the social scale than the would-be acquirer — a good example being Trafalgar's original purchase of Cunard. Hugh Fraser would certainly never have admitted to being a commercial snob, but he coveted Harrods all his life and he got it, much to Tovey's justifiable delight. In a somewhat similar situation, Lord Thomson once told me over lunch in the villa he occupied with Edward Heath in the South of France, that the one newspaper he really wanted to own was the London *Times*. Two years later, he owned it, a fabulous acquisition, but a sickening albatross and the most uncommercial purchase made by that most pragmatic of entrepreneurs. Snob value is occasionally a potent trigger behind a bid, the more so for never being admitted by the acquisitive bidder.

This renowned relationship between Clore and Tovey, when it began, was one of principal and consultant. It was Mr Clore for a while, before Douglas got on to Charles, then they became friends and cronies. This was somewhat unexpected in that Tovey was immensely outgoing, full of the joys of property, always on the move, always on the go, whilst Clore was laconic and parsimonious if not miserly in conversation, and somewhat old-fashioned and cold in his relationships. But Clore saw a sort of genius in the talkative Lloyd George-like property salesman at Healey & Baker. After all, Tovey was fast making Fraser the king of department stores, so why couldn't he do it for Clore as well? Thus began a number of spectacular transactions. Before Tovey the Clore interests, though substantial, were not yet of international consequence. Tovey was to change that significantly, and he deserves every credit for what he achieved.

The morning after their drinks together when Tovey first mentioned True-Form Shoes, he sent Clore a note enclosing the Exchange Telegraph card of the company. It was then one of England's largest shoe retailers. In his covering note he stated that he thought the surplus value over the balance sheet figures for properties, consisting mainly of hundreds of shoe shops around the country, was in excess of £10 million. Tovey received an immediate phone call asking him to a meeting with Clore and Sainer. Within two days the bid had been worked out, organised and declared. The Stock Exchange was duly informed and a letter was duly sent round by hand to the chairman of Freeman, Hardy & Willis. A more galling bolt from the blue had never been received by any board of any British company. Clore's tactics were simple and stunningly effective: a firm immutable decision to go ahead; complete secrecy; and a quick concealed build-up of shares purchased in the market. The first indication of anything afoot was the formal letter to the chairman of the company. Cool nerves were particularly needed during initial adverse press criticism; and Clore in the meantime built up his holding in the company through open purchases in the market. The battle for Freeman, Hardy & Willis was intense, acrimonious and bitter. Clore won. Tovey earned a substantial fee for his firm and he also received a letter of thanks from Clore. It was short and to the point. It thanked Tovey, but also pointed out with deadpan humour that he had slightly over-estimated the surplus.

In the seven-year run-up to the Cotton merger, Clore was busy on all fronts. The year 1953 marked the attempt by Harold Samuel to take over the Savoy Group.* Samuel had accumulated 20% and Clore, who had 9%, suggested that they get together, which was declined, so he sold his holding to Samuel. The Hotels and Restaurants Association expressed 'profound concern' at an attempt by 'outside interest to gain control of the Savoy'. The Bank of England was prompted once again to ask banks and finance companies not to finance takeover endeavours.

Also in 1953, Clore gave a party at his house in Park Street. The Duchess of Kent was the guest of honour and there were acid comments in the press referring to Clore's new social lustre. But it had been forgotten that Francine was well connected and had been on tea terms with Queen Mary, so it should not have been surprising to those who knew of Francine that a sister-in-law of the Queen Mother would be a guest of the Clores. The surprise perhaps reflected a new twist in linking Clore's personal life to his sensational business activities. From then on there were even more frequent mentions of his social activities with numerous photographs highlighting his silver hair and his black tie. But it was soon after this *succès d'estime* that the marriage started breaking up.

In this year too he purchased Bentley Engineering, the leading UK manufacturers of textile machinery. In 1954 he purchased the Curtiss chain of shoe shops. In 1955 J. Sears became Sears Holdings and he purchased the Phillips Brothers shoe chain. In 1956 he went into motor distribution and garages by purchasing Scottish Motor Traction, winning against Hugh Fraser.

In May 1956, his marriage virtually at an end, he went on holiday in *Radiant*, the yacht of his friend Basil Mavroleon and in a rare interview with Frederick Ellis of the *Daily Express* he was quoted as saying that the formula for success was hard work. In the autumn he was still busy; in September he agreed terms to purchase the Manfield shoe factories and shoe shops. In October he purchased the Dolcis shoe chain and he also declared his interest in Mappin & Webb. Before the end of the year the divorce petition against Francine was heard.

In 1957 he applied for planning permission for the new Hilton Hotel in Pitt's Head Mews, Stanhope Row and Hertford Street. In August of that year there was an interesting short piece about him

* The first of the attempts to wrest control of this Group whose arcane voting structure vested in the founding shares arising from D'Oyle Carte not only defeated Samuel but currently has stopped Trust House Forte from having any board representatives although it owns well over half of the entire equity.

in the *Evening Standard*, ostensibly written by Lord Beaverbrook himself. It stated that the true social leaders of the Riviera were Niarchos, Onassis and Clore; all held court in the Mediterranean: 'Mr Clore is in demand from Monte Carlo to Cannes.' In spite of this gushing comment, it must be stated that after the departure of his wife, Clore's social life, although receiving more attention, declined in quality.

1959 was the year when Sears made its bid for Watneys: five breweries and 3,670 pubs. This bid is now remembered mainly for the sniping and for the Parliamentary comments. It was thought that only brewers could bid for breweries. Colonel Whitbread described non-brewers as 'financial marauders'. Sidney Irving, the Labour member for Dartford, asked the President of the Board of Trade whether he would set up a departmental committee to investigate the operation of takeover bids with a view to recommending such appropriate amendments to the Company Acts as might be necessary in the public interest. He referred to huge untaxed capital profits. The Parliamentary Secretary replied: 'Some bids involve practices which are disliked.' He added with some prescience that the majority of bids had a useful side to them 'and keep directors on their toes'.

By June the Sears' bid was withdrawn with an announcement that this was decided after friendly discussions between the two chairmen. It was the first time Clore had ever retreated in a takeover battle. There have been differing explanations, but I suspect the true reason was that Clore wanted the Stag Brewery only, for redevelopment, and not the pubs. I remember going to the Stag Brewery in Victoria in order to interview Simon Combe, the chairman of Watneys, in his old-fashioned comfortable office which had a couple of black family deed boxes by his desk. He was the epitome of the traditional brewer, the gentleman businessman who, having learned with great surprise that his company had considerable undervalued property assets, wanted to keep it that way.

Clore lost Watneys but gained control of Mappin & Webb and Lewis & Burroughs. He then became the proud owner of the Stype Estate with its thousands of acres nestling near Hungerford. With the Stype Estate he also purchased a prize flock of Hampshire Down sheep which won two first prizes in the same year at the Bath & West.

That was far from all. It was in September of that year that an announcement was made. It was in respect of Clore's property company, City & Central. It was floated on the Stock Exchange by way of an offer for sale handled by Philip Hill. This was the first time Clore had used any issue house other than his own Investment Registry. The loan stock was neat and perfectly tidy, very Clore-like, as arranged by Douglas Tovey. Ten million pounds from the Legal & General for thirty years with interest at 5.5% for the first ten years, 5.7% for the next ten years and 6% for the final ten years.

Two weeks later on 14 October 1959 Mappin & Webb made a successful bid for the Royal jewellers, Garrards.

1960 was another good year. City & Central acquired Metrovincial Properties and with it Archie Sherman and Eddie Footring. The board of City & Central had lacked full-time property expertise and Archie Sherman, suggested to Clore by Tovey, provided consummate property expertise. Also with the acquisition came Suburb Leaseholds owning a substantial part of the Hampstead Garden Suburb comprising a veritable self-contained garden city. On the twentieth of the same month he sold Lewis & Burroughs to a consortium which included Selim Zilkha and Jimmy Goldsmith. This started Zilkha on the road to making the fortunes of Mothercare, whose original name was L. Harris & Co., the pram and baby clothes subsidiary of Lewis & Burroughs: it also started Goldsmith on his own spectacular career. In March, Clore was named the buyer at a record price of £27,000 for an Aberdeen Angus bull. In March too the contract was agreed for the new Hilton Hotel. It had taken eight years to assemble the site and to obtain detailed planning consent, but it took Tovey all of twenty-four hours to raise the £6 million of building finance from the Prudential. Photographs were published of Charles Clore and Conrad Hilton posing on the site. In early May Clore let a new office building, 70/80 Oxford Street, to Colgate-Palmolive.

In June Clore started the development of a new office building and theatre on the old Stoll Theatre site in Kingsway, and also the development of Villiers House in the Strand. In September 1960 he bought 40 Wall Street, at that time one of the tallest office buildings in the world. A fortnight later Douglas Tovey had lunch with him at Stype, his recently acquired Berkshire estate, after seeing Jack Cotton earlier that day at Marlow, to suggest that the two tycoons should merge their property companies.

Chapter Five

All the way to Heaven with the Upward Rent Review

To understand the ethos of Jack Cotton and his partner Charles Clore, and indeed of the other property giants like Samuel of Land Securities and Sidney Mason of Hammersons, it is essential to understand two extraordinary investment phenomena of the fifties: the pension fund and the rent review. They suited each other to perfection; they were indeed tailor-made for each other. On the one hand, immense amounts of new monies were avalanching into the pension funds, on the other, the funds had a desperate need for an acceptable investment receptacle to house these monies, and this receptacle not only had to be able to swallow and digest these enormous quantities of monies, it had to be totally secure and inflation-proof. Clearly, property was the answer, and it became so primarily because the rent review provided the perfect arithmetical fit.

As to these remarkable pension funds I suppose, over the years, apart from John Plender the acknowledged expert, I have become as well acquainted with them as anyone in the City: certainly I have established as many direct pension fund associations and partnerships as anyone. Why these associations? It stemmed, I now see, from my perceiving whilst I was at the *Investors' Chronicle* that an extraordinary investment revolution was taking place under my very nose, and my wanting — and indeed in a tiny way succeeding — to play a part in it.

However it was Jack Cotton above all others who first appreciated that pension funds were tiny acorns compared to the oak trees they would become in five, ten or twenty years' time. Moreover, it was surprising how they were being neglected or ignored by most of the investment world. The City was being extremely tardy in appreciating that the pension fund managers had a pressing and urgent need to seek and find appropriate outlets for immediate and future investment. It was perceived by Cotton that the pension funds would require definite servicing and that a main investment outlet could and should be property. If each side could succeed in understanding the other on property, why could they not, some of us asked, also understand each other on direct investment in unquoted companies in other activities, particularly in venture capital? As the pension funds increased in size they could set aside certain monies for new ventures, they could act as activists themselves, they could apply the entrepreneur's unique skills to their own advantage, as they were learning to do in property.

Subsequently, at Hambros in the Bentworth Group subsidiary, we were the first to transact a direct investment by a pension fund in venture capital. Vista Television, a successful venture capital investment in a new TV rental company, subsequently sold to Radio Rentals and now owned by Thorn, was initially financed by Unilever pension fund money. A few of us realized that it was not only the quantitative amounts of money which comprised the real strength of the pension funds but the fact that these monies were their own, not, as in a bank, other people's money, not, as with insurance companies, other people's premiums. The pension funds knew precisely in advance the actual amount of cash coming in each week and they made their own decisions as to how to spend their own money. This has always been their main strength. It is I believe absolutely appropriate that they should pursue investment routes as catalysts rather than as followers, that they should gradually assume the mantle of venture capitalists themselves so as to take the lead in the creation of wealth which, within a properly functioning, property-owning mixed economy, should derive appropriately from the monies arising from tens of millions of people through their collective pension funds.

The property era of the fifties and sixties and beyond can therefore only be understood within the context of the startling rise to power and the meteoric rise of the pension funds. The inherent funds of the insurance companies could never have been of sufficient quantity on their own to sustain the needs of the property investment and development market in the post-war decade, and the massive rebuilding of Britain's cities, essentially by the private sector, could only have come about because of the overwhelming weight of new monies derived from these mighty pension funds. In reverse, it is difficult to hypothesise whether their monies could have been properly and successfully invested without a real estate market.

None the less, giants or not, huge new monies available or not, without the rent review, property investment could not have competed so well over other types of investments. Without any doubt if there had been no rent review there would certainly not have been a property boom.

At the beginning there were of course no pension funds. The earliest I know of is the Guild of St James which started in 1375. 'If any of the foresaid brotherhood falls into such mischief that he hath naught for old age or able to help himself and have dwelled as the brotherhood for VIII years and done thereto all duties within the time every week after, he shall have of this common-box XIII pence for the terms of his life, or he be recovered of mischief.' Not such a Dark Age after all, but the idea of making provision for retirement did not really take hold until the mid-nineteenth century. The East India Company, the Bank of England, the new gas companies, the new railway companies, began arranging trust funds; today, it is the inalienable right of any citizen of every developed country. Here are some figures concerning the UK pension funds. In 1957 pension funds amounted in total to £2 billion of which property (not counting mortgages) comprised £44 million; in 1980 funds had reached £55.8 billion of which property was £10 billion. Here are some figures of individual pension funds: Barclays Bank pension fund had total funds in 1960 of £55 million; in 1980 the figure was £765 million. The Coal Board's pension funds in 1960 amounted to £52.2 million; in 1980 the figure was £3 billion; today it is £4.3 billion. The estimated total of all pension funds as at the end of 1983 is £100 billion. Notwithstanding these huge totals, the menacing question is what will the liabilities of these funds be to the pensioners in 10 and 20 years time, when the proportion of pensioners has increased alarmingly against the work force which is providing the weekly increments to sustain their retired predecessors. A grim future.

Thus the rent review made investment into property unassailable with its automatic frequency; the shorter the frequency the greater was its value, the better was its investment attraction and the more complete was its appeal. A new investment cult is usually brought into existence by some dynamic spur, and so it was with the rent review in bringing about the property cult. With equities, the previous cult, the spur was the new-fangled doctrine of growth stocks, born of the recognition that the terrible scourge of inflation at 2% or 3% was here to stay which, based on long range forecasts and intricate charts, persuaded fund managers to buy shares at fifty times earnings, with resonant names, now with a hollow ring, like Rolls-Royce and Elliot Automation. Rab Butler who had been brought in as Chancellor of the Exchequer by Churchill in order to halt inflation sadly did not fulfil his promise. His first budget in 1953, according to that extraordinary and most perceptive man, Brendan Bracken, 'did not include cut-backs in expenditure in the expensive apparatus of the Welfare State.' The continuing post-war inflation was aggravated by a series of devastating inflationary wage settlements in the nationalised industries. In July 1953 Bracken wrote that Butler 'will be best remembered as the man who made inflation respectable.'

Whilst inflation was rising in the early fifties to the shocking heights of 4% and 5%, the ubiquitous rent review emerged like a gift from the investment gods, and once appreciated and understood, this fabulous benefaction allowed all those fund managers and property developers who fervently clutched the rent review clause to their bosoms, also to looking upward only to thank the gods in the heavens above for the gift itself.

The simple (in concept, not in definition) rent review has altered the face of the Earth literally. Automatic and semi-automatic upward-only increases at pre-arranged fixed periods: that is the rent review, exactly and exquisitely. That is the gift which probably made more millionaires and multi-millionaires in Britain during one decade, the roaring sixties, than during any other boom in the country's entire history.

Several people claim to have initiated or invented the rent review. An early adherent certainly was the National Coal Board and its pension fund. This fund was amongst the first to invest in property, not surprisingly since the Coal Board's own property personnel also looked after the pension fund's investments. One of those looking after property at the Coal Board was Eric Rutherford Young, who was later to become Jack Cotton's chief surveyor.

The most potent voice of protest came from George Bridge, the general manager of the Legal & General. He was right in the forefront of the institutional switch into property and he spurred, prodded and jolted his joint chief surveyors, John Crickmay and Arthur Green, two most intelligent heavyweights, not only accelerating his society's move into property investment, but also into starting a dialogue with Eric Young with a view to combining forces to get better terms from the property developers and from the retailers.

The main difficulty encountered by Bridge, Young and Crickmay/ Green was that, whilst very few other funds were investing in property on a substantial scale, those which had already switched into property were happy to proceed on ninety-nine-year leasebacks with no rent review. Nevertheless on just such an informal basis their dialogue bore fruit; they decided that as far as their own funds were concerned both Legal & General and the Coal Board would actively insist on some form of rent uplift whenever possible. 'In the light of the growth of the property market over the last thirty years,' Eric Young said, 'it may sound ridiculous to think that we were sweating to get reviews at thirty-three and sixty-six years, but in this way we made a start.'

From the sitting tenants' point of view the picture was very rosy. As property had been let on long leases at fixed rentals, many tenants very often found themselves in possession of substantial profit rents and were able to sell their interests to institutions, picking up a substantial capital gain whilst paying an improved rent at market value. The profit rent aspect created a specialist market in short leaseholds (particularly attractive to the non-tax-paying pension funds), but it also created an awareness of the differences in rental value, these differences between the historic rent and the current rent throwing up tremendous capital values.

Awareness of the real situation in Britain was certainly more alive in the mind of George Bridge than anyone else with the possible exception of George Ross Goobey of the Imperial Tobacco pension fund. Bridge was positively infuriated by the long-term fixed rent, forcing the landlord into a state of defencelessness against inflation and against true growth. Bridge was not prepared to accept the established thinking on fixed returns from gilt-edged stocks. He could see vast sums of money being lost by pensioners and by policy holders if the current dogma was sustained. He exhorted Crickmay and Green to seek out situations where rents could be reviewed, thus starting the Legal & General on its grand upward-only surge into shop properties to the proud unassailable investment position it enjoys today. Indeed, George Bridge, with the courage of the entrepreneur, frequently committed his Society to an agreement in principle before he had obtained formal approval from his own Board. Bridge pushed his views very hard on behalf of his group and succeeded most spectacularly. Arthur Green once told me that he was called to a main board meeting at the behest of George Bridge to answer a query brought up by the chairman, Lord Harcourt. He wanted to know how many of their shop properties showed a return above the magic double digit — over 10%. At this time in the early sixties the Legal & General were already in possession of some of their first rent reviews following Bridge's earlier urgings, and Green could barely restrain his glee. To the utter surprise of the directors ranged around the large board table, he asked, 'Would you like me, Sir, to start with those of our properties showing a return in excess of 25%?'

There are of course numerous other examples of returns of 25% or 50% or 100%. But the rent review put in gear an exquisitely simple device which at one stroke could combat effectively the ravages of inflation and provide a return of true growth in both capital and income terms. The figures arising from a rent review are stunning. Look at it from the lender's or institutional point of view, rather than the developer's, and taking our previous example of a rent of £100,000 and a rent review every fourteen years, this showed that if rent trebled after fourteen years, the developer's net surplus increased from £1 million to £5 million. But this was based on a straight loan. If, however, the institution in making the loan to the property developer, or in buying the freehold and leasing the property back to the owner, also stated that it wished to share in the growth arising out of the rent review, the figures work out like this. Assume that the interest rate was 6.5% and the £100,000 of rent received by the owner was subject to £65,000 which the owner had to pay to the lender — to the National Coal Board pension fund, for example. This is a ratio of 100 to 65. If the rent increased from £100,000 to £300,000, the ratio is then 300 to 65. But, if the lender shared in the growth, the 65 would also treble to 195. The property developer, of course, still did marvellously well; he had an annual surplus of £105,000 instead of £35,000, with no cash investment. But the institution received a return of 19.5% on its original loan, instead of 6.5%. The same principle applies to sale and leasebacks whereby the property owner, in selling the property to an insurance company at a cost of £1 million, would take a leaseback at a rent of £65,000. If the lease taken back was a straight one, then all the benefit would accrue to the original property owner. If the lease had a clause stating that it must receive the same proportion as from the commencement of the lease, the loaning institution did very well indeed with its money. No wonder institutions, once they understood these elementary rent review truisms, found themselves eager to invest into and with the property companies. Most of those people now enjoying their pension and endowments have a lot to be thankful for to these far-sighted institutional thinkers, to the likes of George Bridge, Eric Young (his financial director at the Coal Board), Arthur John, George Ross Goobey, John Crickmay and Arthur Green.

The insurance companies were the first institutions (the very word 'institution' is a relic of nineteenth-century strait-jacketed semantics), and inside their vast edifices, at the hub of their activity, were the closet-czars: the regulators, the monitors, the button pressers, the most secret order since the Knights of Malta. In other words — the actuaries. One cannot comment on institutional investment or savings of any sort without referring to these arithmetical assassins of modern man.

Actuaries, devastating in their caution and their doom-laden prognostications, have always killed people off before their time. The word 'actuarial' is one of the most lethal in the entire language and, pleasant as most actuaries seem personally, they have for generations been executioners by administration. Any scintilla of miscalculation by an actuary can lead to a future catastrophe; they deal with hundreds of millions of pounds, their slightest error only becoming evident years later. Their task is of course not easy. After all they have to work out the current value of the premiums or weekly pensions paid in against commitments that have to be paid out years later. Of course, no actuary, indeed nobody, can state what the rates of inflation will be in the next ten or twenty years. One can only forecast. As a result actuaries tend to become less concerned with rates of inflation and more concerned with the likely long-term 'real' return on existing and future investments, which are far easier to forecast and adjust. We are now at a stage when the assumptions made in the past are being tested and paid for in real money terms which has already meant misery for tens of thousands of pensioners. In the early years of insurance companies and pension funds, with inflation at nil or thereabouts and with the amounts involved very much smaller, the problems of future liabilities were not readily apparent. It is my belief that they still aren't, although the recent attempt by British Airways to purchase the liability of the indexed linked part of their pension fund is an indication of the growing realisation of the danger. The actuaries who made those early calculations and those early decisions are now happily retired, enjoying their own pension benefits. Other than war, shortage of food, disease or a nuclear mishap, the greatest possible disaster for mankind may well arise when these actuarial calculations explode. Meanwhile, the entire developed world is ruled by honourable but unknown men who are not even subject to an independent audit; most of the population have never even met an actuary. These invisible men work out the rates, make their calculations, present complex tables of figures which are agreed by committees, trustees, boards, civil servants and government ministers. Few of these, if any, understand actuaries' assumptions, or how their figures are arrived at. Yet the decisions made are monumental. There is not even an elementary checking system so that the public or the decision makers can be assured that what has been approved is going to work and that what was approved last year or a decade ago is still on the right track. Figures are accepted by serious and responsible people as gospel. Elementary accountability simply does not exist. Parliament discusses pensions without basic knowledge of the underlying criteria. (But tell an MP how his own pension is affected and he will react like a scalded cat.) It is no better in industry which traditionally seems to be behind the times, particularly in the use of the new emerging skills, enterprises and professions. For example, although a large industrial company might employ tens of thousands of people, how many have a personnel or labour expert on the main board? Although computers are the main arteries of business life, how many have a member of the board with knowledgeable data processing capability? Lots of engineers, marketing experts, accountants, even financial experts, but no expert on vital aspects of a company's existence. The situation is bizarre. There is not one major industrial company, and very few banks, very few insurance companies, which have an actuary on the board to advise specifically on the enormous decisions being made on pension funds and pension rights. It is equally rare that the actuary is called to a board to explain and describe his views and statements. Actuaries ought to be flushed out. They should come into the open, not be left in dark corners playing around with hordes of figures, making calculations which, if they ever become miscalculations, could break the company they work for, or ruin its employees, or bankrupt a local authority or, indeed, the country. No annual report of any enterprise from the largest to the smallest should be presented without clear details of pension liabilities and without a full report by the company's own or consulting actuary in clear language, supported by an independent actuarial report.

On the other side of the coin, the investment managers, many of whom qualified as actuaries, the men who have to decide how to invest the funds, are an altogether different breed. They have to be, for there cannot be closet fund managers; they are far too exposed and rightly so. But reporting systems and accountability did and do vary enormously. So whilst huge gushing streams of pensioners' monies were roaring in for investment each day, it was amazing to find during this revolutionary period that in many cases the investment manager himself was virtually in sole charge of tens or hundreds of millions of pounds, reporting normally to his committee which was invariably chaired by his finance director, which in turn meant that he might be reporting to one man. The power of some of these managers was vast, with very few people really knowing what was happening — a feature of all revolutions. Most pension funds, pre- and post-war, were administered by insurance companies. If a pension fund was self-administered, the responsibilities were normally divided, with one man in charge of the pensions payable whilst another was in charge of investments, their activities run separately and mostly in isolation. Both men were usually responsible to the finance director or secretary of the company; there was usually an investment committee, but it met rarely. Another curious anomaly was that pension funds were guaranteed by the parent company. Not once had any of these guarantees been called upon. The normal guarantee was a 5% return, the parent company making up any short-fall to the fund. The financial crash of 1974 brought this invisible danger to the fore when some industrial companies were forced to transfer very substantial amounts of money out of their profits in order to put their pension funds into real solvency rather than technical solvency.

None of these institutions worked in the same way. Management structures, procedures, policies, salaries, all seemed to be different. At the *Chronicle*, as its property editor, I had to learn how to find my way around the institutional highways and by-ways, and Harold Wincott advised me that there was no better method than to start with the insurance companies on whom the managers of the pension funds had to lean heavily for guidance in their early years. The insurance companies — the doyen of institutional cadres born out of Victorian thrift, Scottish scepticism and middle-class opportunism — were the first savings institutions available to guard the upright church-goers against all mortal terrors, but not, of course, against any acts of God. Their Head Offices were designed to look like gloomy cathedrals, extolling their bureaucratic faith in savings. Yet by the mid-twentieth century, at the administrative level, the insurance companies too were extraordinarily fractured and archaic in the way they operated and managed their pension departments and property investments, which was not of much help to the pension funds learning to get their own administration in order.

After a year or so at the *Chronicle*, with guidance from senior colleagues, I started finding my way around the investment circles.

I had maintained detailed notes of all institutional property interests and I published in the *Chronicle* a list of the institutional connections between property companies and insurance companies and pension funds. It provoked an immediate reaction. Few people, even amongst the cognoscenti, had appreciated the magnitude of these new and recent associations. I received numerous calls from fund managers who on seeing the list had woken up to the horrifying fact that they were lagging behind a seminal investment shift. Several of the accepting houses also got in touch, reflecting an appallingly belated interest. Many of the brokers, and one or two jobbers too, came to the conclusion that they were neglecting an important aspect of investment and, for the first time, real competition from other brokers was being encountered by Read Hurst-Brown.* Over the next few months I was inundated with requests to give talks and lectures and was even asked to be interviewed by other financial journalists — all of which I refused. I had many invitations for lunch, all of which I accepted (the best of City lunches were then the best in Europe), and I was literally besieged by offers of jobs or partnerships or directorships, one or two of which, in a desultory way, I looked into. Desultory because I was already making up my mind on my next step, a move into the hurly-burly of property development and finance — an association with Jack Cotton.

One day late in 1960, during Jack's honeymoon with Charles, he invited me to lunch. It was on this occasion that he urged me to join him as his adviser on financial matters, working directly with him from his Dorchester suite. My immediate response was to say yes, that nothing would give me more pleasure, even if it meant working in the uncommercial ambience of Number 120. But I murmured that I was put off by his recent merger with Charles Clore. 'Don't let

---

* Read Hurst-Brown later merged with Rowe and Pitman. Although the competition has increased, they are still, I believe, the leading experts on property companies.

Charles worry you,' he said to me, 'he and I are good friends and you will also be friends when you get to know him better!'

These were oddly prophetic words, in more ways than either of us could have imagined. We discussed how we might work together, with me concentrating on the financing strategy, particularly of new acquisitions. He accepted that I would not stay too long — perhaps two or three years — as he knew I wished to work in the City, and already he was suggesting one of his own merchant banks, Hambros. I told him that I intended visiting New York for some months. We agreed to work out our housekeeping arrangements when I returned and, as he would also shortly be in New York, we would get together there for dinner and a further chat. He suggested that when I was in New York, I had to meet his New York partner, Erwin Wolfson, and his great friend, Peter Folliss — Hambros' man in New York, dear 'Peetah' who had recently been responsible with Hambros and Barclays and Schroders in raising the equity finance for Cotton's joint development with Erwin Wolfson — the Pan-American building in Park Avenue. 'See you in New York and bless you, dear boy,' were Cotton's parting words.

Chapter Six

New York, New York

In the middle of the Cotton-Clore merger mania, Nadia and I duly set off for New York. After lunch with my parents at Claridge's, we motored down to Southampton to sail on the *Queen Mary*. Nadia had travelled extensively in the United States on several Royal Ballet tours, but I'd only been once before on my 'grand tour' when I had come down from Cambridge. The Royal Ballet was embarking on one of its marathons, starting in New York and then performing in Chicago, Los Angeles, Dallas, Houston, New Orleans, Atlanta, Washington. I was going to do some work, meet a considerable number of people, see a lot of ballet and opera, have a holiday, go to a large number of parties, and prepare for my new job with the two Cs.

A few days before we sailed, I had had dinner with Felix Fenston in his spacious, ornate house in Hill Street, festooned with hunting trophies, stuffed animals and shooting impedimenta. On this particular evening he was in good form, which meant that as one of London's finest hosts he made his guests feel easy and comfortable, keeping his sharp dialectic armoury at bay. In New York he knew that many introductions had been made by my father, by Cotton, by others, and many letters had been written. Felix growled: 'Whatever you do, you have got to go and see Big Bill Zeckendorf, and I want you to meet him through me. I insist on arranging it. If you think you or I have got brains, wait till you meet him. Fantastic. But . . .' there was usually a but with Felix, 'don't do business with him. He is going to fall flat on his face.' What a prediction.

Without a doubt the most fascinating man I met in New York was Big Bill Zeckendorf. He was, I discovered, the magnet for all visitors to New York; indeed, if a British property developer returned from America without seeing Big Bill, it would have been like returning from Athens without having seen the Acropolis. Zeckendorf's brain was overwhelming; so were his manners, which were expansive, entirely natural and suffused with enormous southern charm. The Zeckendorfs had originally come from Europe in the mid-nineteenth century and had started business in Tucson, Arizona. Big Bill had all the assurance and confidence of the true entrepreneur. His personality was gentle and well-defined but his persuasiveness was so compelling that not even the most hardbitten banker could remain unmoved. He was the most astute and imaginative salesman and deal-maker and financier the American property world had ever known. In his early thirties, some twenty years before I met him, he was already known as the Grand Old Man of New York real estate, with the unprecedented honour for one so young of having an extended profile in the *New Yorker*, probably initiated by the added celebration he had earned in assembling the UN site, an enterprise which only one man could ever have achieved; and fortunately the Rockefellers had sought out that one man. Years earlier, originally working for others, he had taken control of an old-established firm of real estate brokers with the improbable name of Webb & Knapp, whose partners had included James Landauer, the very broker who brought the Pan-Am building to Jack Cotton and the very same firm which sold it to the Metropolitan Life for the record figure of $400 million twenty two years later. Zeckendorf in no time at all transformed Webb & Knapp from an inactive New York broker to the leading property developer in the US. He worked from lavish offices at the top of his building on Madison Avenue. It was the talk of Manhattan. The reception room done in tawny reds and greens was the size of a concert hall; in the centre, from floor to ceiling, was a huge space-age circle of burnished steel with only one door leading to it. This was the door to Big Bill's office. Inside this inner circle was a huge desk with surrounding chairs and a circular lift in the same gleaming steel; the lift ascended to the next floor where he had a luncheon room, also circular, and a terrace with circular tubs. The real miniature Japanese trees were not circular. Nor was his head; it was a computer. He was able to calculate anything in that wonderful head of his. He could evaluate the fourth mortgage on a building, substitute other security charged on another property, pay off the loans on that property from the proceeds of sale of a third property also encumbered by mortgages and, whilst working this out in marvellous precision with a bewildered protagonist, he could excuse himself most courteously to take a telephone call involving a similar problem. I know because more than once I sat in his office, in stunned admiration, listening to his amazing financial pyrotechnics.

A great amount has been talked and written about Big Bill Zeckendorf, much of it inaccurate and much of it by people plainly jealous of him. As the emperor of New York real estate and, in fact, not only of New York but of the whole of the United States, from a period just after the war until the mid sixties, he was easily superior to any other American developer. Each one of his property schemes was beautifully conceived. He was a true Rembrandt, forming and defining the character of a deal by one brush-stroke, by one phone call. He was a builder on an epic scale; his vision of resurrecting downtown areas was well before his time, his matching of commercial tenants to embryonic projects was extraordinarily intuitive, his feeling for good design was remarkable — I. M. Pei, the great architect, was Big Bill's protégé and still acknowledges his gratitude and admiration. With one deal after another coming from his property emporium, 343 Madison Avenue became one of the best-known addresses in the United States.

Zeckendorf was an insatiable deal-maker. His fertile mind was never at rest. It was always dreaming up deals, negotiating deals, implementing deals and then renegotiating deals. As one New York investment banker said to me, Big Bill could not see the wood for the deals. This of course was the trouble. Zeckendorf was more obsessed with making deals than with making money. Consequently he had — and had to have in order to survive — a manic need to borrow. His incessant push to obtain money against under-geared assets, against any form of unencumbered equity was incredible. His style of borrowing, his means of borrowing, his never-ending methods of borrowing, his complexity of borrowing, was a work of art. Inevitably it was this aspect of his flawed genius which finally destroyed him. Finance is oxygen; it creates and sustains the bones of assets and the flesh of earnings. It is the fresh air, the breath of business. Zeckendorf, one of the greatest-ever talents in the world of property, suffered from an ungovernable urge to over-borrow. He could not bear to own an asset on which he had not already borrowed up to the hilt; he could not abide any combination of assets on which there had not been every conceivable borrowing. Assets were not there to increase their value, to earn revenue, to add to the equity; they existed in Zeckendorf's mind to be borrowed against. They had to be squeezed for every bit of borrowing in a series of manoeuvres which only his fabulously fertile mind could possibly dream up. His borrowing finally choked him and made him bankrupt.*

He was a big man in every way; he dealt in big accounts, with the biggest companies — Alcoa, US Steel, Bethlehem Steel. His company's failure was the biggest corporate bankruptcy in the US of the time. Yet well after much richer developers who used to look down upon him have been entirely forgotten, the powerful United States institutions and corporations with whom Big Bill did business still speak highly of him today.

As usual, the Royal Ballet season at the Met was an inspiring success, always then, and alas no longer, an indication of a top New York season. The repertoire included *La Fille Mal Gardée* which, when it opened at the Royal Opera House, was immediately hailed as a masterpiece by the critics and the public alike. It was a wonderful work, lyrical and romantic, marvellously inspired with some of the most inventive dancing I'd seen and vital characters rather than the more usual ballet stereotypes. It was Frederick Ashton's best work, and in creating the leading role for Nadia he brought out all her joy in dancing and acting. No one could see the ballet without feeling more cheerful, more happy and more well-disposed towards humanity.

In those early sixties, New York was full of excitement. It was a vintage period, one of New York's very best; which meant that it was in the middle of a bull market. Xerox, Polaroid and IBM, at 60, 80, 100 times earnings, were like Greek gods reflecting the pounding rhythm of a Croesus-rich city bustling with enormous optimism. If Wall Street was happy, New York was happy, and even the parties given by the UN Ambassadors exuded that peculiar New York aroma which comes from a cheerful Wall Street. Seats at theatres were unavailable; restaurants were packed; Spyros Skouras, who, with his wife Saroula, took us to several spectacular parties, was planning to spend a small country's GNP on a film called *Cleopatra*; old New Yorkers gave 'small intimate' dinner parties in their luxurious apartments for fifty or a hundred people, the real catches being nervy Wall Street brokers and bankers rather than politicians and social lions. Money was the fuel and lubrication of the entire system, and one could see that the New Yorkers' honest, unstinting admiration for the efficacy and power of money was what gave them

* He died years later, bowed but not broken, aware of his fatal weakness and still unrepentant, still proud of his achievements (described with great candour in his memoirs, a copy of which he sent me with the generous inscription: 'To my friend Charles with great esteem').

their unique assurance, sometimes sharp, always forward-looking, which took everyone along in its heady adoration of the virtues of making it and having it and spending it.

Jack Cotton was in New York for a brief trip ensconced in his usual suite at the Waldorf Towers, where Clore also kept a suite. As a feeble joke, which just about bears repeating because of Cotton's riposte, I suggested to Jack that he should always conduct his business with Clore at the Waldorf because as both of them would be on the same premises they couldn't therefore disagree. Jack's immediate retort was that as he and Clore had suites in different parts of the building there was a floor in the argument. For Jack there was of course that extra thrill; he could look at the Pan-Am's structure from his window.

Architects in New York had never been so busy; buildings were going up everywhere, exceptionally good design was in evidence and what was more, major tenants were insisting upon it. David Rockefeller was trying to stop the up-town exodus to Park Avenue with plans for the new Chase Manhattan office building. (My brother Max, at Skidmore, Owings & Merrill — the Chase architects — was working with Gordon Bunshaft on this remarkable building and seemed to be spending as much time designing ashtrays and furniture as working on the structure.) Even budget-conscious corporations were caught in the mood and started looking for new corporate headquarters named after their companies. Rents were going up to record levels, finance was easy. It was a time when the Lever Brothers' building, completed only a few years earlier, was already middle-aged, hardly recognisable among the thrusting, lively sparkle of Palmolive, Union Carbide, Seagrams. Like the baronial keeps of the Middle Ages, the buildings reflected the strengths of these huge hierarchical corporations; ironically, with the architects' penchant for curtain-walling, they also reflected the strengths of their neighbours and competitors.

My discussions with the bankers and the institutions were engrossing. On real estate I found the approach in New York utterly different from our own. In England, a loan on a building was made on the inherent rental value, which formed the basis of the value of the building, whilst in America a loan was made against the covenant of the tenant with no concern about what rent was paid: if General Motors wanted to borrow on a building, the loan was fixed on the covenant of General Motors; it was not fixed on the size or the location or the market value or the rental of the building; this was in practical terms quite irrelevant to the US lenders. In England, institutions and the banks never went out of their way to lend to customers; soliciting and actually wanting to do business was not part of the British style. In America, the institutions and the banks believed that they were there in order to do business, in order to lend money, and they went out to lend it; business-getting was a positive policy. In England, institutions did not discuss their plans or their transactions with other institutions; it was bad manners even to regard them as competitors. In England the Victorians, those wonderfully successful hypocrites, had laid it down that borrowing was a sin and a vice, and a borrower was made to feel as if he were shaming his family or country. In America, borrowers were the salt of the earth, they were welcomed with open arms, with red carpets, and were encouraged to borrow for acquisitions, for inventory, for new plant, for anything. In England, institutional management structures and control systems and procedures were either old-fashioned, or were built around a personality. The American institutions, on the other hand, applied considerable professionalism to their systems, their people were well-trained, competent and properly motivated. In England, the institutions behaved like sheep and, because of their lack of communication and consequent timidity, there was an innate sense of insecurity. In America the institutions had ample assurance and confidence and were prepared to do anything as long as it made commercial sense and was legal. Yet in England there were innovators like Bridge, like Ross Goobey, like Edward Plumridge, who led the sheep into new fields, whilst in the US there were and are fewer innovators.

As to real estate itself, conditions in the USA as against the UK could not have been more different, considering it was the same commercial activity. Even now these basic differences are not fully recognised. The most important factor in US real estate is that the Americans quite rightly give a term of life to a building. The British do not. In America, therefore, a building is depreciated and this can be applied in several different ways. In Britain one cannot depreciate a building, other than a factory. Buildings are supposed to last forever. Not being able to depreciate buildings is poison to property investment, especially in an era of high interest rates, and this was one of the prime contributing causes of the near-death of the property market in the financial crash of 1974, working with deadly effect on the property companies' traditional disregard of cash flow. It is amazing that even now depreciation is not allowable: the authorities still apparently believe that a building, like land, is everlasting, confusing the site and the structure built on top of it. Every other asset in a balance sheet is depreciated — but not a building. How can any corporation establish its *raison d'être* on the assumption that its assets will always remain intact and that repayments can only be made out of monies from new loans based on new valuations, which they hope will always be higher? I had incidentally taken up this point early on in 1959 in the *Investors' Chronicle* in analysing the accounts of Land Securities Limited. Harold Samuel's company had raised its famous sum of £20 million with full City approval and the company did not need to show whence its capital repayments would derive; it clearly wasn't going to come out of natural cash flow. In the United States, property investment is cash flow. Take the example of a building which has a cost of $10 million. With accelerated depreciation in the early years allowed to all new owners of new buildings and new owners of old buildings, a rate of 8% can be applied. This throws off $800,000 which is itself set off against the rent. Assume the rent is $600,000. Not only is there a carry-forward loss of $200,000, but there is $600,000 of post-tax cash sitting in the bank. This same process applies for the next year and for the next few years. However, the excessive mobility of US property ownership and its basic weakness in terms of investment also arise from this factor, for each new owner can and will take the maximum depreciation. It pays to be a new owner, not for property reasons but for tax reasons. This is the pendulum swinging in the other direction, with the result that the weakness of US real estate comes from the over-emphasis of the tax implications, a trend which was thankfully reversed in the late seventies when the US investors discovered the benefits of a genuine investment programme.

On the other hand, when it came to taking an international view, I found the US institutions extremely narrow-minded — as they still are today. There was a blinkered chauvinism, a total lack of interest in anything outside America. Why bother about overseas? Very few of the American funds had any equities or interests outside North America. In discussing our British techniques of property financing, I found polite boredom; they didn't like long leases, they were not at all sure of rent review clauses or fully insured and full repairing leases. The sale and leaseback principle was all right, but they preferred first or second or third mortgages; they spurned equity associations; their job as they saw it was to obtain the maximum rate of interest on a loan with the maximum safety and that was that. They had too much money to invest and it had to be invested rapidly and competently. Property investment companies? What was the point of them? In all of Wall Street you could count the number of listed property companies on one hand.

But above all I was impressed, and I still am, by the sheer difference in size. Here is a simple example, showing also the difference in scale between Europe and the UK. At that time the largest pension fund on the continent of Europe was the Dutch Mineworkers' pension fund, standing at about £100 million, the Royal Dutch Shell pension fund was about £80 million, Unilever N V about the same, the Montedison pension fund in Italy was also about £80 million, the largest in Italy. Nestlé were the largest in Switzerland at around £60 million. If one added up the funds of all the major continental institutions the total arrived at was less than the fund of our own largest insurance company, the Prudential, which stood at that time at approximately £2,000 million. Yet if one added together the total funds of the major United Kingdom insurance companies, the total arrived at was less than the fund of one single New York insurance company, the Metropolitan Life, at that time standing at about $20 billion.

As with Wall Street, real estate was going through a boom period. More major projects were envisaged, planned and built than at any previous period in the city's history. New York was also having its first hotel boom since the depression, a sure sign of property overheating. There is an old real-estate adage which declares that you must always sell your real estate when hotels are being built, the reason being that the market has overheated and boiled over if a developer can actually finance such a nefarious thing as a hotel. Easy or soft lending has always created second-rate property and third-rate loans. Recently however, travel and tourism has established itself as a major growth industry, and indeed I now believe that the security of income for an institution from a lease on a properly operated hotel can match that of other commercial buildings. One of the few property companies then listed on the New York Stock Exchange and owning a large number of well-let but undistinguished office buildings was the big Uris Corporation. Harold Uris, an upper-class New York businessman, proud of his half-ownership with Rockefellers of the New York Hilton, showed me round when it was nearly completed. Workmen were tacking down carpets, curtains were being fixed, furniture was stacked in every corner awaiting the decorators. Being involved in an hotel was something new for Harold. I mentioned the old adage and he laughed. In 1973 the greatly respected Uris Corporation fell on hard times, much to my personal sorrow and regret.

The imposing Pan-American building on Grand Central Station, astride Park Avenue, which would inevitably block the old magnificent New York vista, was going to soar up as high as the Pan-Am Clippers — to the irritation and disgust of many New Yorkers who declared they would never fly Pan-American again. You would be able to check in downstairs, use the heliport on the top of the building and check out several hours later in London, all by courtesy of Pan-American. This seemed fine for the travellers, but the local New Yorkers, living and working near the building, were openly speculating on what would happen if a helicopter fell off the top of the building.*

Whilst this great phoenix of a building was beginning its new life, Erwin Wolfson, its creator and its inspiration, was dying of cancer. Wolfson was not only a substantial property developer in New York but was also the owner of Diesel Construction, a large building company. He had put up dozens of skyscrapers, but the Pan-American building was his dream, his major opus. And just when it was ready for the first great performance, the actual signing of the finance agreement, he found himself in embarrassing need of $20 million of risk money, $140 million in today's money. What had happened was that his major tenant, Pan-American Airways, headed by the wily Juan Trippe, was suddenly not yet quite ready to sign. Trippe also wanted a 10% option on the stock of the company. Without the airline's definite signed commitment, the whole elaborate financing package would fall to the ground like a pack of cards. Wolfson was desperate, he would do anything to realise his dream, except to make an arrangement with another US entrepreneur; that was too much for his inordinate pride. Big business, like life, is made up of chances. By chance, James Landauer, ex-Webb & Knapp, now the respected consultant in his own business, arranged to meet Cotton in Nassau through Peter Folliss. Every winter Landauer went to Lyford Cay, frequently playing golf with Peter Folliss who went to Nassau each month to chair the directors'

* A helicopter of New York Airways did belly-flop years later on the top of the building and fall off the side, causing fatal injuries and considerable protest and concern.

meeting of Bidco, a Bahamian trust company having Barclays DCO, Hambros and others as shareholders. Once one of the regular rich exiles on the Union Castle mail boats to South Africa for the winter, Jack Cotton had by now forsaken that country and instead wintered in the Bahamas. In buying Lord Iliffe's lovely house on the beach he demonstrated once again his flair for acquiring and living in well located buildings.

Peter Folliss and Jim Landauer talked to Cotton. What better venue for idle chatter than on the pink Bahamian beach? What better object of discussion for Cotton, England's foremost property developer, than the prospect of developing, on Grand Central Station, one of Manhattan's largest office buildings?

Cotton was instantly intrigued by the idea of the Pan-American building. One night, long after the deal, when Jack, Peter and I were having a drink together in his suite in the Waldorf Towers, looking out towards The Building, I asked Jack how long it had taken him to make his decision on the Pan-Am. He looked at me, sucking his inevitable cigar, and in his gravelly, trenchant voice said, 'It took me a long time,' further pause for another ecstatic draw on the Monte Cristo, 'exactly ten seconds.' 'Why so long?' said Peter, laughing. 'Dear Peetah, I had to finish drawing on my cigar before I said yes, didn't I?' Why the inexorable certainty to go ahead? 'Well,' said Jack, 'when I first talked to Erwin on the telephone before meeting him in New York, I wanted confirmation on one point only. I asked him, is it on the Grand Central Station, or is it near Grand Central? Erwin told me, "On, not near." On was all I wanted to know.' Peter had, of course, heard all this many times before, but he listened to it amiably, as he did to all Jack's stories.

As I learnt later when I got to know him better and when I developed a great affection for him, Folliss's problem was that he relied on the old-fashioned virtues, firmly conducting business on the basic lines of fair play, an irrelevant anachronism in the savage commercialism of Wall Street. If it were not for Folliss, I very much doubt whether Cotton would have entered the US property market, and if Cotton had not become involved in the Pan-Am building I also doubt whether Clore, so much attracted by the magnetism of Manhattan, would have been drawn to merge with him. That first talk between Cotton, Landauer and Folliss at Lord Iliffe's house sowed the historic seeds, not only of Cotton's involvement with the Pan-Am building, but also of his later involvement with Clore.

Folliss, dependable and bright with a sort of bulldog persistence, had the air of a golden boy, and Jack Cotton adored him as a younger brother. When Cotton eventually resigned, dear Peetah, the loyal buddy, the strong man who had worked in intelligence during the war, broke up and wept; he knew the resignation would kill Jack. The last time I saw Peter Folliss was many years later, just a few weeks before his own death, in 1970. We had dinner together; we talked about Hambros, about the Pan-Am building and about the two tycoons. We were both very aware that my growing friendship with Clore which was as much a surprise to him as it was to me had somehow come between us.

From 1960 onwards, Peter Folliss was pursued by Clore in New York because he was glamorous, because he knew Kennedy and was a social member of the Camelot set, and because he went to the best parties. Folliss was always wary of what he called the 'Clore time bomb' and constantly warned Jack, who took no notice. This man who created the momentous Pan-Am transaction for Jack, was as good-looking as a film star, tall, well-built, with an amiable and strong face. During the war whilst in intelligence he had met Sir Charles Hambro and Harry Sporborg. Later he became an investment banker in New York with the old Empire Trust until he was appointed Hambros' top man in New York after they had purchased Laidlaws, an investment bank which he had introduced to them. He was one of the best liked, most popular Englishmen in Wall Street. He was, however, an enigma to many people in London and I think the reason may have been that he had discarded England in preference to New York. How could an Englishman possibly prefer New York to London? In those days it was rather frowned upon. Suspicions of Peter troubled some people in the City, but not Sir Charles Hambro, the then chairman of Hambros, nor Lord Seebohm, the chairman of Barclays Bank DCO, nor Geoffrey Kitchen, the chairman of the Pearl Assurance, all great supporters. Nor at any time did it ever trouble Jack Cotton. These men not only recognised his qualities of integrity, loyalty and business acumen, but they also had a great fondness for him, particularly Cotton. After Cotton died, Folliss continued establishing the Hambros Laidlaw business in New York, but his zest for life was never the same.

On a Sunday in October 1970 some two years later, Peter, a good golfer, died of a heart attack on the Deepdene Course in New York. The next day, a ghastly depressing Monday, I happened to be lunching at the Savoy Grill. At a nearby table was Geoffrey Kitchen. He got up when he saw me to ask me whether I had heard about

Peter. I said I had. I suddenly found I had tears in my eyes. I was terribly embarrassed. I looked at Geoffrey and found that this great insurance magnate was also in tears.

The planning of the Pan-Am building was American efficiency *par excellence*. The foundations had to be secured between railway tracks under the station; trains were arriving and departing every eight seconds so the rate of piling had to be worked out to a split microsecond, with the work commencing at 6.30 in the morning. The long steel beams could only be brought in when actually required because there was nowhere to put them, so special trucks had been designed to make the deliveries. Being extra long, their route to the site had to be worked out exactly, so that each truck driver knew not only every inch of the route but the precise degree of steering to use at each corner, and arrived on the site at the very second when it was planned. This really was American engineering know-how and planning at its most admirable. It took only eighteen months to start and complete the huge structure, with its two and a half million square feet, nearly ten times the size of Centre Point.

From the beginning on this New York trip, Bill Jr was more than helpful in suggesting and arranging introductions to the US institutions. Later, as I describe below, I had to negotiate with him on behalf of City Centre and realized why financiers, bankers and institutions had such a regard for him. Whereas his father swayed the world by sheer strength of personality, brains and imagination, Bill Jr in his wake quietly picked up the debris, never complaining, always positive, always creating a new strong financial environment, to be plundered once again by his father. Bill Jr has sometimes been underrated, but not by those who knew him well. Certainly not by his father who was saved time and time again by his son's brilliant, patient and fastidious solutions. In New York, it was generally thought that Bill Jr was the lucky son of a great father. Far from it. In many respects, it was the other way round.

Big Bill Zeckendorf, like Jack Cotton, was a remarkable property pioneer. His penchant for having associations and partners was no less advanced, and for a while during the latter part of 1960, around the time of the merger, until the early summer of 1961, Zeckendorf, Cotton and Clore were very much in each other's sights.

At a certain stage during the various wheelings and dealings stimulated by the insistent glamour of the Pan-Am building, which seemed to have an unsettling influence on the judgments and ambitions of those who came within its Anglo-American shadow,

Cotton asked me to look into the Zeckendorf figures and prepare a report. Subsequently Bill Jr and I attempted in several meetings to reach an accommodation, but we both knew it was a waste of time. For though Clore seemed to be keen, Cotton was not even lukewarm. Perhaps it was because he was intuitively aware that in looking at the Zeckendorf syndrome there were one or two ominous similarities to his own. Perhaps too, in looking at Zeckendorf himself, he realized that here was an expert property man very much in the same league as himself, and that, he probably thought, could only lead to a frontal collision. Moreover, Erwin Wolfson supported by Peter Folliss was dead set against any association; in no way did Wolfson want his new personal link with Cotton obscured or molested in any way.

Cotton had an early foray on Zeckendorf's magnificent Place Ville-Marie project and, but for a snag over Bank of England consent, he might well have proceeded — though Bill Jr had his doubts. So once Cotton said that he was out, Bill Jr rapidly concluded a deal through Kenneth Keith (now Lord Keith) and Harry Moore with the Philip Hill/Eagle Star stable. This was the beginning of the celebrated Canadian Tri-Zec Corporation which later led to a full-scale association between the Philip Hill consortium and the Zeckendorfs.

A get-together of Zeckendorf with two such powerful entrepreneurs as Cotton and Clore was not a truly workable idea; what Big Bill needed was financial expertise rather than property expertise, and in discovering Kenneth Keith and his colleagues Bill Jr thought he had found the ideal financial set-up. In the event, it did not succeed. Despite the strong blandishments of Keith and Bill Jr, not even their combined forces could curb Big Bill. When the deal was signed, Keith was quoted as saying that Zeckendorf was their partner, but that he would be kept in a straitjacket. Keith was right to want to encapsulate the more flamboyant excesses of Zeckendorf's creative genius. Everyone, particularly Zeckendorf's own friends and allies, hoped that this time he would be restrained. But Big Bill was in a buffalo charge, he was irresistible, and no one could stop his downfall. The resonances between Cotton, with Clore wanting an orderly expansion, and Zeckendorf, with Keith wanting the same thing, are haunting.

The greatest irony, however, an almost misty part today of the Pan-Am legend, is that as usual Big Bill had been on the scene before anyone else, and unfortunately, once again, he was not in at the financial kill. Very early on, long before anyone else including Erwin Wolfson, he had conceived the idea of a building on Grand Central Station, and he even went as far as getting I. M. Pei to produce the preliminary plans; it was a very slim, very high, very elegant circular tower. With this imaginative design there would have been no blocking effect on Park Avenue, but it was destined that there was not to be a Pei in the sky above Grand Central.

One of Big Bill's better deals was 40 Wall Street, sold by him to Charles Clore in September 1960. Previously occupied by the Chase Manhattan, the building comprised one million square feet in seventy-one storeys; it was at the time the tallest building in Wall Street. It was a good seller's deal though not a particularly good buy, as a considerable amount of money was required for new air-conditioning and lifts to compete with the modern buildings going up around it.

Clore, however, was pleased with his 40 Wall Street purchase even after the refurbishment estimates, when his immediate reaction was to look at Bill Sr with renewed respect. He had told Tovey he wanted the biggest aspidistra in the world, something special for his company, and he got it. But he knew it was second best. The Pan-Am building was the star project which had captured the imagination of everyone in New York and in London. But it wasn't his; it was Jack Cotton's. This gnawed at his competitive ambitions. When the Tovey merger suggestion was first mooted, the Pan-Am building loomed largest in his mind; he saw the merger in the context of being an indirect owner of the most talked-about and most written-about building in New York. The enormous publicity engendered by this building on both sides of the Atlantic certainly turned Jack Cotton's head but it also affected the cold Mr Clore. He didn't want to be left out, having watched Cotton's dazzling ascent in 1959 with growing interest. When Tovey's idea was first expressed it could not have been better timed. Clore's business metabolism was already attuned to a positive response. Each tycoon, for reasons which suited his own particular needs at that moment, was ready to merge with the other. Tovey, I suspect, realised this and, with that rare touch of the true catalyst, planted his idea at the perfect psychological moment.

Chapter Seven

The Marriage Broker

Without any doubt the most extraordinary merger Tovey or anyone else for that matter ever dreamed up was the merger of Jack Cotton and Charles Clore. Even conceived in an aeroplane 40,000 feet above the earth it was certainly not a match made in heaven. The idea itself was created solely by Douglas Tovey. He was not only the marriage broker; he also implemented it and carried it through with tremendous imagination and professionalism. It is now a celebrated story, quoted and requoted in newspapers, journals, books and discussed in its day in bankers' parlours, boardrooms and executive suites in many of the financial centres of the world. It has been described to me by numerous people, including Cotton and Clore. Recently Tovey and I talked about it and he said, 'Let me describe it for you as it was.' So here it is in Tovey's own words.

'I had to make periodic visits to New York in 1959/1960 in connection with the management of 40 Wall Street, and it was when returning by air from one of these visits that I had time quietly to ruminate about the future. It seemed to me rather foolish for my partner Aubrey Orchard-Lisle to be scouring the property world for suitable projects for Jack Cotton and for me to be doing the same thing for Charles Clore, whilst at the same time, both of us were sitting in adjoining rooms at 29 St George Street, W1. What a good idea it would be to try and marry Jack and Charles, and merge the two companies. I felt it would have the approval of the City establishment, and the support of the institutions who were major shareholders in both companies. Also it would enable my partner Aubrey and myself to continue our future efforts and be working for the same cause.

'My plane landed at Heathrow on a Saturday evening and I went to my country house, Highmoor Park, Henley-on-Thames (my home then was in Bishops Avenue, Hampstead). That evening I telephoned Jack Cotton at his Marlow home and made arrangements to call the following morning at about 11.00 a.m. I also phoned Charles at Stype Grange [near Hungerford] and arranged to lunch there with him. I told each person I had one of my bright ideas to discuss, but I did not say what, contrary to subsequent press reports, nor did I mention the matter to my partner, Aubrey, who also had a Thames-side house at Marlow, opposite Cotton's house at that time.

'On Sunday morning I went over to Marlow. Jack was poorly and in bed. We had the usual gin and tonic and I then put my plan to Jack. He was immediately interested, particularly when I pointed out that the combined companies would then be the largest property empire in the world, relegating Harold Samuel's Land Securities to second place.

'Before meeting Jack I had carefully studied the balance sheets of both companies and I decided that a fair price would be a "one for one" deal, although Jack's shares at the time were substantially higher than those of Charles Clore, but the Clore company had, I considered, in the main better prospects and was undervalued by the Stock Exchange.

'Jack asked what terms I had in mind, and when I said "one for one", he took it calmly and asked to be excused from the room for a few minutes. I later suspected that he had gone to his study to phone his financial wizard, Lindgren.

'Jack returned to the room, shook hands and said: "OK, it's 'one for one', but I don't think you will get Charles to agree, particularly as I insist that I be chairman of the combined company".

'After another gin and tonic I left and went straight to Stype and had lunch with Charles, who was alone and also not too well, suffering considerable pain from a slipped disc.

'After lunch sitting in his study by the fire, Charles said, "Well, what's this bright idea?"

'I then told Charles the whole story, even to the fact that Jack must be the chairman etcetera. It took Charles a few seconds to think, and he then said: "I agree. Furthermore I'll even be Jack's office boy for 72/- per share."

'And so I had pulled off a £75 million idea. Charles finally said: "I'll tell Leonard Sainer to tidy the deal up in the morning."

'I phoned Jack that evening and told him Charles had agreed his terms. The deal was announced to the Stock Exchange a few days later. My fees were paid by Jack Cotton.'

To many people the merger appeared outlandish, if not bizarre. Anderson's deputy at the *Chronicle*, the late John Cobb, who was an astute observer of the City scene, came into my office as soon as he heard the news and said the only possible name now surely for Cotton and Clore was the Clots. But the idea for the merger was by no means clottish. It could actually have worked, and been made to work, if something as elementary as the mechanics for decision-making between the two tycoons had been properly worked out, notwithstanding the fact that Cotton made a fateful blunder, of which more later, within the first few months of their new relationship when he deliberately misplaced Clore at an important lunch in New York. It was absolutely crucial that their decision-making be put on a sound basis, for everyone knew that the most difficult hurdle to overcome in the marriage would be the agreed method of restraint upon Jack's lifelong habit of committing first and financing second. Though this was not in itself an unacceptable method of operation, making commitments without prior financing was to Clore like a red rag to a bull. An open-ended financial situation was diametrically opposed to his lifelong habit, indeed his fear, of never going out of his depth. Jack Cotton's particular weakness was known to all, and every effort should have been engineered to circumvent it, or better, immunise it. The City questioned the merger on the differences in the personalities, but the property community knew better. It was not a question of personalities, the two Cs would get on because business is business and they were both consummate entrepreneurs. But the property experts questioned the operational set-up. When Clore first told Sherman and Footring, his two full-time executives in City & Central, these two shrewd operators responded with only one question: 'Will it work, Mr Clore?' What they meant was, 'Who will say no?' not 'Do you like each other?' Many amongst the cognoscenti believed that with the correct checks and balances it could have worked. Both protagonists were shrewd and intelligent; they were very aware of the real dangers. If the merger was going to be a success each of them knew that there would have to be give and take. But one thing Clore couldn't possibly take would be unfinanced commitments.

Just as Lindgren had a key role to play as Cotton's right hand man which he did with exemplary patience and tenacity, but whose advice did not have sufficient influence, Sainer played his key role as Clore's right-hand man to perfection, where his advice was never ignored. His function was to carry out Clore's wishes, commands, decisions. But did he, deep down, really want Clore to amalgamate his own well-run property company with that of Jack Cotton? Until the merger the sensational growth of Sears was due in no small part to the remarkable association of Clore and Sainer, each seemingly in perfect tandem with the other. It was a very workable, very effective relationship, one of the most effective in British industry. It had been in smooth existence for years. Few if any mistakes had been made. Sainer felt comfortable in his role, further cosseted by the fact that his own law firm was growing rapidly and solidly, attracting many other important clients who recognised the superior intelligence and outstanding ability of Clore's exceptional number two.

But the merger with Cotton was different; it would be the first time that Clore would have an equal partner. Leonard Sainer himself was Sainer to Charles Clore, not Leonard; that came much later. He was the lawyer, the subordinate, not the partner. He was on limited social terms with Clore, attending the occasional cocktail party or business lunch at his house in London. It was a close but detached relationship. As for the very rich Archie Sherman who ran the Clore property empire, he too was not considered a partner, never mind an equal partner: he was a working director and shareholder. There were no partners working full-time in the Clore empire; there were paid directors who were also rich shareholders; there were subordinates and only subordinates. They called him Mr Clore; they doffed their caps even though they might run subsidiaries with tens of thousands of people answering to them, even though they were themselves multi-millionaires. On their side they respected Mr Clore because once he was assured that they were competent and reliable he left them alone.

Now with Jack Cotton, however, it was very much equal partners; it was Jack and Charles, arm in arm, they were married, they were going to bed together. Cotton was famous, he was Big Daddy, he was powerful, he had mighty institutions on his board. He was very much on the same level as Clore. From a corporate point of view, too, as the City had already whispered, there was an obvious alternative to a merger with Cotton. Clore's company was a neat tidy operation, with monthly board meetings, excellent progress reports, first-rate management, stable sure growth. Who knows, the City sages prophesied, one day it could become the property division of Sears — acquired for shares. Then Clore could be an even larger shareholder in his own conglomerate. With a property division Sears would have even greater solidity, especially if Sherman, one of the best property brains in the country, continued to lead the property division. Consequently, leaving aside the personalities there must have been serious objections to the merger. The possible acquisition in due course by Sears of Clore's own property company would have struck the right note, it would have had the authentic ring, the clear intellectual grasp of Sainer at his best, always encompassing Clore's ambitions within the most effective corporate structure. Clore himself as he became older was increasingly reluctant to pay anything over the market price, and indeed came to believe that any price wanted by a seller was already too high. Consequently, he missed many marvellous acquisition opportunities, in particular he missed the chance to become one of the largest food retailers in the country. It was a situation in which I was involved in 1970, initiated by Jasper Knight. I had discussions with Unilever regarding the purchase from them of their controlling stake in Allied Suppliers which owned and operated a considerable number of supermarkets. I brought Clore in as the buyer. The negotiations proceeded well until, suddenly, the talks were called off. Clore explained to me that he had decided against it as the consideration was going to be in Sears shares, not in cash, and the shares were standing at a low level. I told Clore that he was making a big mistake and Clore told me that I didn't know what I was talking about. Subsequently Jimmy Goldsmith purchased Allied Suppliers, which thus became the cornerstone of his empire, taking him in one grand leap onto the levels of big business. Subsequently also Clore realised what an error had been made and joining me into it observed on many occasions at dinner tables in London that Goldsmith's good fortune had been created by a couple of proper Charlies, i.e. Charles Clore and Charles Gordon.

The history of Sears after the superb acquisition of Selfridges in 1965 lacked the dynamic thrust of the earlier years, demonstrating not only the consequences of his over-caution, but also some of the after-effects of the failure of the Cotton merger. It has virtually been forgotten that until the City Centre merger, Clore was known not only as an industrialist and as a financier but also as a property man, and that after Cotton's resignation Charles was never again looked upon as a property man. Clore and I discussed his property ambitions frequently, and as the years rolled by after Cotton's death it was more and more apparent to me that his most bitter regret was that he had failed in his ambition to be a major property force.

The mechanism set up to operate the relationship between the two tycoons was based on the idea that a committee would suffice. Neither Cotton nor Clore had ever been or ever could be a committee man. They knew it and everyone else involved knew it. No business, certainly not a dynamic property development company, could be run by a committee. Yet an executive committee was formed, made up of Jack Cotton and Freddie Lindgren, and Charles Clore and Leonard Sainer. The quartet would meet once a week, every Monday at 10 a.m. at the Dorchester. It had been set up to run a huge commercial entity, yet only one of its members, Jack Cotton, was full-time. It was decided that a new headquarters would be based at Park Place, St James's. Little, however, was done to coordinate the management of the merged company, little was done to reorganise the administration, scant attention was given to laying down the proper lines of command. Despite the fact that the other members of the board were aware of Jack's weak organisation and unrestrained flurry of commitments, few management procedures were laid down. What was acceptable in City Centre before the merger, what worked before the merger with Cotton conducting his affairs in his own idiosyncratic disorganised though vastly successful fashion, was clearly not appropriate after the merger, especially if this idiosyncratic method, inimical to the orderly and tidy nature of Clore, was not subject to definite restraints. Years later, in his laconic manner, Charles said 'Jack understood property. Early on we should have curbed him. We left it late. That's all.'

The strengths and weaknesses of the separate companies and of the two men who formed and headed their separate corporations were different, but they were essentially complementary. Together there could have been added strength. What was lacking, it seems to me, was a sensible mechanism. One cannot overly blame Clore. He was expecting management as well as genius from Cotton.

Tovey saw and apprehended the kernel of success, he saw that each side could complement omissions and gaps in the other, he saw that if sufficient effort was made Cotton and Clore could have a workable relationship. This is borne out by looking at the way each company operated. City Centre was a sprawling set-up with several separate offices in London and Birmingham and undefined functions, performed by directors of subsidiary companies and by Jack Cotton & Partners in Birmingham. Secretarial services were carried out by the group secretary, by the company accountant and by Lindgren's firm, Clark Battam. Property management services were performed by agents, or by the directors and staff of the subsidiaries, or by the group secretary. The first-ever group surveyor, Eric Young, had only been appointed a few months before the merger. The chairman, the stellar presence working from the Dorchester, was making decisions and making commitments with no formal procedures to implement them; Eric Young described the organisation soon after his appointment as 'a veritable mess'. Very few notes were made of any of Cotton's meetings, some of which were of great importance. He simply relied on his amazing memory. Board meetings were intermittent and nearly all of the members were in any event non-executive; although the institutional directors, George Bridge of the Legal & General and Edward Plumridge of the Pearl, were concerned at the lack of organisation and the paucity of even the most elementary paperwork, they went no further than recommending that a group surveyor be appointed. One of the benefits they were obviously anticipating from the merger was that administration would improve. Many entrepreneurs are untidy, believing that this is a patent manifestation of their genius, so they tend to rely on their talents, memories and charisma to get them through. For a private company this is bad enough, but in a public company it is deplorable. Some entrepreneurs go further and tend to instill the feeling amongst their colleagues and associates that being orderly is incompatible with their creativity, that they should not be restrained and shackled. They also tend to despise a tidy approach, seeing it as a substitute for talent and as an impediment blocking their own supernatural powers. Entrepreneurs should at the least be sensible enough to have full-time managers who can interpret and guide and channel their undoubted talents into the mainstream of good administration and good organisation. The art of big business is the marrying of entrepreneurial talent with professional management.

No business can survive for long without proper leadership. The man at the top, whether he is a commercial bureaucrat or a one-off entrepreneur, has to lead his organisation. Heads of companies with no entrepreneurial skill themselves or with no skill in monitoring or handling entrepreneurs will eventually lead their companies up blind alleys, just as entrepreneurs heading their companies with no skill to manage and no capacity to take on first-rate management, will do the same. It is a very rare bird indeed who can do both. Sir Val Duncan, who built up Rio Tinto Zinc from a £3 million neglected South of Spain mining company to one of the world's largest, was one such man; another was Sir Joseph Lockwood of EMI who took over His Master's Voice on the verge of bankruptcy and built it up to a market capitalisation of £200 million when he retired twenty years later; another is Mark Weinberg, who founded Hambro Life and who within only a few years brought Hambro Life to a market value of £500 million, more than twice the market value of the bank itself; and another was Sir Maxwell Joseph, a great entrepreneur who built up Grand Metropolitan into one of the largest companies in Europe employing consummate skill in organising first-rate business bureaucracy under him. Tragically Cotton was not one of these rare birds. He was an entrepreneur *par excellence* with immense vision and with profound understanding of property, but he had very little idea of how to set up a team to manage an expanding enterprise. What he was best at was perceiving which property situation should be exploited and knowing how best to exploit it from a financial and real estate point of view. As the controlling chairman of City Centre he ran his company with flair and flamboyance and with impunity. After the merger with Clore it was essential that a management device be installed to process his decisions. This would have allowed him to execute his undoubted talents, whilst others could have cleared up after him. In setting up the Monday committee this was not provided. On the contrary, the committee itself acted against Cotton's nature and forced him to spend more of his own time on administration, creating more confusion rather than less, so he spent more time seeking to justify his actions to the committee and eventually to his own main board. Moreover he reacted strongly against verbal strictures, and he rushed ever more headlong into new ventures, some of which lacked his marvellous feel and intuition; then, as his confidence diminished, he attempted to shore it up by a helter-skelter of activity, designed also in his mind to shore up his partnership with Clore. Of course it did the reverse. It was inevitable that there would be a convergence between his increasing deal-making and his increasing administrative chores.

At City & Central on the other hand, the small Clore-led board ran a very tight ship. Sherman as the expert property man and Footring as the expert lawyer operated the company from a small well-directed office in Hay Hill with consummate efficiency. Sherman, who had a charming disposition towards extreme parsimony, who hated overheads as a necessary but evil ingredient in business, who took a bus rather than a taxi, was a most effective property money-maker, specialising in shop reversions which would bring in hefty surpluses in five, seven, fourteen, twenty-one years' time. Footring, in charge of the conveyancing and the legal administration, had a sparse competent touch. Clore and Sainer had to ratify everything at their regular monthly board meetings; nothing escaped their attention nor their scrutiny. Their style of work could not have been more different from Cotton's.

The two companies also had completely different property policies. City Centre was expanding by purchasing sites for development and by purchasing portfolios with development potential. Cotton thought in terms of development of sites, of new buildings, whereas Clore, though not uninterested in development (indeed his initial portfolio included some brilliant developments), preferred reversions. His policy was inclined to classic, well-let investment properties with superb Sherman-type reversions to come. The Hampstead Garden Suburb acquisition was a typical City & Central acquisition; it was one which Cotton would have turned down before breakfast; it was too long-term, too boring, too residential.

Cotton had expanded on the then orthodox policy of deficit financing, of debiting all the costs of the development to the capital cost of the project, an accounting procedure now considered improvident but recognised and authorised in the fifties and early sixties. Clore, however, expanded by judicious selection: existing investments against new developments. The two companies also had completely different financing policies. City Centre raised finance by associating with institutions and securing the finance on new developments through giving away part of the equity. This was a new method at the time, of which Cotton was the pioneer. Today it is virtually the only means available, other than a forward sale to the institutions or a side-by-side arrangement or a rights issue. Clore, however, only liked to borrow against his existing assets — the key to his takeover technique. He bought existing undervalued assets and after revaluation and refinancing they underpinned further purchases. He gave nothing away. Both methods were sound, were indeed complementary to each other.

Yet the combination of the two groups *was* essentially workable. The intrinsic recipe for the merger was a good one, and there were sufficient ingredients to have made it work. It didn't work for two simple reasons, one that Cotton's management follow-through was weak, and two, that an adequate mechanism had not been constructed to control and channel his undoubted property genius. A serious contributory factor was that Clore's City & Central board remained unchanged and was not enlarged by the addition of Cotton.

From that Sunday morning at Marlow, from the moment Tovey first broached the subject, Jack Cotton was a man possessed, all thoughts concentrating solely on the wide-angled potential of his merger with Charles Clore. He was in tremendous spirits, not concerned at all with the minutiae, not concerned at all with the *modus operandi*. His mind dwelt only on the good things to arise from the possible merger, the glamour, the press, the scale. He talked to his cronies in Birmingham; to Freddie Lindgren, to Edward Plumridge of the Pearl Assurance, to George Bridge of the Legal & General, to Aubrey Orchard-Lisle, to Harry Sporborg of Hambros, to Freddie Seebohm of Barclays, to Eric Rutherford Young, to Isadore Kerman, and to Peter Folliss. The responses were mostly negative, with several dire warnings of disaster. But Jack was not disposed to listen to anyone.

Eric Young was to move from the Dorchester to the new HQ at Park Place, together with his staff and his filing cabinets, thus freeing space for Jeremy, Cotton's youngest son, to work for a while with his father. Jack Cotton did not want Young to go. Young said to Cotton, 'Jack, either I build up a team to look after the group's properties or I stay at the Dorchester to look after you.' Cotton assented, on condition that Young came to see him each evening at 6 p.m. At the end of September, during one of these encounters whilst Jack was changing for dinner, Eric sat in his bedroom suite nursing his gin and tonic. Jack asked him: 'If I were to marry Charles, what would you think about it?' Eric, who had met Charles Clore several times during his Coal Board days, said, 'You know exactly what I think, Jack. It'll be all right as long as you wear the trousers.' At that point, Eric recalled, Jack had one leg in his trousers and, hitching up his fly, he declared laughing, 'That is exactly what I am going to do.'

The merger discussions following Tovey's historic Sunday match-making were conducted in great secrecy. Eric Young was already perturbed. Though he was chief surveyor to the group, he wasn't asked to check the portfolio valuation of either City Centre or City & Central, nor asked to report at any of the later formal meetings with accountants, stockbrokers and bankers. Kerman also observes that Jack brought in no advisers. He had already made up his mind to go ahead and there were to be no pre-contract negotiations. In Kerman's view Jack's overwhelming drive at that time was not so much to get into bed with Clore but to be bigger than Harold Samuel: 'It was his fixation. In Jack's mind merging with Charles would make him bigger than Harold.' He is also of the opinion that Jack's unstoppable megalomania which developed after the Pan-Am announcement also spurred on his Samuel fixation. 'Before that he was quiet and effective behind the scenes. The Pan-Am was the turning point — the television interviews went to his head. They actually came down to Marlow, to photograph and interview him. He was showing the UK flag in the US. From the day he returned from New York, after the Pan-Am signing, he could only think of publicity, of getting bigger and that meant getting bigger than Harold Samuel.'

Isadore Kerman used all his efforts to dissuade Jack from going ahead with the merger but he refused to listen. But Kerman stressed the one point of extreme danger to Jack that he would have to understand that he could not possibly continue to run his business as before. The informal communication between Cotton, Lindgren, Plumridge and himself would be no more. Kerman impressed upon Jack that his method of work would have to change, because Clore would insist upon it. Jack was deaf to his advice, but worse, he made it clear to Kerman that he did not see any reason why he should change his ways. 'Charles must take me as I am.' This was euphoric bluster. Deep down Cotton wanted restraint. He needed it emotionally, he possibly thought it would be imposed in some gracious, acceptable way. Like a spoiled child wanting discipline his excesses were part of trying to attract attention. Early on it could have been done elegantly and effectively.

Bill Zeckendorf Jr recalls an incident at a cocktail party during the merger fever, just before the actual announcement. He and his father were in London having their discussions with Kenneth Keith on Place Ville-Marie, and they attended a party given by Mrs Evelyn Sharp — the owner of several New York hotels subsequently purchased by the Zeckendorfs — for her many English friends at Claridge's. 'Suddenly half way through the evening,' Bill Jr recounts, 'when Charles and Jack saw Dad, they both came towards us and took us over to a corner of the room. They said they wanted to tell us something very confidential. Cotton held up his glass. "Bill," he said, "We would like you to be one of the first to know that Charles and I have decided to get married." We drank their health and as Jack and Charles walked off together arm-in-arm, Dad said to me, "It will break up in a fist fight in six weeks."'

Folliss, in a last attempt to stop Jack from going ahead, flew over from New York. He was particularly concerned because of his personal responsibility to the banks on the Pan-Am financing. He

90

spent one uninterrupted day with Cotton, strenuously trying to dissuade him. He pointed out that the banks in Wall Street and the institutions in New York would not care for the merger, that since the Pan-American financing they had got used to the Cotton balance sheet, that Sir Charles Hambro, chairman of Hambros Bank, might be averse to it, that Erwin Wolfson disliked Clore, that he was utterly convinced that Cotton would not get on with Clore. And so it went on; Cotton listened, smoking his cigar. Folliss later told me that Jack's final comment was, 'Peetah, you are wrong. Leave it to me, leave it to Big Daddy. If necessary I will kill Clore with kindness.' This was the epitaph that should have been on Jack's tombstone.

Folliss gave up. He realised there was not the slightest chance of changing Jack's mind, and it was from this moment that the daily transatlantic calls from Cotton to Folliss commenced. Cotton normally called Folliss around midnight, when most of his friends would have departed from the Dorchester suite, when Folliss on the other side of the Atlantic would have returned to his Park Avenue apartment from his Wall Street office, having had a drink with friends at the Knickerbocker on the way home. Folliss would receive a blow-by-blow account of the day's happenings. These daily calls from the Dorchester stopped abruptly the day Jack resigned and then they took place in reverse: 'Dear Peetah' calling up every day enquiring about the health of his dearest friend.

In the meantime, there were distinct leaks about the impending merger in the City, leaks that today would have started a hundred Stock Exchange enquiries. City & Central had started its quoted life at 125p in September 1959; it had jumped to 180p by the year's end and levelled off at 200p. City Centre was 275p in September 1959, it went over 300p during the next three months on the Pan-Am excitement, by June 1960 it was around 275p again, against City & Central's stable 200p. But then the fireworks began. From the beginning of September, after Douglas Tovey's historic Sunday manoeuvre, City & Central jumped from 200p to over 250p by the end of the month. It started hitting the 300p mark within two weeks against City Centre's 325p. On 24 October, the day before the official announcement City & Central was 350p against City Centre's 365p. Clore's company had risen by 75% in under thirty days.

The official announcement of the merger was made on 25th October. Of all the consequent formal merger documents the one to my mind which is the most fascinating in the light of events is the formal letter from Charles Clore sent to the shareholders of his company City & Central. In this document 'Properties' refers to Cotton's City Centre and 'Investments' to City & Central. The section of Clore's letter headed 'Advantages of Amalgamation' reads as follows:

(a) Properties and Investments as amalgamated will be the largest property holding and development group in the United Kingdom.
(b) Both Companies at present enjoy strong financial links with some of the major insurance companies and other large institutional investors, and the new group is expected to be able to employ these connections to greater advantage.
(c) The policy of both Companies of acquiring, both in the United Kingdom and abroad, sites suitable for development and investment, will be given greater scope by the combined resources of the new group.
(d) The experience and management of the two Companies can be pooled to the benefit of the new group.

In one year the value of Clore's company had almost trebled. During the same year Cotton's company had increased 33% in value. Both companies were fairly valued before the news of the merger; but the hysteria induced by the merger fever ignored values, the shares of City Centre shot up to the stars and were never again to be as high as they were at the pre-merger level.

The media gave the announcement of the merger the full treatment. Photographs of a beaming, genuinely happy Cotton and a smiling though sombre Clore were spilled over all the front pages. The favourite photograph was one which had the marriage broker, an exuberant Douglas Tovey, standing between the bride and bridegroom.

The board of City Centre, now the parent company, was enlarged by the addition of Clore as deputy chairman, by Sainer as a vice-chairman (with Lindgren) and by Archie Sherman. But the board of City & Central remained unchanged. No one joined the board; not even Cotton. This was unprecedented. The new subsidiary given the same value as its parent company by the bid terms was going to be run precisely as before, in Clore's distinctive management style, with the same unaltered board. In other words, Clore was saying, 'Keep off.' The merger would not amount to one iota of change in the running of his own company, despite the fact that it had been taken over. This was a major error on Clore's part, for it is my belief that if Cotton had attended the subsidiary City & Central board meetings, he would have been exposed to orderliness, he would have quickly realised what a good chief executive Eddie Footring would have made, and the formal monthly contact would have made it easier to develop administrative procedures acceptable to Cotton himself, and to place the executive committee into better perspective.

But at the parent company, City Centre, Cotton's company, there were fundamental changes. Though the new executive committee and the board meetings would still take place for the time being in Cotton's Dorchester suite, the new headquarters would be set up in Park Place, St James's, housing to begin with the separate offices of Cotton's sprawling empire and later all the staff at the Dorchester other than his secretary — but including Eric Young and his staff. The new committee would meet regularly each week. The executive committee would start having an agenda and minutes. It would conform to the conventional formalities. These were the same conventional formalities which would soon be forming a noose around Jack's neck. But he was unaware of any possible future constraints. For Jack this was a period of euphoria.

By a sequence of events which, looking back, were not as coincidental as they seemed at the time, the marriage itself was agreed and announced the day before a great London luncheon. This luncheon had been fixed weeks in advance with great care, solely to mark the financing of the Pan-American building. Erwin Wolfson over from New York sat at the top table and he joined in the merger festivities passively, courteously and sadly, glowering disconsolately and feeling neglected, almost like a discarded mistress.

Many of the luminaries of the City and the property world had been invited for the lunch. Not to have been asked was the deepest possible commercial slur. This was a lunch which had originally been organised to celebrate a major deal on a single building. It is strange to think today that five or six hundred fairly to very important people could be invited to an elaborate lunch at a London hotel merely for this reason alone. It didn't seem strange then. England was just emerging from the drabness of the immediate post-war years; spending money was part of the Tory ethic and property men were far from the ogres or monsters as supposed later, though the first political whiffs had emerged, ironically enough, on Cotton's own Monico site. Within the ambience of this extraordinary lunch, the British property man was 'part' of the export trade, he was an equal to the dollar titans across the Atlantic and he was exporting his superior property skills. Property and property men were good for national self-esteem and self-confidence.

The real trouble with this celebration was that, as events turned out, the guests found they were not celebrating the consummation of a mere stupendous, $100 million, sixty-storey Manhattan office building project, but the consummation of a property marriage, the merger of two separate and colossal property interests, the marriage of Jack Cotton to Charles Clore; the marriage of ebullience to reticence, of the brilliant twinkle to the glare of a searchlight, of tactical inspiration to strategic power, of concentrated specialisation to diversified conglomeration, of kind-hearted, extravagant decency to reserved, tough-minded ruthlessness. It was the marriage of the public man to the private man, of Big Daddy to the Godfather.

At the lunch in the vast clattering Ballroom, Erwin Wolfson felt and looked utterly upstaged and utterly deflated by the merger mania. He stood up and made his speech: though professional, it was hollow and flat. Jack's answer was well constructed, paying tribute where it was due, particularly towards Wolfson, with graceful remarks about the turn of events which had caused the lunch to be a double event. Charles Clore's speech was the most succinct speech I'd ever heard, very characteristic of the man. It electrified the room with its deadly shaft of humour and stark realism. 'Jack and I agreed our terms and we decided to get married. I was asked last night what I thought about our marriage. I replied, "I will let you know in the morning." Thank you, ladies and gentlemen.' There was laughter and clapping, but no one was able to overlook the chilling undertones.

At the feast Charles Clore sat next to Sir Charles Hambro. This was the first time they had met. The chairman of Sears Holdings, the diminutive Jew from the East End of London, now one of the country's outstanding industrialists, and the tall banker from Hambros, Eton and the rest, chairman of his family bank, the largest and then the most prestigious merchant bank in the City of London. On several occasions in the intervening years since their first conversation at the top table, Clore has told me how astonished he was to hear from Hambro that his association with Cotton was of very recent origin. Hambro, the upper-class merchant banker, hardly knew Cotton, who had somehow given Clore the clear impression that he and Charles Hambro were old pals. This exaggeration on

Cotton's part, and Clore's discovery at the lunch that the Hambro connection was so new, was a warning signal for Clore and was to have an important bearing on his judgment of Cotton.

Chapter Eight

'I Will Let You Know in the Morning'

I hadn't seen Cotton for some months and had lunch with him immediately after my return from New York. He could not have been more affable. He told me that he was extremely pleased that he had inveigled Eric Young — who was settling down well — to join him from the Coal Board. He wanted me to start work as soon as possible and to be based at the Dorchester until such minor matters as offices and secretaries were settled. As for terms, that was easy: how much did I want? Neither of us was particularly bothered and Jack said we could leave that till later. He wanted me to meet Clore.

Two days later, Clore and I met in his office. It was the first time we had been alone together. His personal offices were just a 100 yards from the Park Lane entrance to Cotton's Dorchester suite and 300 yards from his own house at Number 95 Park Street. Very neat, very organised. Clore's room was on the first floor, large, uncluttered and practical, no papers. I sat opposite him. He was quietly truculent. 'Well, Jack tells me that you are going to join us.' 'Yes,' I replied. Long silence. 'He says you are bloody clever. I've read your stuff in the *Chronicle*. Let me tell you, you're not as clever as you think you are.' His abruptness and shock tactics had a definite appeal. We discussed terms. 'What do you want?' 'Well, it's not a question of salary, but capital.' I said. Silence. 'Sainer will phone you.' That was all. He got up and I got up. 'Do you like paintings?' he asked. 'Yes.' 'You must come round and see the paintings in my house. Goodbye.' As interviews go, it was unusual. He said what he had to say and that was enough. As I was to learn later, he had the knack of hitting the nail very directly and simply on the head with the minimum of effort; he said what he thought and didn't beat about the bush, not caring how rude or disagreeable he was in the process. He was also right about me; I wasn't as clever as I thought I was. I never have been.

Later we were to become intimate friends. Yet soon after this interview and for two years or more, we were hardly on speaking terms; he was fighting Jack Cotton coldly and implacably whilst I was supporting Jack Cotton with all the effort I could muster. It was the beginning of 1961. I started work on Monday. My title was something vaguely financial. I was directly responsible to Jack Cotton. I was not on the payroll, I had no salary and still no capital incentive. This was to be discussed with Sainer. I had no office, but could use Eric Young's next to Cotton's in the Dorchester. I had left the *Investors' Chronicle* with sadness but no regrets. Charles Anderson, who had started me off, was sorry to see me go and wished me the best in my new career. He was a good teacher, as was Wincott, and I felt grateful to both of them for the opportunities they had given me and for their constant support. I was anxious to be on the other side, the side that created the news for the journalists and for the public, the side responsible for the results in the balance sheets, which hitherto I'd merely been analysing and interpreting.

We lived at Bruton Place just off Berkeley Square, in a typical Mayfair mews house on three floors. At the top in a spacious sunny room was housed Nadia's collection of ballet costumes, *objets*, books and photographs. (I had the chance myself of adding a unique, evocative costume to her collection; it was Nijinsky's original Petroushka costume designed by Benois in orange and red satin squares with a white blouse and the original boots.) Photographs and designs of the great dancers were on the walls. Many of these were close friends of Nadia's and they had affectionate messages written on them. In one corner were the ballet shoes she had given me when I first met her as an undergraduate in Cambridge, and below them was Alexandra Danilova's make-up box which the great ballerina on her retirement had given to Nadia. In another corner on a small table was a bronze of Pavlova together with her personal icon. These had been bestowed on Anton Dolin by Pavlova's husband and Dolin, that great dancer, had given them to Nadia. This room was one of the loveliest I had ever known or been in. In the mornings I would frequently sit and read there instead of in my study before going to work.

On my first Monday morning before going to the Dorchester, I was in the 'Nijinsky' room, re-reading the balance sheet of a company called City of London Real Property. CLRP was the most blue-blooded of all property companies and for the best possible reason, because its portfolio was blue-blooded. It was a fabulous portfolio of properties almost all of them in the City of London, almost all of them first-rate superbly let office buildings. CLRP owned property which was impossible to buy: pure gold, properties which never came on to the market, properties which were not for selling, only for keeping and keeping permanently. CLRP was most definitely in a class of its own amongst property companies, it quietly enjoyed its enviable reputation, it knew it had the best. It scorned new property developments — it did not, it believed, require to be involved in that kind of inferior, trendy activity.

In 1941, during one of the worst London blitzes, through an uncanny stroke of bad luck which later turned out to be an equally uncanny commercial blessing, a German aeroplane had dropped its bombs in a line from the Thames, up Mincing Lane, across Bishopsgate and Cannon Street to St Paul's, and every bomb fell on a building owned by CLRP. Their buildings were subsequently amongst the first new office buildings to re-appear in the City after 1945. Such are the fortunes of war.

CLRP ran its affairs in its own way; it had its own cleaning staff and services, it had its own janitors and its own refurbishing firm. The chairman was a true autocrat and the chief executive, Donald Nixon, visibly glowed with the great pride he had in his job and his company. When I first looked into CLRP at the *Chronicle*, I was struck by the pride felt in its portfolio by all levels of management and staff in their company. CLRP was an integral part of the City establishment, an unassailable bastion, whose armorial balance sheet would grow to greater and greater strengths, especially as all its wonderful reversions fell in. It was a company which would always look down from its buildings at the upstarts around it. In analysing its accounts I had invariably taken a very strong bullish view of CLRP, declaring that its shares should always be bought, that they would always be undervalued by the very nature of the reversions arising from its unequalled investment properties, that no institution should be without its large *tranche* of CLRP shares. The company was always at the top of my list for long-term investment; the best that money could buy. There were certainly other companies with excellent City properties. There was the giant Land Securities, master-minded by the inscrutable Harold Samuel, there was the tiny City Offices controlled from Palmerston House by an old Greek City family called Rodocanachi, there was Regis with its Plantation House at over 400,000 sq ft, then the second largest office building in the City after Bucklersbury House. But there was no portfolio in the country, not even that of the Prudential, which could possibly compare with the quality and size of CLRP's in the City of London.

Yet extraordinarily, almost indecently, soon after their merger, a bid was declared by Cotton and Clore for CLRP. As the joyous marriage dance between Cotton and Clore continued to the background of press adulation, as honeymoon-like emotional decisions were made before breakfast, as pragmatic thought flew out of the first floor of the Dorchester suite to be drowned in the Serpentine opposite, this crazy bid for CLRP had actually been made. In normal circumstances it could never have got to first base; it was the sort of fantasy acquisition no board would seriously have entertained, no financial adviser would have countenanced, no broker would have approved. But in early February 1961 the board of City Centre Properties, its principals enraptured with each other's entrepreneurial glamour and sex appeal and its institutional representatives caught up in the contagious honeymoon emotion, actually made an overt, formal bid for CLRP.

The City as a whole could not have been more affronted. The cheek, the audacity. Who do these vulgar chaps think they are? They must be mad; what sheer impudence. Perhaps Cotton and Clore should be called Clots after all. The press was shocked; for the first time Cotton got an unenthusiastic reaction from the press. The opening shots of attack by City Centre and defence by CLRP were fired on each side.

The first announcement had been made by City Centre a week or so before I joined them, but what intrigued me most of all was how on earth this lunatic bid had ever got off the ground in the first place. There must have been a special reason. Apart from CLRP's board and its own advisers, I probably knew more about CLRP's financing and properties than anyone else in the City, and now on this particular Monday, my first day of work, Cotton was going to brief me as an insider entitled to privileged information. I sat in the Nijinsky room refreshing my memory. The CLRP balance sheet was a thing of beauty. The gorgeous properties were in at book value, the financing was long-term at historically low interest rates; there was a significant under-borrowing and under-gearing helped by a recent rights issue raising several millions from its shareholders. The rights issue had not at the time seemed necessary and I remembered there were whispers that one of the largest shareholders and a member of the board had been critical of his colleagues. I finished reading the figures and walked to the Dorchester.

When I arrived there, Denise Tapper told me that Jack was engaged in the boardroom with Clore, Sainer and Lindgren, his regular Monday morning executive committee. She took me to the office of Eric Young, Cotton's new colleague, on the other side of the lobby. His room was more incongruous than bizarre, decorated as a bedroom and furnished as an office, one of its doors leading into a blue-tiled bathroom neatly stacked with filing cabinets, and a further door leading to other small ex-bedrooms, the offices of his secretary and his assistants; but somehow it seemed acceptable in the atmosphere of the Dorchester. Eric and I had a desultory conversation. He said that as one of Jack's boys I should expect to sit around from time to time, his meetings were flexible and he assured me that, although the general set-up was easy-going, there was a lot of work to do, perhaps too much, but I was welcome to use his office and staff any time I wished. He was busy drawing up the first detailed schedule of the group's portfolio; it would not include Clore's City & Central as they were running things on their own and although he was group surveyor he had no cognisance over them. He complained that there were no adequate systems, no procedures, not even essential documentation, and that what did exist was housed in different offices. He was finding it very difficult getting things in order and though he liked the Dorchester he was looking forward to moving to the new HQ in Park Place despite Jack's disapproval. At the Coal Board, he said, the systems had been orderly, he was proud of the work he had done there and was determined to bring the same order to City Centre, but his trouble was that Jack continually dumped new proposals on his desk. He was inundated, working enormously long hours, but he enjoyed it because it was fun. Jack was a real inspiration. And what was I going to do?

I wondered how on earth Cotton had possibly managed before Eric Young arrived and I also wondered how my own appointment would fit into this amorphous set-up. I was not a professional accountant, nor for that matter a professional financial adviser. What was I? An expert on property shares and on property financing; but this was not a recognised profession. I was not going to fit into any conventional management structure. Nor did I wish to; any contribution I was to make would have to come from my own initiative and resolution as a budding entrepreneur. Indeed Eric Young sensed this very early on in our relationship and, just as I looked to him on all property matters, he looked to me when it came to financing and acquisitions and takeovers. He may not have known the value of a convertible debenture, but he certainly knew the value of a building.

After a while, Denise Tapper came in to say that Jack would see me. Eric said he would be joining us later for lunch. It was part of Jack's natural manner to make everyone feel genuinely welcome. After the pleasantries, he asked, 'What do you think of CLRP? Don't tell me,' he added quickly, 'I can see you don't like it.' I asked him how it had started. He told me that Aubrey Orchard-Lisle had recently met Christopher Reeves at a dinner party, and Reeves had there and then indicated to Orchard-Lisle that he would welcome an offer for his shares; he wished to sell because he was fed up with the management. Christopher Reeves controlled directly or through his trusts nearly 20% of the total capital of CLRP. Aubrey mentioned the conversation to Jack who went into action immediately, although Clore was away in New York. He got hold of Reeves and made a firm arrangement whereby Reeves would sell his shares on condition that a bid was made for the whole company. Reeves, it sounded like Kit Reeves, who was odd man out on the board. There were numerous Reeves in the City; all part of a distinguished City family, aldermen, members of liveries, City property owners, they were so ingrained in the City they had probably walked from Southwark to Canterbury. Was this another Reeve's Tale? Cotton said no, Reeves had made an unequivocal promise to him at his meeting to accept any reasonable offer made by City Centre on behalf of his and his trusts' holdings. 'He gave me his word,' said Cotton. Had Jack been in touch with Reeves since the bid was made? Yes, he had spoken to Reeves after the announcement of the bid was made. I asked Jack if I could enquire whether it was the same difficult Reeves I had heard about in the City. 'Go ahead, my boy. Bless you.' Cotton was quite unperturbed. Someone, an impeccable City gentleman, had given his word; this was quite enough for him. This was the way he did his business.

Of more immediacy Cotton made it clear to me that he urgently wanted me to prepare my own calculations on the CLRP bid terms. What he wanted were estimates of the true income and the value of the shares based on different bid terms and the way the City Centre balance sheet and profit and loss accounts would look after the takeover. He told me to be ready to discuss my figures with Hambros and Schroders when required by him. A meeting had been called for the next morning at 9.00 a.m. on the CLRP bid and he wanted me there. It was the first to be called since Clore's return. He expected these takeover meetings to take place most mornings until he had acquired CLRP. He needed the figures by 6.00 p.m. that day, and they were so confidential that Miss Tapper would type them and I was not to talk to anyone about them unless instructed by him. Subject closed. We were going to lunch downstairs. Eric was going to join us, it was to be just the three of us. He wanted to talk about Walter Flack.

This first conversation about CLRP took place in the spacious boardroom of his suite, a room which will always remain vividly in my memory. One of its doors led through an ante-room to his personal bedroom suite, another door opened on to a central lobby. From that lobby there were doors leading to Miss Tapper's office, to the large drawing room which housed the Renoirs and the Rembrandt, to Eric Young's offices and to the formal front door of Number 120. Jack Cotton's own bedroom suite could be reached from both the main lobby and from the boardroom, and it also had its own separate front door. The proportions of the boardroom itself were perfect, with large windows in a bay looking down over Park Lane and across Hyde Park. In a corner by the window was his desk. He would sit there with his back to Hyde Park when he dictated his correspondence and when he was on the telephone. There were reams of paper in fairly neat piles on the desk; only Miss Tapper could ever find the papers he wanted.

The most crucial and vital instrument of work for Jack Cotton was not his telephone, but his bulky red *Economist* diary. It would always be by his side, on the boardroom table or on the desk; every entry was made in that diary, nothing was left out. All invitations were pinned to the relevant pages, and later, as the year progressed towards June and July there were as many invitations pinned to each page as there were entries. June was the season, Jack's season. It was Ascot and it was during Royal Ascot week on Thursday, Ladies' Day, that Jack gave his celebrated annual party on the riverside lawn of his house at Marlow. A splendid occasion, the long June evening, pretty clothes, grey Ascot suits, most of the guests flushed with the excitement of the day and the never-ending champagne. I am quite sure that there were more Rolls Royces outside Jack Cotton's house in Marlow on Ladies' Day than outside any other place at any other time throughout the country. He was a most popular host.

In the middle of his boardroom was a large Chippendale table with comfortable chairs. It would seat fourteen for a large meeting and was normally arranged for ten. Cotton liked sitting at the head of the table, near his desk. On the walls behind him were the most ravishing Fantin-Latour flower paintings. There were some days when the Fantin-Latours seemed more alive than the real flowers. And there were always real fresh flowers in the suite, a profusion of them, home-grown and brought directly from Marlow in their hundreds by Browning, Jack's chauffeur, in the larger of the two Rolls, the number JC 1 of course, the second Rolls JC 2, the personal fleet ending at JC 9 with a shooting-brake. The Dorchester suite had five Fantin-Latours in all; Cotton loved flowers and seemed to love flower paintings as much or even more. At Marlow he grew thousands of tulips of varying shades, and just as he could recall his bridge hands and every one of his leases, he could just as easily recall the exact number of every shade of tulip he had grown each year at Marlow. At the other end of the boardroom, opposite the windows by the door leading to his bedroom suite, was an ornate walnut cabinet, which served two purposes, both practical. One purpose was to house the plans and designs of buildings and projects, the other was to house the drinks.

During Jack Cotton's later years it used to be said by many that he drank far too much. There is no doubt that he was a heavy drinker and that in the final year or so before he resigned he drank to excess, and then mostly in the evenings. Sir Charles Villiers recalls that in the mid-fifties, at his first lunch at Helbert Wagg, Cotton held up his wine glass and said, 'My father always said I had a weakness. I know I have an Achilles heel. And this is what it is.' Before the actual battle with Clore, before his nerves went, he was able to contain this propensity in spite of a rather light head. One gin and tonic before lunch would be enough to go straight to his head. Indeed he deprecated hard day-time drinking and was vexed and sad when he realised that Walter Flack had his first large scotch at ten in the morning. Drink never affected Cotton's judgment, but rather, it affected the judgment that others had of him.

Eric came in to join us and brought his new employer up to date on several matters which had occurred that morning. Then a wave of the arm from Cotton towards us — the boys — 'Denise, tell them downstairs that we are coming down. Come along, come along,' with his arms outstretched, pushing us forward in front of him. His suite was at the far end of the hotel. We went downstairs and walked through the main ballroom to the restaurant. Whenever there was a formal luncheon in the ballroom we would walk through the kitchen, to the delight of the chefs. The staff at the Dorchester seemed to have a particular affection for this friendly property tycoon, who would enter any room as if he was a star facing his audience, looking round appraising with a sharp eye who was there and who would recognise him. He was always recognised. Coming into the restaurant that day he was greeted or waved to by several people at several tables. A large number of people would specifically go to the Dorchester for lunch and hope to greet the great man himself and possibly have a chance to talk to him. We sat down at his table, ordered our food, and Jack started his peroration about Walter Flack and his company, Murrayfield Estates Limited. As Eric and I listened little did we realise that Walter would be the first one to fire the opening shots against Jack in his conflict with Clore, and if we had known I doubt whether the outcome would have been any different. After lunch I got down to the CLRP figures.

The CLRP takeover meetings were the first truly formal business meetings I had ever attended. I had been to some of my father's company meetings, but that was a medium-sized, unquoted family business. This formal meeting, convened to discuss the progress of the takeover of CLRP, was utterly different. On my second day at City Centre early next morning, I was apprehensive and mildly agog. I did not expect to have anything to say and although I was present mainly as a spectator, I was now on the other side of the fence. Instead of writing about other people's decisions and negotiations and bids, here I was, able to witness the real thing; I was to be part of the side which caused the action.

I had checked about Reeves; it was of course the same difficult Reeves. I wanted to inform Jack before the takeover meeting and, on going into the boardroom, found him engaged in a conversation with Plumridge. He, on seeing me, showed complete surprise. Jack told him that I had joined the group on the financial side, but clearly Plumridge had known nothing about it until that moment. Plum was the head of investments at Pearl Assurance as well as a director of City Centre; he was an acknowledged expert on financing and on investments. He and his chairman Geoffrey Kitchen, amongst the first to support Cotton, were now reaping the harvest of those golden seeds. Financial matters concerning City Centre would above all be Plumridge's province. Of all the non-executive directors, I would be working more closely with him than any of the others. Finance was his purview and yet he hadn't even been informed of my appointment. Cotton's system of communication was very strange.

Before I could tackle Jack on the Reeves situation, Harry Sporborg entered the room. A director of Hambros, the joint financial advisers with Schroders to City Centre, Sporborg was also Jules Thorn's and Earl Fitzwilliam's adviser. He was an ex-solicitor out of Slaughter & May, a wartime friend of Sir Charles Hambro and one of the first City lawyers to break ranks and join the board of an accepting house. Charles Villiers of Schroders would not be coming because Schroders, who were also advisers to CLRP, had to stand down. As a managing director of Helbert Wagg, a City issuing house built up by Lionel Fraser with spectacular success, and recently taken over by Schroders, Charles Villiers had been Jack Cotton's first City financial adviser. The lawyers then came into the room consisting of a couple of partners from Linklaters & Paine, the solicitors to City Centre. Then Freddie Lindgren. David Finney was next; he was the senior partner of Finney Ross, auditors to City Centre, small wiry, Scottish and shrewd.*

Clore and Sainer then came in and the meeting started immediately. The discussions centred on the bid terms and the financial implications to City Centre. Most of the talking came from the lawyers and from Sporborg. He was professional, well-versed in the intricacies of the bid itself and well-acquainted with the strength and weakness of his client's balance sheet, but I soon formed the impression that most of the people around the table had only a hazy idea of CLRP, the company they actually intended to acquire. Incredible, but true. As I was to learn later in my career, comparatively little is normally known of the victim or candidate by the bidder, that is little knowledge outside the Extel card, the report and accounts and elementary research. In a sense this is inevitable by the very nature of things; the need for secrecy is paramount in takeovers and one can't easily make a proper investigation without disclosing one's intentions. Even where terms are agreed in a friendly merger, it is not normally possible, especially in the time involved, for either side to evaluate all the facts properly. For a successful takeover, swiftness is all. If too much time is taken management becomes severely troubled, leaks occur, tactical advantages, particularly of surprise, vanish. In most takeovers, mergers, and bids as I

* An adviser to many, including the three Ogilvy brothers, David, Angus and Jamie, he advised them all on their initial careers with immense perception; David, now Lord Airlie, going into banking with Schroders, where he is now chairman, Angus going into investment with Harley Drayton and Jamie going into stockbroking where he is now a partner at Rowe & Pitman.

was to discover, not only is a disproportionate element of luck required, but the bids themselves have in many instances been made for the wrong reasons: expansion for expansion's sake with no industrial logic or planning; personal or social ambitions of the chairman or his colleagues on the board; surprise and anger at someone else's bid. Too few bids are based on sound commercial sense.

But here we were in this splendid boardroom in Jack Cotton's suite with some important men in the City advising the largest property development company in the world on its bid to acquire the highest quality property investment company in the world — and none of the people around the table, with the exception possibly of Plumridge, really knew anything in depth about the company they wished to purchase. The personages at the meeting clearly thought it was a very good buy at the right price, but they did not know all the salient facts. The discussion that morning ended with the decision to meet again at the same time, 10.00 a.m., the next morning.

Everyone got up to take their leave. Jack talked to Charles Clore quietly in the corner by his desk. Plumridge suggested that he and I have lunch together. I thanked him warmly; he had obviously reconciled himself to Jack's unwitting or deliberate forgetfulness. I went across to speak to Jack about Reeves and mentioned that it would be embarrassing if Reeves provoked a chargeable situation. Jack said that would be an impossible outcome. Reeves would certainly keep his word and comply with the City Centre offer. Clore ignored Cotton and me, turned to Sainer and asked him to come back from the door. He asked Sainer whether Reeves could change his mind. Sainer said of course — there was no legal commitment. 'I'll get it from him,' said Cotton. 'Quite right,' replied Clore and then he left with Sainer and that was that.

Cotton told Tapper to arrange that he saw Reeves as quickly as possible. Reeves was unavailable. Not in his office. Try again, Tapper. Reeves could still not be reached. It transpired he was out of town, and no, his office didn't know when they could reach him. All the classic symptoms of deliberate unavailability. Cotton became anxious for the first time. He eventually tracked him down and Reeves told Cotton that, although he was not going to go back on his word, he had been talking to the trustees and so on. After ten days, on 13 February, this almost grotesque takeover atttempt, which had gone into top gear at the start, fizzled out dismally to the complete discredit of City Centre. *The Times'* comment on the bid was acidly incisive: it 'carried the hallmarks of haste and even disharmony in the way it was dispatched from the City Centre headquarters. It has been an unfortunate beginning for the new combine and it may possibly point to the sort of management problems that can arise when two large, enterprising and individualistic companies amalgamate.' Christopher Reeves resigned from the CLRP board on 21 February. The Reeves share situation which started the bid certainly was compelling but the desire to go ahead came about because the initial impetus from Jack was to shock and to astonish, not to succeed and to win. In the end, Reeves had broken his promise to Jack, and this was bad luck for Jack more than bad judgment. But bad luck was what this partnership could well do without at this time. Some weeks later one Sunday at a dinner in Marlow, Clore commented to Aubrey Orchard-Lisle: 'Jack made a big mistake with Reeves.' Aubrey said, 'Not necessarily. If a well-known City gentleman says something, you don't expect him to break his word.' Clore said, 'It's a pity I was in the States when it was set up. Jack did it the wrong way. I would have bought Reeves' shares straight away for cash and then made the bid.' To this day Aubrey and others in the Cotton camp regret that Clore, the takeover king, was away when the bid was made, because going the Clore route, the two tycoons would certainly have won CLRP. Hindsight is the step-brother of failure, but this is one occasion when one can be forgiven for ruminating on what might have happened if Clore, by chance, had not been in New York at that crucial moment when the CLRP bid got under way.

I referred earlier to two main causes for the failure of the Cotton-Clore merger, one being the lack of a proper mechanism to harness Jack's zeal. The other was Jack Cotton's extraordinary behaviour towards Charles Clore at the lunch in March 1961 held to celebrate the signing of the major tenant, Pan-American Airways, at the Waldorf Astoria in New York.

It all arose from Cotton's catastrophic discourtesy in the way he had seated Charles Clore. Folliss believed that Clore was perfectly justified in his reaction, which only made Jack Cotton that much more angry. The lunch was as lavish as any given in New York, but no amount of lavishness could disguise Jack's incredible and quite deliberate gaffe. Considerable trouble had been taken over the planning of the lunch, over the guest list and particularly over the placement. As usual with City Centre, everyone was going to be there, including Rockefeller, Dewey, Wagner and so on. The top table was large, but not that large, and it was here that Jack made one of the biggest mistakes of his life, a mistake which finally led to his eventual demise. It was a mistake utterly out of character — for he did something which was unpleasant and uncharitable. He deliberately decided, in an odd mixture of jealousy, insecurity and euphoria, that Charles Clore would not sit at the top table. If anyone had a right to sit with the dignitaries it was Clore, a joint leading shareholder with Cotton and the deputy chairman of the parent company, although admittedly not on the board of the actual company owning the building. But Jack declared that he should be seated in the body of the hall, his technical rationale was that only the directors of the corporation owning the Pan-Am building should sit on the dais. There was admittedly a faint gleam of propriety in this reasoning, but it was a ghastly error. Peter Folliss knew it was going to cause serious trouble. It did.

Young Bill Zeckendorf was at the lunch, seated next to Clore. He was astonished that Clore was not at the top table. Clore was more than astonished. He was livid. 'What a bastard!' he kept muttering to Zeckendorf. 'What's Jack playing at? What a bastard.'* Bill has recalled this incident and Clore's fury to me on more than one occasion for he believes it was the first menacing sign that the two tycoons would fight to the death, for if Jack could possibly do something as banally stupid as this there was absolutely no chance for the merger. In his view it was all over at that lunch.

But what about the Pan-Am building itself? There was to be a huge concourse with shops, restaurants and escalators leading to different floors and to the Grand Central Station. There was a bank of twenty-six lifts. The Sky Club, restricted to chairmen and chief executives and so on, was on the fifty-sixth floor of the building. The Pan-American Airways executive suite was superbly fitted out. In the boardroom looking down most of Manhattan, a staggering vista, the rich upholstered beige chairs had the directors' names deeply embossed on the sumptuous Connolly hide. This was where the great Mr Juan Trippe ruled his empire. When on one occasion Trippe took several of us around on a tour, I asked him whether the

---

* Neither Cotton nor Clore was scatological. 'Bastard' — meaning a creep or a rotter, almost but not quite a shit — was Clore's favourite expletive, directed at anyone and everyone. His second favourite was 'potz', an East End Jewish epithet meaning an idiot.

unembossed unnamed chairs in the boardroom indicated that one or other of his executive directors was going to be fired. 'Oh yes,' Trippe replied, poker-faced. Being the man he was, I still don't know whether he was serious or joking. Folliss thought probably both.

The Pan-Am structure was a massive single tower edifice with a huge podium, a tribute to the technical genius of the Americans; it would never fall down, the underneath was solid Gropius.* As far as Jack Cotton was concerned, he owned not half of the building, but all the building. It was his building — after all, he had financed it with risk money raised on his name, not on Erwin's. Although it required all the great authority of Sir Charles Hambro, accompanied by Peter Folliss and supported by Villiers of Schroders and by Seebohm of Barclays Bank to raise the ante of $20 million, it was raised very quickly, a convincing reflection of the City's confidence in Cotton. He had immense pride in 'his' building and felt that not even Charles Clore could have transacted the deal so rapidly and efficiently. As far as Juan Trippe was concerned, however, the building belonged neither to Erwin Wolfson nor to Jack Cotton. It was his building, it was the Pan-American Airways Building, the headquarters of the Trippe airline which he had started himself forty years earlier and which he had built up into the best airline in the world, the airline which was the pioneer of new flights, of new aeroplanes, of new techniques. The building was a fitting symbol of the strength and reputation of his airline. It was a tribute also to Juan Trippe himself, the founder, the chairman and the chief executive. Juan Trippe, distinguished, tall, slim, looking like everyone's image of the head of a great US corporation, had immense pride in 'his' building. He was of course the major tenant, and in

* One night in the suite, Peter Folliss and I were invited to join Jack for dinner with Gropius and his wife. Gropius was anyone's idea of an architectural genius and here he was in the flesh, the majestic architectural man himself. Both Folliss and I were rather overwhelmed.
  Suddenly Peter asked Gropius, what made a very high building stay up? A very, very good question, Gropius replied, whilst Cotton moved his gaze from Gropius to me, saying, in effect, 'You don't know why sky-scrapers stay up, either, but at least Peter had the guts to ask.' I listened to Gropius who addressed Folliss directly. 'Imagine a tall tree, it has roots, it sways in the wind. It will fall down at any time if its undergrowth is weak. With tall buildings it is a matter of what you put underneath, not only what you put on top. Now ask me what goes on underneath. . . .'

addition, he had negotiated not only the right to own 10% of the equity, but split 5% from Cotton and 5% from Wolfson. This was a late concession, reluctantly granted by the other two: irritating and a nuisance, seemingly not too important at the time. But shrewd Mr Trippe knew with sublime timing exactly what he was doing — it made him kingpin and, years later, after he bought out the original partners, it was the borrowing derived from his building which saved his airline from bankruptcy in 1970 and the sale of his building in 1980 which saved it from bankruptcy a second time.

Erwin Wolfson, who quite clearly thought of it as 'his' building too, had the morose appearance of a teutonic physicist. He had a first-rate mind and looked as if he would have been happier lecturing on neutrons than studying the plans of a new building. His general intellectual demeanour set him apart from other New York property men. He was fully aware of this and made a strength of it when negotiating with the banks and with the insurance companies. He got on well with Cotton, though their actual relationship was comparatively short-lived. If Wolfson had lived longer, I doubt whether they would have maintained their very cordial and warm regard for each other at the same intensity. Wolfson was an earnest, thorough, fastidious man, utterly devoid of humour, not really able to appreciate Cotton's natural bonhomie and frequent flashes of wit.

Whilst the building was going up, Wolfson discovered he had cancer. When he knew he was going to die, Wolfson conducted the last year of his life with great dignity. He was passionately concerned with all aspects of his estate and particularly of his monument which would be dealt with in a proper manner. His wife Rose was sensible enough to comprehend the stark, unexpected problems, and in a curious way around this time she turned to Nadia and me for friendship. Wolfson, dying in his lovely house in Rye, brooded upon the building for which he had imperial pride. He had obtained the site from New York Central, he had implemented the project, he had built up the professional team, appointed the architects, negotiated the lease with the major tenant. Grateful as he was to Jack Cotton, the British side had merely provided the cash and a certain amount of moral support and glamour. The building was his monument, not anyone else's and no one was going to deprive him of his due credit. Indeed one of his last wishes was to see his Pan-Am building before he died, and, accompanied by a medical team, he was taken in a helicopter to fly over the site. Rose saw this very clearly and immediately after his death in June 1961 acted upon it. Today,

110

when you walk through the huge, cathedral-like grey marble lobby of the Pan-Am, there is a larger-than-life bust of Wolfson, not concealed in a corner, but unmistakeably in the middle of the lobby, looking down at all passers-by, at the millions of Grand Central commuters. It is not a particularly distinguished piece of sculpture, but it does bring out forcibly the Wolfson character of intensity and concentration. There he is, inside his own building, staring at you, formidable and still brooding. A plaque simply states that he was the founder of the building. But that huge bronze replica of the conceiver of that building, entombed in that vast lobby, says far more than any plaque.

The two tycoons were Englishmen. They both lived in England, their company was a UK company; but the New York property scene, and in particular the Pan-Am building, was ever-present in their minds. This building, in its way representing their own personal wealth and strength to powerful rich New Yorkers, motivated all their responses during this period. It was extraordinary how the building affected everyone connected with it. To me it will always be a building that had a strange emanation and foreboding of danger, and tragically its history seems to bear this out, with too many of the leading characters connected with it dying well before their time, and indeed with the airline itself, seeming to meet new problems the moment it moved into the building.

Peter Folliss, too, very nearly lost his own financial benefit on the building. Jack was generous almost to a fault to all his friends and acquaintances, both in and out of business. He was not generous for any personal gain, nor to create obligations. He gave because he was naturally charitable, and he gave because he believed in dispensing his obligations to others. He recognised that if it had not been for Peter Folliss, he would not have had the Pan-American building. Not only did 'dear Peetah' make the initial introduction, but he also organised the initial financing with Hambros and Barclays Bank. Jack got Erwin to agree that Peter should have a $1 million stake in the building, payable over twenty years as a fee or salary by the corporation owning the building. It was an arrangement known to all, approved by all.

After Erwin's and Jack's deaths, a serious threat arose from the Wolfson side that Peter's fee would not be paid. I had just arrived from London and Peter and I were having drinks at the Knickerbocker when he told me about it. I was surprised, as I knew that Rose Wolfson had gone to inordinate lengths to carry out all Erwin's wishes, promises and commitments. Clearly, newer advisers were intervening — Peter confirmed this. I told him he was like a gentile Daniel in a den of Jewish lions and I would jump in with him. He remonstrated, but I knew that he was a deeply worried man. I telephoned Rose there and then and arranged to see her with her new adviser next day, declining to tell her what it was about. When we met, she was pale and fidgety, but as precisely courteous as usual. 'What is it Charles?' 'It is Peter and his fee,' I replied. And then I explained that I had myself been at the meetings when it was discussed with Erwin's full agreement and that, irrespective of formal documentation, it was a definite commitment. I looked pointedly at the adviser who, as a tough abrasive New Yorker, would only understand tough abrasive dialogue, and added that I would state this in any court or at any press conference. He believed me. Either way Rose would have done the right thing. Peter thought so too. Months after, when it was all fixed up and signed, Peter sent me a graceful letter of thanks, signed Daniel Folliss.

One of Clore's first reactions after the Pan-Am lunch was to bring up the appointment of a full-time chief executive. He wanted to separate this function and role from that of the chairman. Jack agreed half-heartedly, and despite pressure from Kerman did not take the suggestion terribly seriously. The real question was: what sort of man could be induced to take on the job of chief executive of a company headed by a super-active chairman and major shareholder, like Jack Cotton, and an uneasy deputy chairman and major shareholder like Charles Clore? Surely no top-level outsider of any calibre would be prepared to take it on. But of course an insider might not only be interested, he might be very enthusiastic. An insider like Walter Flack, for example.

Part II

Interlude

Chapter Nine

Dorchester Suite, Banker's Parlour, Friends, Aides, Cohorts, and Money Men

In describing the earlier careers of Cotton and Clore, I have already introduced Lindgren and Orchard-Lisle behind Cotton and Sainer and Tovey behind Clore. Whereas Clore, following the dictates of his secretive nature, limited himself to a few restricted aides with whom he felt at ease, Cotton, friendly and expansive, at ease with all and mostly at ease with himself, had a seemingly endless number of close relationships. Whereas Clore had a true and most effective right-hand man in Sainer, steadfastly relying upon his competence and not basically taking counsel with anyone else except 'the lawyer' as Clore sometimes (without derision) referred to him, Cotton took counsel from numerous friends. Clore had no need for friends and did not have many until the last decade of his life but Cotton thrived on his friends, could not abide having them away from him, and considered each of them, even the most recent, as one of his closest. Clore only desired and sought an ever-increasing circle of acquaintances, all of whom without exception he used for information and for his social life, but Cotton had a genuine affection for his friends and acquaintances, all of whom he sought to have around him simply because he liked their company. As a result he was always offered new prospects, some of them fabulous bargains which helped build up his fortune, his fame and his reputation. Clore, though also constantly looking for interesting new acquisitions, did not possess Cotton's allure nor the Cotton bonhomie which went down so well in the hurly burly of an active, dynamic property market. But in one important respect they shared a common trait. If either said yes, it was known to be meant irrespective of the amounts involved; throughout the property world their word could be utterly relied upon.

In their entourage during their partnership, fanned by the extraordinary publicity surrounding each of them, there were characters from many walks of life. Clore, hobnobbing with royalty, dukes, society hostesses, upper-class shooting aficionados, racing enthusiasts and owners (for he enjoyed racing and breeding), not neglecting his wide circle of rich Jewish contacts, many of whom he had known since his East End boyhood, could also number leading bankers and captains of industry among his circle. Cotton's life was more limited. He didn't shoot, he didn't go racing except for Ascot. He enjoyed the occasional dinner party, not the grand ones frequented by Charles Clore, but gregarious friendly dinners given by lawyers, doctors, wealthy estate agents, property entrepreneurs. In stepping out in London Clore, fond of the theatre, ballet, new restaurants, night clubs, went frequently, rarely staying at home. Cotton, though also fond of the theatre, rarely went, and though a sometime cello player at school he had no particular interest in music. He never, for example, went to any of Nadia's performances at the Royal Opera House; Clore, on the other hand, went out of his way to see her dance. As they both gave generously to charities, many of their friends were like-minded, with Clore an active Zionist giving enormous amounts to Israel (which he did with the only evident manifestation of genuine sentiment I ever discerned in him). Some years later, when Nadia and I were his guests in Israel, he was sometimes near to tears in the pride with which he described the achievements of that young nation.

Charles Clore had one listening post in his business career — Leonard Sainer. Cotton did not have one but many — Freddie Lindgren, Aubrey Orchard-Lisle, Isadore Kerman, Peter Folliss, Freddie (now Lord) Seebohm, Sol Joseph, Lewis Civval, Sidney Simon, Geoffrey Kitchen, Louis Freedman the number two to Samuel at Land Securities. But of them all his closest business cohort particularly after Lindgren suffered a set-back in his health was 'Plum', Edward Plumridge, head of investments and later executive director of the Pearl Assurance.

*　　　　*　　　　*

In appearance, Plumridge resembled an amiable, short, slightly plump assistant bank manager; respectable, but undistinguished. He had lost much of his hair, but what remained was slicked over to cover as much of his egg-shaped head as possible. His intelligence and shrewdness were tinged with a charming conviviality. He was devious and crafty, but always in the interests of pragmatism.

116

1. The Dorchester Hotel facing Hyde Park. Cotton's famous suite is on the first floor to the left, above the Park Lane entrance

2. 22 Park Street, Clore's private office: a modest Mayfair mansion around the corner from the Dorchester suite

3. Jack Cotton: invariably the bow tie and matching handkerchief, invariably the warm friendly smile

4. Charles Clore: in the realms of business he regarded insecurity as the main driving force, and as a profound sceptic he exploited to the full this melancholic view of life

5. Jack Cotton with his daughter Jill at her wedding in Birmingham in 1957. The train taking the guests from London was dubbed 'The Champagne Express'

6. Charles Clore on holiday at Megève with his wife Francine, the only love of his life. They were married in 1942 and parted in 1953; after Francine left him no other woman affected him emotionally in any way

7. The marriage: Clore and Cotton with the marriage-broker Douglas Tovey between them, on the day of the announcement of their merger in Charles Clore's drawing room, 95 Park Street. The still life is by Cézanne

8. The honeymoon: the two tycoons toasting each other's acumen at the Dorchester

9. The famous Cummings cartoon

"Are you sure, President de Gaulle, we're negotiating with the right man?"

10. At a formal retail association dinner at the time of the merger announcement
(*left to right*): George Bridge, the innovative general manager of the Legal and
General and their board representative on City Centre Properties; Douglas Tovey the
beaming agent; Hugh Fraser (later Lord Fraser) who eventually obtained his great
prize, Harrods; and Charles Clore and Jack Cotton

11. The Monico site today, still undeveloped. This was Jack Cotton's
biggest blunder. The scheme was virtually destroyed by a press
conference

12. The Pan-American building astride Park Avenue in New York, inspired by Erwin Wolfson, financed by Jack Cotton, tenanted by Juan Trippe

13. 40 Wall Street: when Clore b it, this building was the tallest in downtown Manhattan

14. Big Bill Zeckendorf with his arm round the shoulders of his son Bill Jr, taken on the porch of the Zeckendorf store established in Arizona in 1854 by the first Zeckendorfs, *émigrés* from Russia

Walter Flack, one of the brightest
the property stars. His smile was a
wing Cockney smile, a centuries-old
anese smile, which had encountered
degrees of human failings

16. Edward Plumridge, investment head
and director of the Pearl Assurance, the
institution more closely connected with
Jack Cotton than any other: 'my Plum',
as he was called by Cotton, who would
provoke Cotton's cry of 'Plum the Judas'
during his last days

17. The headquarters of the Pearl Assurance, a huge mausoleum-like
building looking discreetly out onto Holborn with its air of strength and
long-term confidence

18. Eric Young, the group surveyor to City Centre Properties. Jack persuaded Young to join him by telling him that working for him would be fun

19. Felix Fenston, one of the most successful developers during the property boom. 'Jack's not a developer,' he said, 'I am. He's just a bloody genius'

20. Isadore Kerman, Jack's oldest friend who was at school with him in Cheltenham, was his personal solicitor, trustee and counsellor

21. Jocelyn Hambro, deputy chairman and later chairman of the family bank during most of the sixties and seventies. Only Hambros have ever been chairmen of the bank, now headed by Jocelyn's eldest son Rupert

23. Lord Bearsted, the chairman of M. Samuel, the merchant bank on whose board Clore sat with great pride. Bearsted sold a half-interest in the Samuel Estate (11 acres in Mayfair) to City Centre Properties

. Aubrey Orchard-Lisle: in property atters Jack Cotton turned almost clusively to Orchard-Lisle, just as Clore rned to Orchard-Lisle's partner ouglas Tovey

24. Lord Rayne, a property developer par excellence, once dubbed 'Midas' by Charles Clore

25. Leonard Sainer, 'the lawyer', as Clore sometimes referred to him. Always at Clore's side, the perfect Number Two, he was considered one of the cleverest lawyers of his generation – and certainly one of the richest

26. Lord Samuel, the chairman of Land Securities, the largest property investment company in Europe, possibly in the world. City Centre Properties was acquired by Land Securities in 1968

27. Thames Lawn, Marlow, bought by Jack Cotton in 1951: a stately cream villa sitting among thousands of tulips

Jack Cotton's house in Nassau, h he bought from Lord Iliffe. The led straight to the beach

29. Jack with the author on his Nassau beach. Cotton was looking bronzed and fit, but only weeks after this photograph was taken he was dead

30. On holiday on Mustique in 1971, outside the house designed by
Oliver Messel for Nadia Gordon. When this picture was taken, it was
half-built; Clore said, 'Leave it that way.' *From left to right:* Charles
Clore (displaying his Selfridges bag), Lord Dudley, the author, Lady
Dudley, Nadia Gordon and Colin Tennant (Lord Glenconner)

31. Charles Clore, photographed by the author. He said he had never
enjoyed a holiday as much

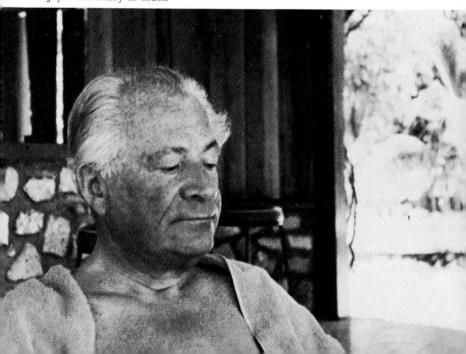

32. Clore and his perfect Jeeves, Kay, who was butler, valet, chauffeur and also loader, photographed at Armanvillier, during a shoot on Edmond de Rothschild's estate

33. Stype Grange, Hungerford, which Clore purchased from Lord Rootes in 1960

34. A detail from 'La Pensée' by Renoir, purchased by Jack Cotton and bequeathed to his daughter Jill, with a value today approaching £2 million. Cotton's other paintings, including his numerous Fantin-Latours, were left to his children to be drawn by lot, so as to avoid any disagreements

35. Nadia Nerina in *Laurentia*, which she danced with Nureyev. This was Clore's favourite ballet photograph, taken during the performance he attended with Max Rayne and the author

Plumridge was most definitely an innate businessman as well as an actuary: a formidable combination in a supporter and a dangerous if not fatal one if and when support were withdrawn.

Plum had decided that it was more convenient for us to lunch together at the Dorchester. He was going to have a private meeting afterwards with Jack before his departure for New York and that ill-fated Waldorf lunch. In briefing me Cotton seemed most anxious about my relationship with Plum stressing very strongly that I should get as close to him as possible. Plum, Cotton insisted, was very shrewd. I would learn a lot from him and should listen to him carefully. 'My Plum' he said with relish and satisfaction. Yet it was Edward Plumridge of the Pearl Assurance, Cotton's closest institutional adherent, 'my Plum', his great confidant and friend, who would provoke Cotton's cry of betrayal, his cry of 'Plum the Judas', during his last days.

Plum and I discussed my functions in the Group. We talked about property shares, about the Pearl Assurance and about institutional connections and about forging new links between City Centre and the major pension funds. Plum had discussed my role with Cotton and I am also quite sure he took him to task for not telling him sooner about my appointment. Plumridge remarked that bearing in mind my own connections and expertise, apart from acquisitions, a concentration on financing in institutional areas was what he and Cotton had in mind. Plum seemed very much in control of his own personal position in City Centre. We talked about Walter Flack; Plum said he was erratic and that he was going to be a problem. He waited for my response, judging my reaction, watching me to see if I was going to show my hand, to see if I were indiscreet, to determine whose side I would be on if the chips were down. Not only an actuary, not only a businessman, I mused, but also a politician.

We then talked about Felix Fenston, Harry Hyams, and of Barranquilla, a company controlled by Hyams, the Pearl Assurance, City Centre and Fenston, the company which is now the property subsidiary of Granada TV. A few years earlier Plum, supported by Kitchen, pushed the Pearl into real estate and with superb judgment (apart from Jack Cotton) backed two of the brightest of the property virtuosi. The first was Harry Hyams, the bearded lone wolf who had made his first million at twenty-one and who in my estimation must have a net worth of over £200 million today. Hyams was the London boy made good, the prodigy who was difficult to get to know, a highly concentrated, single-minded private person with a sensational talent for property. Time spent in his company was usually illuminating, reflecting a humour which is deep and sardonic. He recounted to me once his first-ever rendezvous with Nigel Broakes, the chairman of Trafalgar, who wanted to meet him. Harry, who runs his company on a very tight, lean, low-overhead basis, was in wonder at the spacious Broakes set-up with its large staff. On reaching Broakes' inner sanctum, Hyams said to him, 'You have at least twenty-odd staff out there and at an average annual wage of £5,000 and giving them, say, 20 years' purchase each, I have just passed a capital investment of £2 million. It must be a hard life, Mr Broakes.'

The second virtuoso was Felix Fenston. Felix Fenston was one of the most extraordinary men I ever met, one of the most insufferable and one of the most lovable. A rare individualist, he was stout, strong — able to tear up the London telephone directory at a whim — bearded, a lover of country sports, a great snob, a Scottish earl manqué, and though a man with a gift for friendship, nevertheless argumentative, and overbearing. This was a small price to pay for the pleasure of his company. He went to great lengths to preserve his close friendships and to equal lengths to nourish and cultivate his enmities; no one was a match for him when he was in full spate, vituperative and excoriating, shooting at his adversaries from all sides and angles. Among property developers he was the most social; he knew almost everyone, had numerous acquaintances whom he saw regularly at his shoots and at his grand dinner parties. A sure sign of his affection was his propensity to call on the telephone and mimic anyone from an irate Scottish neighbour complaining about the terrible silence to a frantic financial journalist asking in exquisite Lancashire brogue some inane question like the price of sugar before the Boer War.

Fenston had met Hyams whilst the latter was a junior in a West End real estate agency and they soon started doing deals together. Regrettably, these two talented men had a personal row and they split up. The Pearl was faced with a quandary; which of the entrepreneurs would it back in the future? It decided upon Hyams on a modified basis, but either way, the Pearl's investment in the two ex-partners was showing enormous returns. Hyams later turned to George Wimpey and the Co-op Insurance Company. As a result of their bust-up, the insurance company's position in their joint company, Barranquilla became anomalous and Plumridge told me that he thought Hyams might be willing to sell his shares in the company to City Centre. The market in Barranquilla had always been thin, the purchase of a few hundred shares would send the price soaring. Plumridge asked if I would make an assessment of the company and an evaluation of the shares. It would seem he was already considering me as part of the Cotton financial team.

*   *   *

Soon after this lunch Miss Tapper telephoned me about a meeting she was trying to fix, a meeting which proved the intimacy of Plum's relationship with Cotton. Miss Tapper had been told to get Plumridge, David Finney and myself together for a session with Cotton and she was having a devilish time in finding a convenient date. Plumridge and Finney were extremely busy and Jack's diary was becoming a mess. His great red invitation-laden *Economist* diary could not cope with his ever-increasing commitments. A year earlier his time was already more than taken. Now there were the City Centre executive management meetings, the pension fund meetings, the French, Belgian and Dutch meetings, the regular main board meetings, the subsidiary board meetings, the internal property management meetings, the meetings with the accountants and with lawyers and with tax experts. Then there were the meetings with the banks — the clearing banks and the merchant banks — with the brokers, with the City institutions who were taking a growing interest in his company, with the journalists not only from England and the United States but from all over the world. Then there were the meetings to discuss the new proposals, the new ideas, the new businesses, the new projects, meetings with surveyors, engineers, architects, meetings with other property millionaires, with non-property entrepreneurs, meetings with the chairmen of industrial companies. Then there were the encounters with his own friends, his cronies whom he loved to see, particularly in the evenings, who would drop in for a short while on their way home from work, some staying for dinner, some staying half the night. Then there were his family, his children and his grandchildren. Then there were the friends of friends with impeccable introductions come to meet the great man, come possibly to discuss some business and then the friends of colleagues and the friends of partners. And then there were the overseas visitors, more and more of these from America. They all came to London to see Jack Cotton.

It was a constant procession and Miss Tapper tried to stop the constant flow, to get Jack to cut down. Day after day and week after week the meetings and discussions and encounters went on. 'There is so much to do,' he would protest. 'I must see so and so. I can't let him down.' Miss Tapper complied wearily. Yes, he would go and see his dentist, yes, he would go and have a check-up. He had an exceptionally strong constitution, but no constitution could endure this sort of non-stop regime. Underlying everything was the real pressure, the tension with Clore and the realisation that the partnership was under serious strain. His anxiety was continuous and painful. It began to affect his nervous system. He was beginning to sleep badly and he was sleeping less and less. There was increasing concern from his family and friends.

This urgent meeting which Tapper was trying to arrange was to do with the group's capital and borrowing base. The company had expanded astonishingly. In two years its balance sheet had increased sixfold. An injection of cash was required, the equity base was too small. The idea of unsecured convertible loan stock was fashionable around that time and there had been mutterings about this possibility from Cotton and Clore.

I have never liked and still do not care for convertible stocks; they are bisexual, a hybrid form of finance, neither equity nor loan, a bit of both and in most cases the holders getting the worst features of either. The precise outcome is unknown until the end of the convertible's life, nor can one determine the precise value of a company with convertible stock. It appears as a loan and it could be an equity. The advantages? That equity is not unduly diluted, interest payable is lower than normal rates, security is less rigid when offered and the convertible stock can be quoted. I have always preferred the plain simplicity of an equity or a loan stock and have never been enamoured of a complicated financial package whose wrapping tends to conceal weaknesses rather than to demonstrate strength.

The meeting was eventually arranged and Cotton, Plumridge, Finney and I sat down round the board table to discuss City Centre's capital base. Plumridge was in favour of a huge convertible loan stock amounting to about £50 million with very attractive convertible rights, perhaps full conversion with a very low interest rate, much lower than the prevailing rate, perhaps as low as 4%. The convertible loan stock would be taken up readily, he thought, as both Cotton and Clore had an impressive following in the market. I expressed my opposing view. I said that a convertible in a property company balance sheet was a comparatively new and unsuitable idea, that until conversion it would always hang on the balance sheet, inhibiting future loans and the future issue of shares, that it would reduce the investment status of the company's shares and the conversion rights would always hang over the market. But above all I thought it was inappropriate for City Centre. At this point in our discussion I could see that Plumridge was becoming restive; Finney was looking at me shrewdly. I continued my peroration, saying that in any event it was inappropriate for City Centre because far more than half of the equity was owned by Cotton, Clore, the institutions and other directors, so any issue of any sort was already basically underwritten. There was no need to have any worries about whether it would be a success or not. City Centre, I said, should have a conventional rights issue. This would provide sufficient cash for the company's coffers, but more vital, the equity base would be greatly strengthened and the balance sheet would be considerably cleaner and stronger. David Finney expressed his agreement and I felt encouraged. But the sour look on Plumridge's face presaged the difficulties to come. He countered by insisting that anyone who put up money now would want an immediate return of at least 4%; they would not be satisfied with a dividend return which would be much less than that. Cotton said he would have a further talk with Plum who would also sound out Hambros and Schroders.

A week later Cotton, eyeing me gently from across the boardroom table, asked very deferentially whether I would mind if he kept me out of the capital financing plan. He knew it was a direct and important part of my own function for City Centre and that if I were kept out of this particular fund-raising it was a veritable slap in the face. He said it was because I was not in favour of a convertible whilst Plum definitely was. Charles Clore, he stressed, was also strongly in favour. The rights battle was lost. I realised that as far as corporate finance was concerned, Clore was not as sophisticated as I had supposed, that in this instance his desire for an immediate higher return had clouded his view. Plum subsequently launched the plan as if he were the ordained financial director of City Centre, not the investment manager of the Pearl Assurance. He went round the City and spoke to the merchant banks, the clearing bankers, the pension funds, the insurance companies and the brokers himself.

Plum was totally committed and saw to all the underwriting details. He hoped that the Pearl would take up more than its due proportion but his colleagues dug in their heels. This was a signal to him that his propinquity to Cotton was not in total favour with his own people. It was also, Jack thought, a signal to him that Plum would always be totally loyal to him. To Jack this sort of dedicated support from an institutional man on his board was sheer balm.

Within a year the convertible issue proved a dismal failure, a perpetual drag on the company's earnings. It made any further financing, including the issue of new shares, far more difficult or downright impossible. Some of the problems arising from it led eventually to the sale years later of City Centre to Harold Samuel. Put another way, if there had been a conventional rights issue, instead of the convertible, the balance sheet and the profit-and-loss account would have been considerably stronger and the board of City Centre, post-Cotton, might have had more confidence in going it alone. I was not overly glad to have been proved right. The cul-de-sacs of commercial life are littered with people who have been right. Being right is not enough; one must also be on the winning side. And to be on the winning side one has to rely on manoeuvres, on manipulations, on intrigues, on judgments like Finney's, not merely on the merit or the soundness of one's own argument or logical position.

Not only did this provide an insight in the way Plumridge and Cotton worked together, it also shed light on the way Clore's financial mind worked, and illustrated once again that his aims were avaricious. Clore was won over by Plumridge's argument that he would receive an immediate return on his money, whereas on a normal rights issue, the dividend return would be far less if not minimal. As a short-term argument it was unassailable and it neatly captured Clore's innate greed. What they forgot or wished to ignore was that the value of the convertible rested on the value of their shares, and that value was considerably jeopardised by the issue of the convertible.

*　　　　*　　　　*

I was starting to find my feet and hit my stride. I still had no office; I would sit in Jack Cotton's boardroom or drawing room or in Eric Young's old room. I was also working without remuneration. So Leonard Sainer, 'the lawyer', and I arranged to have our first discussion at his offices at Titmuss Sainer & Webb in Serjeant's Inn. There were no Titmusses nor any Webbs but there were two Sainers in the firm, the other being one of his two sisters. The Sainers, products of a sound working-class Jewish background similar to Clore's, were then in middle age and unmarried; all three still are. Right in the middle of the Spey row in June 1971, when Sainer acted as my solicitor, his mother died and he was completely shaken. It is a very rare thing indeed for Sainer to show any emotion and the only other occasion I saw him overcome was at Charles Clore's funeral in 1979, when he was visibly moved, a sobbing associate bereft without his chief.

Sainer is a modern product of the ancient Rabbinical schools, where hairs which had already been split a thousand times were split again to the finest point of dialectic discipline and interpretation. For centuries, Jewish scholars with remarkable memories and physical stamina would spend most of their long days and nights reading and re-reading the Talmud, knowing all of its three million words by heart, arguing over all of its philosophical and theological and pragmatic aspects. These men could explain a whole new vista of philosophic or religious thought on the inflection or interpretation of one word. Their object was and is to comprehend the morality of life. The Talmud is profoundly practical. In order to live you have to survive, in order to survive you have to learn. No wonder the old Rabbis' modern offspring made fabulous physicists, teachers and jurists. Sainer, though not Rabbinical, has that type of mind and it serves him well. His is a practical intelligence which avoids irrelevancies with distaste, always working to interpret the salient points and to implement them towards a successful conclusion. He had always been at Clore's side, advising, counselling and faithfully following his orders and exhortations, the immensely capable number two. During our initial talk in his office, it went through my mind that what probably made him such a perfect number two was that he knew his own limitations and strengths precisely.

Sainer was at great pains to explain to me that less than a quarter of his firm's work was involved with Clore's interests. He was equally at pains to point out that he had many other clients, some very distinguished, and he was proud of the size and reputation of his firm. He was justified in feeling so; it had not been easy to develop a law practice after the war and especially difficult to establish one with such an outstanding reputation. Perhaps it was his good fortune or Clore's calculation that brought the two together. It was however very much to Sainer's credit that he didn't leave the law in order to join Clore full-time, clearly aware that if he did, his loss of independence might undermine the excellent relationship he

123

had. So he concentrated on his professional practice and caused it to go from strength to strength. Yet he was always known, and referred to, as Clore's right-hand man. In the process he also became one of the richest lawyers in the country.

In his office, with his numerous neat pending trays, Sainer, a tall imposing person, sat behind his desk seemingly tired and weary, with layers of skin draped round his eyes, but the liveliness of his brain belied his appearance. We agreed that my title would be financial consultant to City Centre, and we just as soon agreed my remuneration. But we had reached no conclusion on my capital incentive. I had not, of course, expected this from the company itself, but both Cotton and Clore had known from the beginning that I looked to them to grant me an option on some of their City Centre shares. Cotton had already accepted the principle and had made the point to Clore. Sainer would not go along with it and said that it was very different for Clore because of the nature of the Clore trusts and that if Jack Cotton wanted to do something with me on his own side, that was up to him. It was a good diplomatic *démarche*, which we both recognised. Then out of the blue, Sainer made a surprising suggestion. Would I be interested in basing myself at Investment Registry, the new-issue house owned by Clore and situated in Grafton Street, off Berkeley Square? Investment Registry was known, in that slightly derogatory description used by the City, as a West End finance house to make it clear to all and sundry that it was not part of the City establishment. Indeed, in the early years of Clore's career he was known exclusively as a West End financier. Curiously, Investment Registry later became part of Hill Samuel, itself the result of a merger in 1965 between Philip Hill, Higginson — another West End house headed by Kenneth Keith — and the prestigious M. Samuel & Co. headed by Lord Bearsted. Investment Registry had become extremely well-known because it had acted as the issue house in all of Clore's takeover bids. Sainer's suggestion had some merit: the Dorchester suite, apart from not being really suitable, was not large enough to provide me with a permanent office. Investment Registry was also situated near Berkeley Square where I lived and was only a short walk from the Dorchester. Sainer said that there might even be some interesting transactions I might do together with Investment Registry. Our talk ended and we parted with a certain amount of mutual respect and a certain amount of mutual wariness.

Cotton was almost beside himself with joy that I had been asked to be housed in the Clore stronghold. I found at Investment Registry once I based myself there that Roland de Rougemont, who ran it, and his colleagues, in particular his deputy Charles Wilson, were friendly and helpful, providing me with all the services I required. Until I moved into Hambros Bank some months later, this was where I had my office. Soon after I settled there I phoned Clore on some matter. He was out. Next morning I was at Investment Registry unusually early, well before 9.00 a.m. Clore returned my call. I was surprised by the quick return and its timing. I was to learn later that if Mr Clore says he will get in touch with you at 3.45 p.m. six months hence, you can rest assured that at 3.45 p.m. six months hence, you will receive a telephone call from Mr Clore. He was fastidious about keeping his commitments, no matter how trivial.

Whilst Jack was still purring with delight, Roland de Rougemont brought me a potentially large shop development in Richmond. Cotton thought it interesting and consequently some days later Archie Sherman, Douglas Tovey and I drove in Douglas's huge Rolls DT 1000, out to Richmond. On the way back Douglas and Archie played a business game which I suppose only a dozen or so people in the country could have played. It was devastating in its simplicity. All it required was an encyclopaedic knowledge of the shop properties of the country. Douglas to Archie: '163 High Street, Slough?' Slight pause, then Archie to Douglas: '£5,250.' (A nought can now be put on these rents.) Tovey: 'Right.' Archie to Douglas: '34 Prince's Street, Edinburgh?' Douglas to Archie: '£4,450.' Then Archie Sherman would say, 'Right', or, 'No, £4,650.' When they disagreed there would then be a long scholarly discussion. They were playing the game of shop rental values. Each of them seemed to know the precise rental value of every shop in every high street in the country; what was more, they also seemed to know who were the tenants, who were the previous tenants and what the previous tenants had paid in rent. Afterwards, Douglas confided to me that he thought the most erudite of them all was Archie, the man he had personally recommended to Clore to run his property company. Their extraordinary knowledge was distilled over decades. In property terms their knowledge represented enormous money-making potential, not only for themselves, but for their clients or partners. With experts of this calibre, no wonder the British property man was considered the best in the world.

*   *   *

What was particularly fascinating to me in the discussions I had with the different pension funds I was trying to encourage to associate with City Centre was just how different they were. This was apparent not only in their internal structure and in their style and policy, but also in the vast range of calibre and character of the personnel.

At the ICI fund, the now well-known Norman Freeman who took early retirement from his position in 1972, was sleek, expensively dressed and self-assured. He invariably wore bright striped ties, a Freudian sign of outward candour and inner secretiveness. Ten years later, in Spey, I learnt what a talented demolition expert he was. When we first met, he suggested that we have lunch at the Savoy Grill, a surprising venue which would have been the last choice of any other fund manager. In my dealings with ICI at that time and later, I never met anyone else from his company, no other colleague except an odd assistant called Dobbie. He never introduced me to any of his trustees. I was never asked to any meeting with his investment committees and I don't recall Jack Cotton either meeting anyone from ICI except Freeman. This was Freeman's personal style.

At Unilever the man who called all the shots was Jasper Knight, a craggy, hulking man, looking every inch the oarsman he had been at Eton. An accountant by profession, he had risen to the top of Unilever, where his father had been before him, to become its finance director. Most people working under him either disliked him or were scared of him. Knight enjoyed being with merchant bankers and entrepreneurs. He took an immediate liking to Cotton and very much wanted to push his pension fund into property, so terms were soon agreed for an association with City Centre. During the negotiations he made it clear to me that it was he who made all the decisions, that he was the big white chief of the investment committee and that he regarded his investment manager, Andrews, whose reputation in pension fund circles was very high, as merely a technician. There was no need for me to meet Andrews, he told me, and I didn't. In fact it was nearly three years later, long after the City Centre deal with Unilever, when we formed a joint company at Hambros with the Unilever pension fund, that I finally met Andrews and his assistant, William Broadfield. Rather late in the day, Unilever started looking for Knight's successor. He and his board made a brilliant choice which as it turned out was pure luck.

126

With some diffidence Lord Poole, then chairman of Lazards who were the traditional financial advisers to Unilever, suggested that Unilever might consider Cob Stenham who was his son-in-law. After Stenham's appointment, Jasper Knight joined the board of one of the subsidiaries of Spey, where it soon became apparent that a recent illness had transformed him from an agreeable difficult man to a disagreeable impossible man.

George Ross Goobey of the Imperial Tobacco pension fund was the best known spokesman for the pension fund industry. The press respected him as the father of the equity cult and Ross Goobey, with his frayed military look accentuated by his adjutant moustache, spoke, lectured and pontificated against gilts and for equities with utter confidence and always with good sense. It was usually the same speech, but no worse for its repetition because the direct benefits arising from his crusade probably made hundreds of millions of pounds for millions of pensioners as numerous fund managers influenced by his arguments got out of fixed interest and government bonds into what were then inflation-proof equities. The investment world might well erect a monument to George Ross Goobey for the vital role he played in the history of investments. His investment policy at Imperial Tobacco required real courage, for in the early fifties equities were regarded with almost as much distaste as properties were ten years later. Ross Goobey not only switched from gilts into equities into property before most other institutions. He was also the first ever pension fund manager to be appointed to the board of his parent company, much to the chagrin of other managers who had ambitions in that direction. He was outstanding, and when he started looking into the intricacies of property financing he took to them like a duck to water. Both Eric Young and I soon discovered after the initial discussion between Imperial Tobacco and City Centre on the Royal Garden Hotel site in Kensington which eventually involved the Pearl and ICI too, that it was one of the most complex transactions any of us had ever encountered. I still believe that the only man who really understood that particular situation was George Ross Goobey.*

* Ross Goobey and I still find amusement in a ludicrous negotiation we attempted when I was at Hambros Bank. We were proposing to have a joint company between Bentworth and his Imperial Tobacco pension fund. It was to be 85/15. 'Well, I am glad we have sorted out the terms,' said Ross Goobey. 'So am I,' I replied. 'And I am glad, George, that you're happy with your 15%.' 'Oh no, Charles, it is you I hope who are happy with your 15%.' George was always ahead of his time.

After moving into Grafton Street, I still seemed to be spending as much time at the Dorchester as before, but the negotiations with the pension funds were beginning to bear fruit. Apart from Freeman, Knight and Ross Goobey, I also initiated talks with the managers of several of the pension funds of the nationalised industries. All were interested in varying degrees in wishing to associate with City Centre. None of them was put off by the fame of the two tycoons nor indeed by the Dorchester. In fact, with the ICI fund, at their internal meeting held to discuss the loan to Cotton and Clore, the comment from the employees' representative, an ardent trade unionist, was, let's get together with these two chaps, perhaps they can make some money for us as well.

In these meetings with the funds we discussed rent reviews and rental values, sales and leasebacks, the investment status of the different types of commercial properties, the advantages of shops against office buildings, office buildings against industrial premises, the principles on the valuation of property, the strength of covenants, building costs, interest rates, security requirements, the sharing of profits, loan capital, debentures, redemption yields, capital conversion factors. We would go over the growth rates of property investment companies for five, ten, fifteen years. We would work out the returns on fourteen, twenty-one, or forty-two year leases on new buildings at varying rental values, at varying interest rates with or without an equity participation in the actual development or in the company making the development or in the quoted parent company. We looked at all forms of leaseback arrangements, of joint participations, associations and partnerships, many of these possibilities being innovative, with the best ideas coming from the fund managers themselves. The discussions were challenging and not academic or theoretical at all. We were exploring new ground in property financing and in property investment, the objective being a definite commercial association and partnership. We argued over our calculations to test the efficiency of one method of financing our partnership against another, and as our discussions proceeded, it was apparent that the fund managers were becoming increasingly convinced that property investment could provide the best combination of a definite, rising, secure, recurring income with increasing capital growth. What could possibly be better than a lease signed with an undoubted covenant like Marks & Spencer or Barclays Bank for forty-two years with rent reviews? There was also at this time a prevading confidence that demand, though erratic, would

128

persist, that rents would go up not down, and that any dangers would be in changes in taxation. There were few political clouds on the horizon, no pressure to legislate against property; the property industry was recognised as a serious and important activity, not a social aberration nor a social monstrosity. And the property developer himself, typified by Jack Cotton, was earning some respect with the recognition that he had a social function to perform: bombed town centres had to be replaced, local authorities had to increase revenues. The commercial and political atmosphere within which these discussions with the funds took place was agreeable and stable.

The formula which finally emerged between City Centre and the pension funds, as devised basically by Cotton and Plumridge, was as follows: a small £100 corporation, the Joint Company (JC),* would be formed with the equity owned 70% by City Centre and 30% by the pension fund.

---

* Having established the principle that the fund would advance all the finance required and would own the property, the Joint Company would take a leaseback from the fund at 6% on the total monies advanced. This lease would be for ninety-nine years. Ignoring tax, the fund would receive 30% of the profits of the corporation (i.e. the surplus over 6%) and City Centre would receive 70%. If a £5 million building was let offering a yield of 10%, i.e. £500,000, the fund would receive 6% on its £5 million, i.e. £300,000 or an initial return to the fund of 7.2% on its investment. This is made up of 6% plus 1.2%, being 30% of the balance of four points between the 10% yield on the property, and the 6% payable to the fund. On a tenant's review in fourteen years' time, resulting in a doubled return of 20% on cost, the fund would still receive its 6% plus 30% of the difference between 6 and 20, i.e. 30% of 14, giving it a total return of 10.2%. If on the tenant's rent review the fund was to receive the same proportion of revenue throughout, i.e. 60% of the gross revenue before the 30/70 shareout, it would receive 60% of £1 million, i.e. £600,000 plus 30% of £400,000, i.e. £120,000 totalling £720,000 or returning 14%. City Centre would receive £140,000 per year in the first fourteen years and £490,000 in the second fourteen years, or £280,000 if the fund received the same proportion of revenue on its initial investment throughout.

Looking at these arrangements in the context of the transactions made by institutions later in the sixties and seventies and today, it would appear, depending upon the division of the rent review, to be ludicrously weighted in City Centre's favour. But it should be remembered that during this period it was still possible to borrow straight twenty-five year loans at a current interest rate of less than 6% with no equity for the institutions. Some institutions were happy to commit funds at, say, 5% to a property company secured on the completed development, with their equity aspect only comprising the purchase of shares in the quoted parent company, these shares being issued at the market

The first two Joint Companies agreed to in principle were with the Unilever and ICI pension funds. From the inception of these associations, there was one inalienable principle insisted upon by Jack Cotton which later became the hallmark of negotiations, dealings and agreements with pension funds by others, including myself, over the years. This was that the terms of the association would be agreed first and that finance would only be committed or advanced by the fund after the trustees had specifically approved a particular investment. To my mind, it is a principle which should pertain to any association between an institution and its partner; a very proper two-stage principle. However it became an enormous bone of contention between Clore and Cotton. Clore approached an institution exclusively for a specific proposition, wanting a binding commitment straight away. When the 45 Park Lane project was being discussed at the City Centre board meeting, Clore asked where the money was coming from. Cotton replied from a pension fund and referred to the letter of intent from ICI. 'That's a letter, that's not money,' was Clore's retort. They were of course both right, they were both expressing their different financing philosophies.

Another crucial principle engendered by Cotton in respect of pension fund associations was that, after making the investment, the fund should thereafter monitor the investment and be encouraged to receive data on a regular basis. Cotton firmly believed that a fund should be intimately concerned with its investment. Ironically it was this thinking which he failed to implement properly for like many

price or on option at an agreed price. The method evolved by City Centre gave the institution a direct stake in the particular development it was being asked to finance. It was in a strong position as it owned the freehold, subject to a leaseback, and it owned 30% of the equity of the £100 Joint Company which owned the lease. The fund owned the property from the beginning, it took no risk — City Centre having to pay the initial 6% come what may — the security was sound and it also received an immediate above-average return for its money. All the work, site assembly, planning approval, project management and letting was done by the City Centre professional, no fees being charged to the Joint Company by City Centre itself, only actual disbursements. In the meantime, the fund could learn about property developments from City Centre at no cost to itself and could decide whether and when to establish its own property department. The main advantage to City Centre was that it could finance its developments fully without any cash commitment and without weakening its balance sheet. City Centre could plan ahead and could organise its development programme efficiently and without borrowing restrictions. The one risk for the fund was that it was relying entirely on the calibre of the management.

outstanding persuaders, negotiators and pioneers, his natural form of communicating was in person, by telephone or round a table. Data, memoranda, telexes, copy letters were far inferior, in his mind, as an administrative process than speaking to someone directly. Because of his memory, facts and occurrences were indelibly registered in his own personal information retrieval system. The theory, none the less, was that once the institution had paid its money for an investment, it should not abdicate its own management responsibilities. Rather, that was when the responsibilities should commence. Cotton contended that whether an investor likes it or not, in every act of investment there is an endemic and responsive interest in management. The investor should have as much access and information as possible and should not take a back seat. If costs are incurred in monitoring, too bad, the costs are inevitable and necessary. If a fund has tens of millions of pounds of investments, what is the relevance of an additional overhead, of say, £25,000 to £50,000 for a full-time expert? As a result of my own early lessons from Cotton, I stolidly implemented the same principles in all my own transactions with pension funds. Indeed, going further, I insisted that not only should each fund have representatives on the boards, but that one or other of its investment staff should attend internal management meetings and receive copies of all internal paperwork on the joint ventures. There were protests certainly. It was asserted that it was not the responsibility of the fund, that its responsibility ended once the decision was made to invest and that thereafter its only concern was whether to stay in or to get out. It was declared that the amounts of monies being invested in these joint associations were small in relation to the whole and that staff spending a disproportionate amount of time on investment surveillance and in communication with management could not be justified. Over the years, as more and more arrangements have been negotiated with the pension funds by entrepreneurs, by banks, by corporations, as moods have changed, as the funds' investment personnel has grown, as the funds have become more experienced, wiser, more confident, these protestations have inevitably died down. Jack Cotton was very much on the right track. Prudent investment requires continuous analysis not only of data but of management; the very act of investment means getting involved in management. The owners of most businesses are the pensioners and the policy holders; the working representatives of the pension funds, the investment managers and their colleagues, should therefore learn to act as

131

owners on behalf of their members and should select the managements they intend to support with special care and watch them like hawks thereafter. That the intimate and continuous management participation by pension funds is gaining ground is, in my view, a sign of maturity and an indication of a more responsible attitude on the part of the institutional investor.

*   *   *

Of all the younger property tycoons, the one for whom Clore had the most respect was Max Rayne, now Lord Rayne. This respect as always with Clore emanated from Rayne's talent as a money maker. He was amongst the most brilliant of the new-rich property developers, easily on a par with Felix Fenston and Harry Hyams. If Rayne had only stuck to property he would today be a world beater, but he developed a taste for extra-curricular investments. His company, London Merchant Securities, extremely active with its developments mostly north and east of Oxford Street, had recently financed a whisky distillery in Scotland, named Invergordon, which seemed an amusing diversion for its abstemious chairman. This same non-property investment though initially a great success was to lose his company many millions.

In those days his most noticeable quality apart from his astuteness, was his desire to be liked, and he was very much on his best behaviour and always anxious about his appearance, dressing carefully and neatly. Dapper, short, good-looking with slightly wary eyes, he was known in those days, by no means disparagingly, as the poor man's Charles Clore. He had already extended his interests in the theatre, particularly in the ballet, and though he then knew relatively few people in the arts, he soon started forming new associations and friends and developed an active social life. Once he gave a party for Nadia in his house after one of her performances at the Royal Opera House around the time Nureyev first arrived in London. This was almost the earliest occasion when that talented, moody Russian dissident was seen in the flesh. (When I first met Nureyev some weeks before, I discovered that almost the only English words he could utter were 'tax free' and I knew then that he would go a long way.) Rayne's house is built on a hill overlooking Golders Green, a heavily populated Jewish suburb. The house itself is beautifully designed and its contents are a vivid indication of Rayne's inherent good taste. His superb collection included one of the most stunning paintings I had ever seen, a Monet water-lily, lit by a single shaft of light which illuminated not only the painting but whoever was looking at it; Titian, Degas, Rodin nearby all paled against this purity. Rayne himself was always an agreeable companion, slightly ill at ease after his first marriage broke up, but totally immersed in his business and in his growing social life. These were the years of Rayne's greatest growth, before his whisky fiasco and other forays into non-property diversions. His capacity for making money was such that even Charles Clore dubbed him 'Midas', and it was said that he was making up to £1 million a month, tax-free.

One evening whilst Jack was out at dinner and we were sitting in the drawing room admiring his Rembrandt, the wise face looking at us as if fully aware of what lay in store, Peter Folliss and I gloomily discussed Cotton's future. Peter and I were going to the Mirabelle for dinner, where Max Rayne was joining us. Rayne had returned that day from New York, where, he told me earlier, he had done a 'marvellous deal'. He was anxious to talk about it, and I surmised that he was quite happy for Peter to know as well, because it would seep back to Cotton and Clore and their consequent approbation would give him some sort of extra satisfaction.

Peter was especially miserable because at the City Centre board meeting that morning Jack had waffled and had been far from his best. Clore had asked some pertinent questions and Jack's replies had made his friends on the board squirm. Peter moodily observed that Jack still refused to accept the fact that being chairman and managing director of a corporation such as City Centre was a job for two people. Why did he insist on doing it all himself? We strolled down Curzon Street to the Mirabelle. Mayfair then, before the casinos arrived, the most relaxed urban village in the world, was quiet and restrained. The Hilton's arrogant tower smirked as if it was signalling to us from Clore. Peter and I looked up and smirked back. 'I would never stay there if you paid me,' said Peter with unusual fervour. When we sat down at the Mirabelle, the *maître d'* put Peter's drink on the table without asking.

As usual, Max Rayne turned up late, making his entrance on the soles of his feet, looking right and left to see who else was in the restaurant and, as usual, apologising courteously and effusively for his tardiness. When he told us that his big New York deal was with Zeckendorf, both Peter and I burst out laughing. Surely Max knew better. Big Bill always got the better part of any deal. Rayne earnestly explained that this one was different. It was. He had bought an hotel, the Savoy Plaza on Fifth Avenue, opposite the Plaza Hotel. It was owned by the Zeckendorf Hotel Corporation. He explained that Zeckendorf had obtained a tenant — General Motors. Peter and I stopped laughing and listened intently.

Big Bill, once again before anyone else, had perceived the Savoy Plaza as a prize office building fit for the king of corporations, General Motors. He had purchased the property and run out of money, as he always did. This was where Max Rayne had come in. He had taken up a mortgage and with great skill and characteristic commercial elegance had purchased the prior loans until he controlled the property. In due course the Savoy Plaza Hotel was demolished, and in its place there was the white marble General Motors building, thoroughly burnished and quite resplendent and now owned by a British company — Rayne's. In prestige terms it was on a par with the Pan-American building and Rayne was deservedly pleased to stress to us that because it was General Motors the interest rate on the financing was lower than US Treasury bonds. Alas, the building is no longer owned by Rayne's company, he sold it to G.M. Today his company's interest in that building alone would be worth more than half as its entire market value.

Before the Savoy Plaza hotel was demolished, a certain amount of additional cash flow was created for Rayne's company with an ingenious idea. There was a vast amount of hotel paraphernalia with 'SP' — denoting the Savoy Plaza — emblazoned or stitched or engraved, on ashtrays, tablecloths, sheets, pillowcases, crockery, cutlery. Cecilia Bennator, Rayne's clever New York associate, was never one to waste money nor ever at a loss to find an opportunity to make it. Her office got in touch with all those people in the Manhattan telephone directory who had SP as their initials and, touching a latent snobbery, did a roaring trade selling thousands of plates and knives and forks and napkins all marked with their personal insignia. When Clore heard about this, he grunted, 'Midas'.

*   *   *

One morning at the Dorchester, just as I was leaving after our meeting, Jack said, 'Can you stay on? Morris and Joe are coming to see me, you'll enjoy meeting them.' Morris and Joe were Morris Saadi and Joe Green. Some moments later, they both entered the boardroom in a very business-like fashion, hurried and brisk. They shook Jack by the hand and walked quickly round the room, examining the pictures and the furniture as if they were bailiffs. It was the beginning of a celebrated act. Green said, 'Well, let's get on with it Jack, you might have all the time in the world, but you know we're busy people, Morris and I.' From Jack to them: 'Not at all, I've got absolutely nothing to do. Take your time.' And to me: 'Charles, sit at the bottom of the table and listen carefully. You could learn a thing or two from these characters.' Saadi, thin, spare, elegant down to his tiny crocodile moccasins, the diminutive Laurel, puffed out his pigeon chest and sat down on Jack's right, whilst his partner Green, large, out of breath, amiable, the veritable Hardy, sat opposite on Jack's left. Saadi started first. 'Jack, you should know straight away that Joe and I are very fond of you and we are only here today to do you a favour.' Pause. 'Jack, you know, you are a very lucky man, because the deal we are offering you we can do with anyone else at a much higher figure.' Jack sucked on his cigar, his eyes widening in astonishment. 'Believe me, Jack,' Saadi went on, 'we're not only doing you a favour, a really big favour, but you're also going to get this marvellous deal at a very low price.' There was no mention of what the deal was. It was Joe Green's cue. He ignored Jack, looked hard across the table at his plucky little partner. 'Morris, who are you to give our money away? We are not in business to make special prices. Remember we are 50/50. If you want to do Jack a favour and give away any money, it'll have to come out of your fifty.' Jack looked down the table at me, glistening with mirth. Saadi and Green stared at each other across the table, ignoring Jack. 'But Joe,' said Saadi, 'we love doing business with Jack. Let's be generous to him. After all, he's got problems. He's chairman of a great big company. He's got to think of Charlie Clore, of his directors, his insurance companies, his pension funds and his bankers. They must be making his life a misery. Let's do him a good turn.' A deep reluctant sigh of agreement from Joe Green. 'All right, Morris, you've convinced me. I'll go along with you.' The two partners then turned to Jack, who hadn't been there a moment before. It was all good fun and you could see Jack visibly relaxed, his growing tensions forgotten, whilst he and Saadi and Green got down to some tough business talk. The transaction they discussed was far from small and the details were explained professionally. They went over the figures and agreed how they would set about proceeding together. Jack later told me that every transaction he had ever done with this pair had been profitable for all concerned. He explained that Saadi was the property partner and Green was the financial partner. Tweedledum and Tweedledee, Laurel and Hardy. Within the limits they had set for themselves, they were both very clever indeed; and also a very formidable duet.

*　　　*　　　*

There were occasions during this interlude when both sides were together at one party or another, and there would be shafts of the Clore character, usually by way of his inimitable direct cross-questioning and occasionally through his unexpected wit. One such party was when Peter Folliss decided to give his first dinner after the Pan-Am opening. It was at the Dorchester in the Orchid Room. We were thirty or so, and the guests included many of Peter's London friends and acquaintances. As we arrived Jack Cotton took us across to talk to Geoffrey and Joan Kitchen who particularly wanted to meet Nadia. I saw Clore with Angus Ogilvy and Lady Hesketh. He joined us and said to Nadia, 'I saw Fonteyn in *Swan Lake* last night. She was terrific, but I've seen better.' Then, looking down, 'Where did you get those shoes?' 'Raynes,' said Nadia. 'Terrible,' said Clore. Raynes had always made Nadia's shoes, but were not part of his shoe empire. Some time after this we were at Harold and Edna Samuel's yearly party at Claridge's. This event was extremely well organised, a perfect illustration of Samuel's sense of doing everything in a well-ordered manner. Clore was in a group. I said hello. Charles said, 'I was at the ballet last night. Fonteyn was —,' I cut in. 'Charles, it is no good. Nadia is not going to leave Raynes for Dolcis.' He eyed me with amusement. 'We may be friends yet,' he said. From time to time he would display a quick wit. Aubrey Orchard-Lisle told me how, on Clore's first visit to their London house in Aldford Street, he asked to be shown around. Aubrey's wife Bunty had a large dressing room with hundreds of pairs of shoes neatly arranged in the wardrobe. Charles viewed them in amazement. 'Aubrey,' he said, 'you are not married to a woman. You are married to a centipede.'

On another occasion, after Cotton's resignation in the early years of my friendship with Clore, several of us ended the evening at Annabel's. Peter Folliss had already gone home and we were preparing to leave. Charles asked, 'Would you like to meet my new girlfriend?' 'Tomorrow.' 'No,' he said, 'let's go now. She is waiting for me at Park Street.' I was puzzled. A few minutes later he was giving us a nightcap and took us into his drawing-room. 'What do you think of her?' And there she was, beautifully framed, a lovely sensual Renoir brimming with French gaiety and warmth. Nadia turned immediately to the Vuillard on the opposite wall. 'You have known her for a long time, Charles.' We gazed at the Vuillard. It was a large canvas of the painter's own studio, vividly reproducing the paintings on his walls, some of his own, some of his friends'. One of them was the Renoir beauty now on Charles' drawing room wall. Charles said, 'It's good to have her waiting for me,' and darting a penetrating look at me, 'A pity you haven't got your wife's brains.'

As one can imagine, Clore was impervious to the wealth of others. But there was one exception — Edmond de Rothschild, Francine's famous cousin. As Clore would say, it was not only the amount of money Edmond had, it was the quality. Clore was deeply impressed by Edmond's large number of lovely houses, each opulently furnished with priceless paintings, furniture, carpets and *objets*, all previously owned by generations of Rothschilds and by some quirk more frequently bequeathed to Edmond than to any of his Paris cousins. (Once in the seventies, when we were driving into Paris, Clore said, 'This is one of his.' He did not have to mention the name, for by the shorthand of long friendship I knew he was referring to Edmond. 'This' to which he was referring was the outer end of an estate which seemed to run for miles.) Clore, who had one of the better shoots in England, and who entertained his guests on a lavish scale, said that it was nothing to the way Edmond entertained at his shoots. Take his dinner services, Clore would declaim, Edmond has over a hundred separate full dinner sets, each of which can service over a hundred guests, each of which is a collector's item, and each of which is in regular use. He has several large albums with coloured photographs illustrating each service and he flips through them before deciding which is to be used for a particular dinner. 'Edmond is so rich,' Clore said, 'that he has things which not even money can buy,' this last comment being the highest possible accolade which Clore would accord to anything.

Edmond de Rothschild was very rich indeed and it was said, obviously with some exaggeration but not much, that his annual income was larger than the net worth of any other Rothschild. His father was the legendary Maurice, 'the Monster' as he was known because of his monstrous size and appalling personal habits. He was a stock-market operator of genius with no staff and no premises; all he required, he would claim, were the two offices he maintained in his jacket pockets, the one stuffed with the *Wall Street Journal*, the other with the *Financial Times*. Baron Maurice was related to Clore by marriage.

To my mind the most remarkable thing about Edmond himself was not his staggering wealth, but his staggering gift for choosing exceptional people as his closest colleagues, a gift which of course helped to make him even richer. There were three colleagues in particular: George Karlweiss, François Péreire and Ben Jakober. Karlweiss was the nephew of the great Viennese actor. Today he is running Edmond's Banque Privée in Geneva and using his investment flair with extraordinary success. I had first met the latter two, Ben Jakober and François Péreire, a cousin of Edmond's, in London, and immediately fell into friendship with both of them, a friendship which exists just as happily today. Jakober was a serious and superior businessman with a tremendous sense of fun. He retired before he was forty, much to the consternation of Edmond, who kept me up late one night trying to persuade me to get Ben to change his mind (Edmond's consternation was well founded because without Jakober his property empire has lost its dynamism. Jakober meanwhile has become a talented sculptor). As to François Péreire, he is an exceptional man in every way and another of the very few people for whom Clore had immense respect. An outstanding banker and entrepreneur, it was he who made the decision to finance the Club Méditerranée, one of Rothschild's best investments. Edmond was most fortunate to have his cousin François as his closest, earliest colleague. Together they built up his Paris bank, La Compagnie Financière, to its present strength and eminence. In the early sixties Edmond was somewhat off-side to his famous French cousins, and it was François Péreire with his urbanity and culture and sure touch who made Edmond acceptable, to them, to the European banking community, and indeed in those early years to 'the Monster' himself. There is a story of an early transaction concerning Edmond and François when they first started the Compagnie Financière, a story much to Clore's own taste and which he liked telling. Rothschild and Péreire saw an interesting share position in one of Paris's most respected Banque d'Affaires. They approached Maurice who already owned 10% and suggested that if they bought a further 10% father and son would jointly control the bank. Maurice said go ahead and the two of them started collecting the shares on the market. When they had bought their 10% they jubilantly told Maurice. He told them in return that he already knew their purchasing position as he had been peddling his own shares to them through the market.

One day, Ben phoned me. He, Rothschild and Péreire wondered whether Cotton and Clore would like to come over to Paris to see their property developments. It was a very meaningful invitation. I understood immediately that it might have long-term implications. We all duly went over. We saw the properties and had a sumptuous lunch at 47 rue du Faubourg St Honoré, the offices of La Compagnie Financière and another of Edmond's houses. The garden adjoined the garden of another house in the Rue d'Elysées, where Edmond had his main Paris residence. Cotton during the entire day was uneasy and I could not at first understand what was troubling him. Then I realised that it was because, in the intimacy of this small, elegant gathering, Clore, his partner and deputy chairman, on very cousin-like terms with our celebrated host, was clearly number one. Cotton felt put out. By the end of the lunch, I could see that however much Edmond, Charles, Ben, François and I might have wanted an association, Jack had already decided against it.

But for Cotton's recalcitrance and his obvious envy of Clore's French connections, we would I believe have gone into business with Edmond de Rothschild. We were all in tune, except Cotton; he was the odd man out. Usually he would push in Clore's direction, wishing to please his partner, but this was one occasion when he dug his heels in. His rationale had nothing whatsoever to do with the business situation itself, but everything to do with his emotional insecurity whenever Clore was involved.

*　　　*　　　*

Nothing gave him more satisfaction in his relationship with Hambros Bank than my move from the Dorchester suite and Investment Registry to Number 41 Bishopsgate, the Head Office of Hambros Bank and known in every banker's parlour as '41'.

I was to see Sir Charles Hambro at '41' at 3.30 p.m. Peter Folliss and I left together for the bank from the Dorchester. We sat in the Hambros' boardroom on the first floor, next door to a small meeting room which was adjacent to the spacious partners' room. The table was covered with a green baize cloth. The windows were double-glazed but one could still hear the hum of the Bishopsgate traffic. The butler, in pin-striped trousers and with the ironic set grin one sees in all bank butlers, sat us down in large mock-Chippendale chairs. Peter, the nonchalant insider, lit a cigarette and looked at me with a smile. Sir Charles came in.

As I have already observed, one's immediate and lasting impression was of a very formidable presence. Tall, large, well proportioned, immaculate, with a shiny dome-shaped head topping well-formed regular features — no wonder Sir Charles had been such an outstanding intelligence chief during the war, the Germans would run a mile; no wonder that he was one of the most respected men in the City of London; no wonder that people came from across the world to do business with his family bank as they came later with similar respect and admiration towards his cousin Jocelyn.

At tea on this day, Sir Charles Hambro did not waste much time. He said he gathered from Peter and others that I was very useful to Jack Cotton and that I knew a bit about property financing and a bit about property shares. He thought I might be useful to the bank. He looked me straight in the eye with one of the most concentrated glares I had ever seen in my life. 'Come and join us. Jack will provide your rations, we'll provide you with everything else. Let's see how it works, and good luck.'

Jack Cotton, as Sir Charles so amiably put it, was paying my rations and Hambros were providing the services. We were all going to see how it worked out. I wonder how that great merchant banker, if he had lived, would have considered how it had worked out when I left Hambros some six years later.

*   *   *

A meeting had been arranged at the Dorchester. Around the board table apart from Jack Cotton and myself, there were Harry Sporborg, Francis Brandford Griffiths who ran Hambros' office in Paris, Charles Villiers and his colleague at Schroders, Govi Mallinckrodt (a most courteous and charming German who was soon to marry the boss's attractive and intelligent daughter Charmain Schroder. The purpose of the meeting was to discuss property investment on the Continent. A year before, I had written in the *Chronicle* that 'for some years property investors have gone as far afield as Canada, mainly with lamentable short-term results. Yet so far, if one ignores the Murrayfield/City Centre flats deal in Paris, not one of the developers has crossed the Channel and become Common Market minded'. When this article appeared, although it drew a surprisingly

140

quick response from the institutions, brokers and property companies seeking to discuss property investment on the Continent, it was nevertheless another ten years before the British property developer started to conquer Continental fields as Marlborough and Wellington had done centuries earlier. My own interests were and are deeply European. The Common Market had caught my imagination and full support from its earliest days, so that when the European League for Economic Co-operation headed by Geoffrey Rippon so successfully activated its ideas and aims (and deserving a major credit for helping to nudge Britain into the EEC), I enthusiastically supported its operations and donated substantially towards its financial requirements. This was also one area where Cotton and Clore were of like mind. They were both very European-minded. If anything Clore was the more cosmopolitan as a businessman, more interested in the EEC, and as the largest shoe retailer and manufacturer in the United Kingdom more alive to its dangers as well as its strengths.

Our particular meeting in the Dorchester suite was called because I was even more anxious than Jack Cotton to investigate property possibilities on the Continent, and after some discussions between us we had decided that it should be launched through the two joint financial advisers of City Centre, Hambros and Schroders. Jack was as ever concerned with expansion, and moreover the continent of Europe was large enough to lose dear Walter Flack, whom he had in mind to be in charge of the operation, indicating once again that in corporate decision-making, geographical displacement can also be the reason rather than the effect of many top level management appointments. Cotton had already discussed Europe with Clore and he knew that he had his deputy chairman's approval.

The Murrayfield/City Centre flats transaction in Paris had been unique. As recounted by Flack himself, with scant regard to accuracy but with his usual panache, he had gone down the Seine in his new yacht, the *Isambard Brunel* — named for the eminent Victorian engineer and builder, one of Walter Flack's heroes — and had become so utterly bored when the engines broke down opposite the Eiffel Tower that he had jumped on to the quay and bought the first block of flats he saw. Actually, he had been put on to it by his friends, Prince Rupert Loewenstein and Anthony Berry. Some transactions had taken place elsewhere. Metropolitan Estates, now MEPC, was developing property in Toronto, Central & District was developing a new town in Canada, Berkeley Properties owned some buildings in exotic Tampa, City Centre was in Manhattan and Port Elizabeth,

141

Slough Estates was developing tracts of industrial estates outside Melbourne. But the sum total of British property endeavours on the Continent was this one single purchase by Walter Flack, the Boucheron House on Avenue Foch in Paris.

Sporborg and Villiers, both as usual very succinct, agreed at our meeting that we should first make a preliminary study of continental property finance. Each of the two merchant banks envisaged contacting old-established banking friends in the various European countries, friendships which would be strengthened or re-awakened by a new business activity — property — an activity moreover which had international appeal and was easily understood. To these European banking friends they would be talking about an important joint client, City Centre, whose chairman and whose deputy chairman were so well-known that there might even be an element of financial glamour. The Continental banks, by tradition and practice, liked working with institutional shareholders, and City Centre, in addition to the fame of its two controlling shareholders, had some of the more celebrated institutions of Great Britain as shareholders and indeed, alongside Cotton and Clore, their own representatives on the board. What better opportunity of making new banking relationships and renewing old ones?

It made excellent sense to the two merchant banks. It was fascinating to perceive how their collective minds and wisdom were reflected through their respective directors. Inherently each bank thought it was more distinguished than the other, and they were both probably correct because they were not strictly the same animal. Each was controlled by a family, which was where the similarity ended. Most of Schroders was owned by one man, Helmut Schroder, together with his son Bruno and his daughter Charmain, the balance of the equity being held by the public and associates. Leaving ownership aside, the family influence in running the bank was nil. Helmut Schroder lived near Windsor and was a passionate and erudite orchid grower, and Bruno's main occupation was the more than full-time job of coping with his large family trusts. Only Mallinckrodt, the prospective son-in-law, had an executive position in the bank, albeit at that time at a rather lowly level. Now he is not only one of the more important UK directors, he is head of the New York operation. Hambros Bank on the other hand was not controlled by one Hambro, but by several branches of the Hambro family, and the bank was certainly run by the family, consciously and firmly. Of the separate branches in control, Jocelyn Hambro's side was by far the richest. The reason, curiously, was that, some generations earlier, a Hambro making his bequests had left most of the landed estates to the 'lucky' side of the family and most of the bank (which was 'trade') to the 'unlucky' side. Jocelyn's side had inherited most of the bank and Sir Charles Hambro's and Jack Hambro's side had inherited most of the land, virtually all sold before the last war.

In 1961 Jocelyn's father, Olaf, having resigned as chairman for decades, died in harness and his cousin Sir Charles Hambro became chairman; Jack Hambro another cousin became deputy chairman. (Decisions on the entry of partners' sons were made solely by the managers of departments for whom they worked on trial, with no interference from the family, an intelligent and odd method, but true.) Jocelyn's three sons were still at school or university. All of us at Hambros knew the inevitable succession — that after Sir Charles, Jack would be chairman and that after Jack it would be Jocelyn and after Jocelyn it would be Charlie and after Charlie, one of Jocelyn's sons. And so it has been. Jocelyn, who has a marvellous gift for producing just the right phrase or *mot*, in describing how his family bank was run, said sincerely and proudly that it was by 'enlightened nepotism', but with quintessential banking caution the enlightened nepotism only took effect after the Hambro sons were screened and tested by the non-family department heads. Banking is after all about checks and balances.

Just as a Hambro was and definitely would be chairman of Hambros Bank, a Schroder was definitely not nor foreseeably would be chairman of Schroders. Their chairman was in fact an ex-barrister who had specialised in company law: his name — Gordon Richardson, now Lord Richardson. When he was appointed in 1957 at the age of forty-one, it caused a great stir in the City: a complete outsider, a lawyer, no title, no money, not even an Etonian; it was without precedent. He had no banking experience and to cap it all he was coming in at the top. It was an incredible appointment and as it turned out, once he was appointed Chairman a few years later, possibly the best top banking appointment made by anyone at any time in the City of London. Under Gordon Richardson, Schroders undoubtedly became one of the smoothest, best-operated merchant banks in the City: general overall expansion, little publicity, less fanfare, superb results. A natural leader and a natural banker, Richardson also emerged as potentially one of the best Governors of the Bank of England of the century when he left Schroders for the Old Lady. To my mind Schroders, like Hambros and one or two others, has always been the epitome of merchant banking at its best because it was rarely less than professional in any of its manifestations. It remains to be seen whether the new leadership can maintain the standards set by the previous régime, for, in recent years, apart from losing Richardson to the Bank of England, it has lost Villiers (to steel), Murphy (to the NEB), and last but by no means least, the brilliant Wolfensohn (to Salomon Brothers and now to his own investment banking business).

On the corporate finance side, Schroders had a large number of clients, Hambros had very few; in banking, Schroders were relatively small whereas Hambros were relatively large: in America, Schroders were huge, bigger than all the other UK merchant banks put together (and they probably still are), whereas Hambros had only just acquired through Peter Folliss its interests in Laidlaw in New York, a comparatively small investment house. In new issues Schroders had a profitable business through its acquisition of Helbert Wagg, whereas Hambros had a small, almost non-existent new business. On the European front, Hambros was immensely strong in Scandinavia, whereas in the rest of the Continent both banks were about even.

That day at the Dorchester, Cotton, Villiers and Sporborg did all the talking, or rather most of it. Francis Brandford Griffiths also spoke, mostly in an amiable stutter, Govi Mallinckrodt and I kept silent. The consensus was that a team would be set up of the three young ones: we would work together, Mallinckrodt and Brandford Griffiths representing their respective banks and myself representing City Centre. After the meeting Cotton said to me, 'Charles will be pleased about this. I shall tell him about it straight away.'

I had met Mallinckrodt before. He had very graceful manners which were quite natural to him, he was stolid, reliable and thoroughly straightforward. This was the first time, however, that I had really met Francis Brandford Griffiths, Hambros' representative in Paris, with their offices in gilt and cream mock-Louis housed in the Place Vendôme directly opposite the Ritz where Jocelyn and I always stayed, and Clore too at the time. The direct view from the Ritz across the Place to the Hambro offices where we had our various meetings gave Francis five or ten minutes to get his thoughts in order, whilst he watched us walking across for our rendezvous. As the man in Paris, I had naturally expected a suave elegant banker with the air of the experienced man-about-*salons*. Instead he looked like an untidy Humpty Dumpty with a podgy yet pointed face and a

144

roundish head. I soon discovered that Francis usually only stuttered when he had to talk figures and was more than articulate when he talked of people, especially bankers. He was a veritable mine of information, knowing what had occurred in and out of banking parlours for the last five or six decades up to the previous day. He was invariably up to date. He knew the ebbs and flows, the rumours and the counter-rumours, who had been guests for lunch at this bank, at other banks, what they had eaten, the exact year and shipper of the wine, and why they had been invited. He knew who had been excluded from important meetings, which banks would allow their representatives to sit on the boards with other banks and which wouldn't and why they wouldn't; he knew why, after a break in relationships going on for forty or fifty years, a bank had suddenly put a representative on some other forbidden bank's board or subsidiary; he knew why after a short courting period one bank bought a piece of another bank's new venture. He had remarkable knowledge and remarkable verbal stamina. I listened and he talked, and he talked and I listened and he talked, but like the very best Vatican courtier (which role would have suited him to perfection) he was never indiscreet except deliberately.

Jack found Francis a little strange, Charles Clore ignored him, and Walter Flack, when he met him in Paris, found him as curious as a museum piece; but it was readily apparent to anyone who met him that he had extensive if not esoteric banking experience and Jack, always quick to perceive the strengths and potential of a new relationship, took his comments seriously. Francis on his part found the Dorchester entourage strange and disturbing, he was not overwhelmed by the Rembrandt or Renoirs — possibly in his own mind some real or imagined ancestor had owned them — but it was a social and business atmosphere alien to his usual experience. Moreover, he didn't feel at ease with Jack, wilting under that Cotton gaze, for Jack had the unnerving habit of assessing a new acquaintance or reassessing an old one by sucking on his cigar, looking at him levelly and saying nothing. Nevertheless, like all who met Cotton, Francis immediately recognised that here was a major talent and in fully appreciating Cotton's formidable gifts he fully accepted the viability and enormous strength and power of City Centre. However, in merchant banking terms the considered personal judgment which Brandford Griffiths would formulate on Cotton and indeed on Clore would be crucial. It would colour the sensitive and delicate conversations he would make, and would enjoy making, to the chairmen and directors of the banks and others on the Continent, in anticipation and in preparation for our initial visits and discussions and to be followed by later encounters between the legendary Jack Cotton himself and his new Continental associates. Ostensibly Hambros and Schroders were thoroughly committed to City Centre. They therefore 'approved' of Cotton and Clore and, in opening the doors to their banking friends abroad, they were not only sealing the respectability of their client, but were putting at risk what was to them of far greater importance, their own relationships with these banks. It was soon apparent to me that two or three directors at Hambros and Schroders felt uncomfortable about City Centre, their concern centering on the viability of the relationship between Cotton and Clore rather than the viability of their company. At lunches, meetings, dinners, one of them would casually bring up the subject, seeking some sort of reassurance. I hope I provided it by stressing Jack's character and ability and Clore's love for money, an addiction so obsessional that I thought (wrongly, as I realised later) he would never rock the boat because it would lose him money. When any bank introduces its client to another bank, all aspects are considered very carefully, for opening the door to the wrong person could ruin a century's friendship. The door handle is consequently turned very slowly, a whispered question, a sentence or two with the appropriate director, the door now slightly ajar, the initial intro-duction to the customer himself, the telephone call from the foreign bank to 41: 'And how is Jocelyn? We haven't seen him for some time. He must be very busy since Olaf's death. . . .' The checking and re-checking behind the scenes. Then the actual confrontation: the representatives of the client, City Centre, arriving on the scene, flanked by Francis and Govi. It was a ritual as old as Byzantium, as old as the benches or *bancos* in St Mark's Square where European banking had all started in the first place and where it had got its name.

No one can be considered a professional banker unless he is well-versed in this elaborate part of banking foreplay. Francis was a master at it. A bank's greatest possession is its name, not its balance sheet. One false move, one bad introduction, one dicky client and its reputation can be destroyed forever. Francis, fully aware of all the dangers, manipulated Hambros' relationships with great skill. As for me he admitted that his job was extremely easy in making the introductions for he could emphasise that I had been the leading City expert on property shares before being the financial consultant to City Centre. These early Continental excursions, arising from the initial meeting in Jack's Dorchester suite, were beautifully prepared and organised by Brandford Griffiths. In the course of time he and I worked very closely together; in fact after Jocelyn Hambro he became my closest colleague. For years we gossiped together, intrigued together, did deals together. We did so much together we never got to know each other. Such is the nature of a close commercial friendship between colleagues. Nor have I seen him since I left Hambros. But in the European property plans of Jack Cotton and Charles Clore, and in particular in respect of Walter Flack, he had a vital role to play.

*   *   *

Whilst swanning around on the Continent for City Centre with Francis Brandford Griffiths and Govi Mallinckrodt, I got embroiled in and became one of the co-founders of an important property financing company later called Intershop Holdings AG. In Europe the UK property boom was the talking point in all the Continental banking parlours and whilst the British would normally be received fairly frostily, we in the real estate sector found ourselves being sought after, to explain the nature of the boom which intrigued many of the European bankers and the nature of the property men, like Cotton and Clore who were being increasingly featured in the financial pages of the Continental press.

Intershop AG was the brainchild of Dr Hans Braunschweiller, then the general manager, now the chairman and chief executive of the Winterthur Insurance Company. His original idea was to form a Swiss property company which would invest directly in shopping centres and supermarkets throughout Europe. Braunschweiller had already talked in Paris to Ben Jakober, the chief of Edmond de Rothschild's property empire, and also in Amsterdam to Keuning, the head of the Netherlands Overseas Bank.

Keuning, whom I already knew because of our City Centre Europe investigations, arranged that I met Braunschweiller. I liked the concept, so did Cotton, and we both thought that Intershop should finance other developers or retail groups, rather than be a developer or owner itself. Arising from my new experience on City Centre Europe, I also thought that a leading bank from each country in Europe should be asked to become shareholders with representation on the board. I suggested that both Hambros and Schroders might come in from England and that to lend property weight, Jack Cotton might join them, as Intershop was not in conflict with City Centre; on the contrary there would be benefits on both sides. After some meetings Jakober, Keuning, Braunschweiller, Erich Gayler (a distinguished Zurich lawyer) and I, as co-founders, finally agreed the terms round the old Schroders' board table in Fenchurch Street. Gordon Richardson attended an early meeting and he nominated a delightful colleague Bobby Holland to come on the board of Intershop. Apart from Hambros, Schroders, Netherlands Overseas, the Winterthur, La Compagnie Financière (Edmond de Rothschild's bank) and Jack Cotton and myself as large shareholders, the Kredietbank from Belgium, the Lavoro from Italy, the Bayerische Hypothek from Germany, also joined in. We celebrated the start of our own Intershop club in typical Rothschild fashion with a lunch at one of Edmond's celebrated Paris houses. Six large round tables had been laid with magnificent plates and cutlery, and a footman in livery for almost every guest stood behind the beautifully carved chairs. As we entered, Keuning asked me what was the delicious aroma pervading the house. 'Money,' I replied. In the twenty years I have known this humourless man, it was the only time I heard him laugh.

The early years of Intershop were enjoyable mainly because the directors all liked each other. Once every quarter we would meet in a different capital, looked after superbly by the host bank. Over the years Intershop has grown into a thriving business operated from and quoted in Zurich, now involved in shopping centres and supermarkets not only in Europe, but throughout the USA. Meetings of the executive board of Intershop took place monthly in Zurich. We had an extremely good management, led and still led by Jacques Muller, who has become a world expert on shopping centres.

Through these monthly meetings I became immensely fond of Zurich. The city old and new is small, clean, placid, predictable, and its personality, emanating from its honest citizens, is shaped by their total and uncluttered admiration for money, especially if it is money on deposit — an attitude I have always found very cosy and unhypocritical.

If I were asked to describe a Zurich gnome, I could not do better than describe Paul Kern, Hambros' man in Zurich and the first man to tell me that the Cotton/Clore partnership would end in disaster. Certainly when I first met him during this Intershop period at his office in Claridenstrasse behind the Baur au Lac Hotel, I had an immediate feeling that I was in the company of the quintessential Swiss gnome. He was small, with a head that was too large for his body and ears too large for his head. Those ears were veritable antennae, they could hear whispers across boardrooms and through walls and across frontiers more accurately than a short-wave radio. His eyes were Zurich banker's blue, deep and expressionless, watering a little with age, but glimmering, impish and alive, especially when he heard a joke against another bank or another banker. He wore well-cut grey flannel suits, white shirts and restrained ties, a slight English look which he nourished deliberately and with more care than he would ever admit. He usually sat with slightly hunched shoulders, cigarette in his hand and a wicked smile set around an untidy mouth somewhat like a precocious schoolboy. When I first met Kern he was already a legendary character in banking circles. He was an expert on currency and an even greater expert on the psychology of Continental bankers (especially German) which gave him an enormous advantage over his rivals in estimating the value of a currency. He used to say you could evaluate and judge the character and stability of a nation by the character and stability or otherwise of its currency. He fully understood the commercial, economic and political policies which dictated business conditions, but long, long before that he would already have decided what to do from his own spy network, based on incessant phone calls made all over Europe, the high-pitched conversation sounding as if he were deciding what apfelstrudel or gâteau to have for tea. Paul Kern was as wily as a monkey. He hedged every single bet: he was never caught short. He was wonderfully informed but he only told you what he wanted you to know, what he wanted you to pass on, and what he knew you would pass on. He was articulate and accurate but he would deliberately make statements which forced you to doubt what he was saying. He would talk behind anyone's and everyone's back and he took relish in letting you know that this was one of his major pleasures and one of his major weaknesses. He loved gossiping. In fact he was so good at it that he made it an art; he created gossip in front of you like his billowing cigarette smoke, and as one listened to his rasping Germanic English, frequently punctuated by vicious coughs, you wondered if anyone could possibly be more gnome-like or more devilish. He had some endearing qualities because his mischief was more intellectual than personal; calculated as a challenge to one's intellect, to one's own susceptibilities and prejudices. One couldn't trust Paul Kern but he forced you to trust

149

yourself.

He often and openly said that though he was a Hambros man he had more affection for Schroders. I had done an inestimable service, he told me, in bringing the banks somewhat closer through Intershop. It was typical of the man that he would prefer Schroders. But it was also typical of the man that he would be the first to warn me, well before anyone else, that our City Centre Continental plans would come to nothing. He had never met Cotton and Clore, but what marvellous antennae he had.

And when he died he also took his final option. In hedging every bet he lived a Jew and died a Catholic. Charlie Hambro and I flew over together from London to represent Hambros at his funeral in Zurich. I was most impressed by the large number of people by his graveside. It was a Catholic cemetery, but most of the mourners were Jews. Paul Kern had done it again.

*   *   *

Intershop was started soon after I was installed in '41'. Around the same time I founded another important investment vehicle called Bishopsgate Property. About a year later I also started Bentworth Group Holdings, the precursor of Spey, which also involved Hambros. Jack Cotton made personal investments in the first two, and greatly encouraged me with the third. Charles Clore was livid that I had excluded him from all three and carped about it for years after — forgetting that we were hardly on speaking terms during this time.

The idea behind what came to be called Bishopsgate Property had arisen whilst I was still at the *Chronicle*, when dozens of the new-type property companies were coming to the market for public quotations. Their promoters or major shareholders varied from instant property men — entrepreneurs who had wittingly or unwittingly discovered a bandwagon at the beginning of its bullish trip — to professional property owners and family trusts with portfolios assembled and improved over decades and now seeking a public quotation (mostly for estate duty reasons). In every boom there are investors prepared to accept any flotsam offered to them, and I had formed the belief that institutional and private investors ought to be provided with an impeccable property investment outlet which would provide a balanced stable spread in this increasingly popular but still incomprehensible sector of the market. One instance of this incomprehensibility was that some property companies not only refrained from writing off interest charges on properties in the course of development, they followed the practice of adding back the net after-tax amount to the profit and loss account. Unless one understood this practice the profit and loss accounts of all the development property companies and many of the property investment companies were obscure.

Investors required clarity and guidance and I thought that Bishopsgate Property could satisfy that need. The idea was to select a well-balanced group of quoted property shares as the initial portfolio and also to take stakes in selected unquoted growth companies. In the market generally there were dozens of investment trusts, formed mostly before the war. They were of all sorts, directed towards all types of investors, satisfying it would seem almost every conceivable investment need. There was however no investment trust nor any unit trust yet serving the property sector.

The conventional method of forming and establishing an investment trust was for the new trust to issue a prospectus soliciting funds, then for it to purchase holdings through the market or convert an existing private portfolio into a public investment trust. Bishopsgate Property was going to be different; its own shares would be exchanged for the shares owned by large holders in selected property companies, starting off, it was hoped, with £5 million worth of Bishopsgate shares issued in exchange for £5 million worth of shares in selected property companies.

The second distinctive feature in Bishopsgate, its investment policy, was based upon the belief that we should be actively involved in the business of supporting the young Jack Cottons of tomorrow, financing them in their earliest endeavours with Bishopsgate's own resources, arranging and organising finance for them through the institutions, with whom Bishopsgate would be forging new links on their behalf. An endemic part of Bishopsgate therefore was that it would engage in active management, not the then conventional passive type of investment trust management.

I drew up a detailed memorandum on Bishopsgate. I arranged to see Jack Cotton. He sat as usual in his chair at the head of his board table. I was on his left, my favourite position because I could more clearly see the Fantin-Latours by the bay windows overlooking Park Lane. When the sun shone the boardroom was bathed in light and colour, the freshly cut Marlow tulips sparkled from their vases one on each side table, and the Fantin-Latours glowed with quiet beauty and pride. Through the windows Hyde Park itself, with its huge oak trees, a mass of green foliage, seemed inches away. At such times, when the diary was deviously spaced by Tapper so that there was time to spare, when Cotton had perhaps just completed a particularly satisfying transaction or when he had just had a more pleasant encounter with Clore or Sainer, or when he had just agreed to make a charitable gift — at such times when he felt calm and tranquil, his clarity of mind would be well-pitched, his sense of humour would start humming and his natural star quality, radiant and good-natured, would engender a feeling of warm humanity around him. At rare times like this he would shout at Tapper in a more affectionate tone, almost as if to reassure himself that she was still there, then embark in a flash upon new decisions, getting up to telephone Freddie or Aubrey or Plum to suggest a new course of action. At such times one saw the man's genius. It was on one of these serene occasions that Jack Cotton and I discussed what was to become my own first major achievement. 'Dear boy,' he said, 'you know I won't read your memorandum. Just tell me about it. Bless you.' I gave him a run-down. No comment. He was engrossed in his Monte Cristo and gazing at a Fantin-Latour, eyes half-closed. 'Go over the projections again.' Turquoise smoke curled from the Monte Cristo. His eyes were glinting, a sure sign that the computer was working. 'Yes,' he said at length, 'it's okay. You've got it right — by accident of course.' A half-smile, another pause. 'I'll take half a million for the trusts.' I shot out of my seat. 'You heard what I said. I'll take half a million for the trusts.' He leaned back. 'I don't agree with your selection of companies, but you have my support. Speak to Harry Sporborg and you can mention what I have just told you.' He then started talking about the selection of the companies and about his own early days — until we went downstairs to lunch.

*　　*　　*

Jack Cotton had a great deal of faith in people. He was a man who, if he liked you, if he judged you sound, would trust you implicitly. This was probably one of the greatest personality differences of all between him and Clore. Clore whose ambitions and associations were calculated, had very little faith in people. Both men survived on their instincts to a very great degree, but in utterly dissimilar ways. But Cotton's more volatile character could work against you too: if he didn't take to you, if he didn't perceive a like mind, if there were an element of good will or good sense missing, that was it. He would have no part of you.

This disparity of personality was interestingly illuminated in the relations between City Centre and a close neighbour of Hambros, the Bearsted family bank next door but one from '41', M. Samuel & Co. Lord Bearsted, its chairman, came from one of the most distinguished families in the City. His great-grandfather Marcus Samuel had been one of the greatest entrepreneurs in history. Originally an East End dealer in seashells, he had not only started Shell Oil but had also founded the bank — its emblem naturally being a shell too. Bearsted had two younger brothers; but the leading light of the bank, his protégé, was Julian Melchett, a brilliant — and kindly — man whose grandfather Mond was a founder of ICI. The great-grandsons of the two founders of two of the largest companies in the world, both peers of the realm, were partners together in a happy personal and commercial relationship in Bishopsgate.

Clore was particularly drawn to Melchett. He respected his open and intelligent approach to business and was intrigued by the fact that Melchett, a natural aristocrat, was of Jewish origin. One of the results of their friendship was the later purchase by Clore of a holding in M. Samuel which made him the largest shareholder of this august bank after the Samuels themselves. Clore went on to the board; he was now a director of a merchant bank and an accepting house. How proud he was. So proud in fact that he told me about the proposed arrangement before it was announced. Gratuitous information from Clore was unprecedented. We were having one of our first ever lunches together, some weeks after Jack had resigned. He looked hard at me and said, 'I trust you. I'm going to tell you something confidential. I am going to become a shareholder and director of M. Samuel. Listen, when I was a boy, very poor looking for a crust, I would take a bus from the East End and pass the big headquarters of M. Samuel in Bishopsgate, with the shell outside. Now the poor little Jewish boy from the East End is going to be a director of the bank. What do you think? Charles Clore with the great Samuel family. And I couldn't even afford the bus fare.'

In the twenties, Lord Bearsted's father had purchased from the Berkeley family their estate in Mayfair. It extended over Berkeley Square, Bruton Street, Bruton Place, Charles Street and Hill Street. Regrettably, before the war, the Samuels had granted long leases on many of their Mayfair houses which had made individual fortunes for many of their tenants after the war. The Samuel Estate was, like the Sutton Estate, one of the best known of the family-owned estates in London. Lord Bearsted had recently consolidated some of his family property in a new company called Samuel Properties, the main asset being these fabulous Mayfair acres. Lord Bearsted and Jack Cotton talked of a possible merger with City Centre. It was a sensible idea, as Samuel Properties had no development experience and could look to City Centre for this know-how, whereas City Centre could obtain in return a portfolio of Mayfair reversionary properties which it could look after closely for the benefit of its shareholders, including the Samuel family, over future decades. Details of the portfolio were sent to Eric Young, and Cotton asked me to look at the corporate and financing aspects. Samuel Properties had an unbalanced portfolio. If it sold all or part of the estate, its main property asset, to City Centre, it would exchange low-yielding reversionary properties for a large lump of shares and loan stock in City Centre. What the company needed was more property, not less, and more management. Bearsted realised this and talks had been started with Sydney Cowan, a developer, who, together with his partner, Jack Dellal, had built up their own private property company, City & Southern. These two had been introduced to Bearsted by William de Gelsey, a friend of Melchett's and a well-known genial man about town who had recently joined M. Samuel. I looked at the Dellal/Cowan balance sheet and suggested to Cotton that City Centre should acquire Samuel Properties, which could then acquire the Dellal/Cowan company. This way, City Centre would broaden its own equity base, bring in a new impartial partner in Lord Bearsted, whose own presence and authority would balance the relationship between Cotton and Clore. There were attractions to this combination or a similar one, but the stumbling block appeared to be Jack Dellal. During all these manoeuvres, everyone kept on looking at me. Eventually I got the message. It was I who had to speak to Dellal.

I met Dellal for tea in the lounge of the Dorchester; there was no question of inviting him to the suite upstairs. I didn't know what to expect. This was the man dubbed Black Jack by the City and the financial press who later became a leading force at Keyser Ullman. What was the reason for Cotton's antipathy? As I approached him in the lounge, he got up from his seat. He looked like a Soulage painting: swatches of white and black and tan and black. It was inevitable that he would be known as Black Jack. I broached the subject and he roared with laughter. 'What's it all about? All I want is the cash. I don't want any directorship. Why all the fuss? I love Jack Cotton. We all do. He is great for all of us who are in property. Long may he prosper.'

Samuel Properties eventually bought the Dellal company, and Bearsted decided to retain family control of Samuel Properties. But he did sell half his Mayfair Estate to City Centre Properties in exchange for shares. It was regrettable from any point of view that Bearsted did not go on the City Centre board, for his presence and quiet personality and authority would have helped to circumvent some of the later conflicts. Clore, who liked the transaction, would have welcomed Bearsted's presence, and would have been conscious of his bus rides as a child.

*　　*　　*

There were two landmarks in my career with Jack Cotton which stay in my mind particularly. Oddly, they were at opposing ends of the property scale. One was City Centre's interests in the world of car parks, the other its association with an Oxford college; yet both displayed Cotton's vision and his flair for negotiating and dealing with people to a memorable degree.

I had become interested in the problems of traffic and car-parking soon after I started at the *Investors' Chronicle*, but incredible as it may seem, until the sixties no purpose-built underground or multi-level car park had been built in London. London was going through the same problem as any other city in the world, but going through it in a typically muddled fashion whilst the car-owning boom in the Western democracies was causing one of the world's nastiest urban problems. Everyone had a car, it was modern man's Bible; he went nowhere without it. Irreparable decisions were taken, ruining whole residential sections, majestic eighteenth-century streets and quiet squares. St James's Street was made one-way and lost its charm forever. So did Piccadilly; Mayfair became a driver's maze; and when buses were seen in Berkeley Square, the nightingales flew away never to return. Traffic problems however did not fly away; they got worse and worse. Most of the existing car parks were at street level, old bombed sites, leased to National Car Parks Limited, which most car drivers thought was a nationalised company

155

belonging to the state. There were incessant arguments about mechanical systems and inventors and builders came out with dozens of different schemes; only gradually did the planning staffs of the local authorities make some attempt to tackle the parking difficulties. They would purchase the sites, build the car parks, and either lease them to parking operators or operate them themselves. Amongst the first was a car park at Aldersgate in the City, which was successfully tendered for by an entrepreneur called Alex Kaye, who had teamed up with the Meyer brothers of Manhattan, an extremely successful American partnership. The City decided that it would itself operate another new car park, the one built under London Wall; whilst the operating contract for the largest of these early, unfriendly, asphalt monsters, the underground car park beneath Park Lane with space for 1100 cars, was granted to a subsidiary of J. Lyons. (If only the planners had gone down three or four more levels under Hyde Park, learnt indeed from the French, the best engineers in Europe, Central London's parking troubles would have been significantly eased for years.)

From my earliest days at the *Chronicle*, I had been fascinated not only by the obvious boom in the business of car parking, but by its urban aspects, by the design and architectural features, by the operational problems, systems, controls and administration, and of course by the financing. I talked to the planners and the architects about structures and façades. My brother Max had by now left Skidmore, Owings & Merrill in New York and joined two of his Cambridge friends as their partner in London. We got together. On my trips to New York, Chicago, Paris and other towns in America and on the Continent, I made the habit of visiting the city planning departments and looking at the latest designs, investigating the latest operations, studying the methods of financing. I felt that parking was a most essential aspect of property development and that its inclusion in a project would affect future values significantly. Parking had to be taken seriously by the property world, if only out of self-interest. Few were prepared to believe in it. Most of the property developers assumed that it was the responsibility of the local authorities. Anyway, how did one value a car park? It was a downright liability. Valuers and estate agents were also unenlightened, reluctant to put any value on a car park and discouraging their clients from any financial involvements. On the other hand, there were the public and planning authorities clamouring for more facilities. The short-sightedness of the property developers was appalling.

Cotton was aware of my enthusiasm for parking whilst I was still at the *Chronicle*, and when I first started talking about it with Alex Kaye and the Meyer brothers, he encouraged me with a foresight which no other developer at the time could match.

Alex Kaye and I met whilst his Aldersgate car park in the City was nearing completion. His staff had already been trained and his systems had already been organised by his Meyer Brothers partners. Kaye and the Brothers, as they were known, had been very thorough, applying new marketing techniques which are very much the norm today. They had written to every office user in the City, describing the services and the rates, explaining different prices for long-term parking as against daily rates. The figures showed that there would be a profit if 50% capacity was achieved on a five-day week. The lease which Kaye and the Meyers had signed was for ninety-nine years with reviews every twenty-one years. Kaye and I went over the figures carefully. If the rent was static for twenty-one years and charges to customers and other charges went up by 10% or 20% and capacity went beyond his 50% estimate, what then? Very elementary: immense returns. And if charges actually doubled, the profit would go up more than fourfold. The figures were very acceptable indeed.

I eventually met the Meyer brothers through Kaye and sub-sequently met their numerous sons-in-law and nephews. All of them were in the business; not one of the tribe, none of the sons-in-law, was permitted to work outside. It was a real American family business, and every member of the family was, quite literally, a car park fanatic. Well into the small hours they would discuss the merits of one operating system against another, the merits of non-mechanical against mechanical parks (they disliked the latter); incessantly they would discuss cash and cost controls, the different types of ticket machines, security and surveillance. In the years I knew the brothers, all our conversations were centred on parking — any other subject was virtually forbidden. The world to them was one vast car park, and they firmly believed that they had a mission in life — to park every car they could lay their tickets on. As far as they were concerned, General Motors and Ford also had a mission: to manufacture and sell motor cars in order to have them parked, preferably by the brothers.

They abhorred street parking. It was offensive, obscene, it was an open sewer, it was unhygienic. There was only one proper place for a motor car — in a car park — and, understandably, in a Meyers car

157

park. Kaye too was a fanatic on car parking; he had to be, otherwise the Meyers would never have taken him on as a partner. He was already an honorary member of the Meyer family and was known as the sixth Meyer brother. On one occasion in New York, at a meeting at Laidlaw's with the Meyer brothers, Peter Folliss jokingly asked them where they parked their cars. What, give business to a competitor? As they had no downtown car parks, they had arrived in taxis.

The Meyers' company in London was owned by the brothers and by Alex Kaye. It had a tiny capital of £10,000 and a small loan provided by Alex Kaye. But they had a problem. Famous in Manhattan, they were unknown in the United Kingdom; the new company had no standing, no covenant and Kaye's problem was to convince the local authorities and the property developers that they Meyer Brothers in the UK were serious operators. He had obtained the Aldersgate site because of a lucky introduction to the contractor, and now he needed an important financial partner, preferably a financial and property partner. City Centre would be ideal, a tremendous catch, for it would allow Kaye to compete with National Car Parks which already had over half of the market, an astounding near-monopoly. Kaye and I agreed on a deal which was probably one of the best City Centre ever did, relative to the money invested. City Centre purchased 20% of the equity for £2,000 and made a nominal loan of £25,000 for one year. A further 10% of the equity was taken up by Hambros, myself and Peter Folliss — which particularly pleased Jack as it meant that Hambros were now involved in a formal equity association with City Centre for the first time. Jack wanted the City Centre board members to appreciate the importance of car parking in property development, and so had the board approve the investment formally, though it was far too small for their normal consideration. When Meyers was later sold to National Car Parks, City Centre received over a hundred times its original investment of £2,000.

The association with the Meyers worked well. The City Centre board liked it, perhaps because the minuscule loan of £25,000 was rapidly repaid and the company was already paying dividends. Two open sites in Hill Street and Charles Street, Mayfair, part of the Samuel Estate (now half-owned by City Centre), already had the Meyers signs prominently displayed. Felix Fenston, his house adjacent to the Hill Street site, asked for and immediately got from me a parking space for one of his cars: dispensing harmless patronage especially to personal friends is a minor though definite pleasure of commercial life. In addition, I helped arrange that Meyers should obtain the contracts to operate the Hilton car park and that of the Royal Garden Hotel in Kensington. The City Centre subsidiary companies were circularised with details of their parent's new parking involvement; meetings took place with surveyors and architects. As Cotton anticipated, better relations with local authorities on parking requirements benefitted City Centre on its larger projects. For their part, the Meyer brothers were delighted that at last they were being seriously taken by the local authorities and could start beating NCP at its own game.

On the Continent, the parking industry was in its infancy. The Meyer brothers and Kaye were not keen to expand across the Channel, but I took a more positive approach and we found ourselves sitting at meetings in Milan, Brussels, Zurich, Frankfurt, Paris, negotiating for future car-parking sites. How many cars per floor? What were the turning circles? How did the validation system work? What sort of fenestration? Cars were flooding the centre of every city. In Milan the Automobile Club were the historic owners of parking concessions; we discussed the possibility of going into partnership with the Club and covering the whole of Milan. In Paris there were plans for huge car parks under the Champs Elysées and the Place Vendôme; we looked at the plans, talked to the authorities, studied the costs. In Brussels a car park for the central area was being planned and the Kredietbank put us in touch with one of its clients as a possible partner, who himself eventually became the largest operator in Belgium. I could not, however, instill real enthusiasm in the brothers for operations on the Continent, and when they sold their US operation to Hertz Rent-a-Car, the parking plans for the Continent had to be shelved. Then I decided that we at Hambros would start our own parking company. We called it Europarks Limited and went into partnership with Lyons, who had the Park Lane park. We were now in direct competition with National Car Parks in the UK, and on the Continent we were soon operating car parks in Duisburg and Düsseldorf. Subsequently NCP acquired Europarks and the Meyers UK operation. Years later it gave me great pleasure when I purchased half of National Car Parks through Spey Investments, and particular delight to note that amongst the more valuable car parks were those I had started off myself.

The landmark at the other end of the scale concerned Brasenose
College. Opposite the Royal Garden Hotel in Kensington, which had
a Meyers-operated car park, was a property owned by Brasenose
College, Oxford. This is where Cotton had a special interest. Gary
Arnott, my successor at the *Investors' Chronicle*, had spent part of
his post-graduate career at Brasenose and had introduced me to
some of his ex-colleagues including Norman Leyland, by then the
College Bursar. Leyland told me about his college's property in
Kensington and that it suited his College to look into the possibilities
jointly with Cotton. A new principal of the College had just been
appointed, Sir Noel Hall, an economist and previously head of the
Henley Administrative Staff College. Perhaps because of his
management philosophy he was showing an unexpected commercial
interest in his college's property. The more predictable reaction of
the head of an Oxford college to a possible association with a
property tycoon might have been sheer horror. As it was, Noel Hall,
Norman Leyland and an outstanding academic lawyer named
Maudsley wanted to have further talks. Some kind of arrangement
made sense for both sides, as any project involving this large site
would be more viable if it were part of a comprehensive scheme,
rather than a piecemeal development.

Joyce Frankland, widow of a City goldsmith, had in 1586
bequeathed her property in the village of Kensington to Brasenose.
The incidence of England's remarkable social history seeps through
intriguingly whenever one looks at old conveyances and bequests.
Ancient leases bring to life people long dead and forgotten; lands
conveyed through marriage settlements, through dowries, through
bequests, through inheritance, reflect the characters of the people
and the families who became the successive owners. The conveyance
of land is described in quaint or direct or simple or legal English and
describes the heritage of an ancient and noble country more vividly
than any book of history. One can trace a poverty-to-riches story
through twenty generations in hundreds of conveyances, and a
riches-to-poverty story through a single generation, in a single
abrupt and tragic one. It is easy to see how English property law has
enriched the country's basic principles of law over the years, how it
relied on fairness, on what the 'reasonable' man would do. One can

also read into the conveyances the bitterness of family conflict, the greed, the chicanery and hate, and the fortune, good or bad, of battles and wars. One can learn how the landed estates came into being and how the landed gentry increased their holdings by luck or cleverness or marriage, or lost them through stupidity or gambling. One can see how the church built up its great stretches of property and one can see how the seats of learning at Oxford and Cambridge had themselves become amongst the largest of the landowners, some colleges with such formidable holdings that they ranked on a par with the largest landowners in the land.

By the standards of some of the colleges in Oxford, Brasenose was not rich, but it had some splendid endowments, some splendid properties, and thanks to Leyland some splendid equity investments.

History was made, though on a much more modest basis, when Cotton formed a joint company between his own City Centre and this ancient Oxford college. The corporation was called CCP (Brasenose) Limited. It was in reality a terribly small transaction, but when it was announced the press gave it immense prominence. For once Jack was less interested in the press than in the intrinsic association with an Oxford college. Before the conclusion of the deal, numerous meetings had taken place including the occasional dinner at high table. Cotton was invited after the press announcement and said he would be honoured to accept but he would like the date deferred until the proposed joint scheme was well under way. They were pleasant leisurely Oxford encounters. The Royal Ballet regularly visited Oxford and Cambridge each year on its summer tour, and having invariably accompanied Nadia to Cambridge, I now looked forward as well to the visits to Oxford. One year Leyland and his fellow dons gave a party for Nadia in college after *Swan Lake*, and one of our guests was Alan Clore, Charles's son, then up at the same time as my brother David. The party was a great success and when Cotton learnt that Clore's son had attended he questioned me closely as to what sort of person he was. Cotton was already showing signs of undue interest in Clore's personal life.

I wondered how my Brasenose friends would take to Jack Cotton, the nation's foremost property man, and now known even in the sheltered cloisters of Oxford. How would they speak of him to their colleagues? Two utterly different worlds were to meet: the one languid, scholastic, ancient, intellectual, the other dynamic, modern, commercial, pragmatic. And how different as landlords: the college had owned its properties for centuries, whereas City Centre had

161

owned its properties for little more than a decade.

It was arranged that we would have drinks in Cotton's boardroom followed by lunch downstairs in the Dorchester restaurant. I was nervous and went below to meet the Brasenose contingent. I found that they were more nervous than I. They would certainly need a drink. When they came into the suite, they were met by Jack who was at his best. He wore a crisp white shirt, a new spotted bow-tie, a dark blue suit with the ever-present flower in the buttonhole, his glasses were shining, his voluminous black hair neatly in place and his Monte Cristo alight. I made the introductions. Jack behaved like a born diplomat. After greeting each in turn warmly and courteously, offering them drinks and cigars — the latter declined — he talked of the general fears about property developers in general and himself in particular. He said that of course a lot of the fears were justified, particularly where the wrong developments were executed by the wrong developers — the new amateurs.

Jack made the point that property was not just a business; it was a profession. It required a trained, disciplined mind, not merely business ability. The larger property companies were led by men of vision — of whom he hoped he was one — who were aware of their responsibilities not only to their shareholders, but also to the millions of policyholders of the insurance companies supporting the property companies and of the members of the pension funds now doing likewise. There would be a growing bond between property companies, insurance companies and pension funds, and also with local authorities and the large landowners. He was presently having discussions with the Sutton Estate and indeed also with the Church Commissioners concerning land they had owned for centuries in Paddington. 'Like your land, Sir Noel, which your college has owned for several hundred years, but let's talk about that during lunch. Charles here tells me that before we go downstairs you would like to see the paintings.' In describing his paintings, it was apparent to his guests that he loved each one of them and knew a lot more about them than the price he had paid. We moved from the Fantin Latours in the boardroom across the lobby to the drawing-room. We gazed at his Renoir masterpiece, *La Pensée* and at the warm, serene Rembrandt. We then went downstairs to the restaurant, and as we settled down at the table Jack, who had been waved at and greeted in his customary manner by many of the other people having lunch, said to Sir Noel, 'I'll bet our young friend,' pointing at me, 'doesn't know how Brasenose got its name.' I didn't. 'But I'll tell you.' And he did so very eloquently.* Crafty Cotton, I thought, during all the time we had our negotiations and discussions with Brasenose, when he and Eric Young and I had looked at the leases and discussed the possibilities of an association, he had decided to catch me out. I knew why. Some weeks earlier, at breakfast with him in his suite, he asked me to tell him what was in the papers as he hadn't (very rare for him) yet seen the morning press. I told him that the Government had come to the conclusion that he was a major problem. He stopped in his tracks. 'Show me,' he demanded. I passed him one of the newspapers. The headlines read: 'Cotton problem. Government to take action.' He read on. There was unemployment in Lancashire and the Government was prepared to subsidise the cotton mills. 'Very funny. But don't worry,' he said, 'I'll get my own back.' He did, at the Brasenose lunch.

*　　　*　　　*

Every day meetings, discussions, telephone calls, lunches, dinners took place, with friends, aides, cohorts and money men. Every day deals were discussed, plots were hatched, decisions were taken. Every day the net worth of the two tycoons increased. Seven days a week. With the marriage of the two Cs, the price of their shares reached record levels. Jack Cotton and Charles Clore had a lot to be pleased about. But they also had a lot to be worried about. It was apparent to each of them that the honeymoon was over. What lay in store, however, was beyond any of Cotton's worst fears and beyond any of Clore's worst calculations.

* 'Brasenose' is the large brass nose on the front door or gate. There would be an equally large knocker to bang on the nose to attract the gatekeeper or porter. One can see the brass nose in the Hall of the college today, by the High Table above the Principal's place.

Part III

The Divorce

Chapter Ten

Flack by Name and Flack by Nature

Whilst the insiders were aware of the growing strain between the two tycoons, an outer semblance was maintained, sometimes with grim smiles, that the partnership was in effective working order. As expected, Clore had reacted against his notorious *placement* at the Waldorf lunch by examining Cotton's acquisitions far more closely. And he began seeking to impose upon him an orderly commitment procedure by pushing for the appointment of a chief executive. Cotton's response was similar to that of a supplicant wife in a new marriage. Instead of concentrating on making the relationship work, he concentrated exclusively on how he could best please his partner, sincerely believing that the best way of pleasing was to conduct business as usual. So, he engaged in more transactions, more joint companies and more press releases. Cotton's method of appeasement exacerbated what was already becoming a difficult and tense situation, eliciting cold fury from Clore when he would occasionally learn about a new City Centre transaction from his own morning newspaper. Clore insisted upon procedures and upon prior approvals; to his orderly mind, Jack's method was a form of madness. But Jack was incapable of curbing his natural ebullience even to the extent of pausing to talk to Clore before going ahead on a deal. He had a real desire to act as a genuine partner to his deputy chairman but in his wish to earn respect he couldn't comprehend that he was more likely to lose Clore's confidence, the more he endeavoured to impress him by a new transaction which had not been previously discussed.

After I moved into Hambros Bank I spent a great deal of my time on behalf of City Centre Europe, and would be at the Dorchester almost daily to make my reports to Jack. He would listen and then say, 'Terrific my boy, that will please Charles. I will phone him straight away. Tapper . . .' he would shout to Denise, 'get me

Charles.' He would pick up the telephone and recount my news. On many occasions the conversations were short. One could almost hear Clore saying, 'Good, good . . . let's discuss it at the next meeting.' Tensions mounted, and as Clore's doubts did likewise, Cotton made even more determined efforts to prove to Clore that he was mistaken in having any doubts about him. From the beginning Jack had decided his tactics — he was going to kill Clore with kindness. But the telephone conversations inevitably became shorter and Clore was more often 'out'. Sweat would sometimes appear on Cotton's brow. His enthusiasm would chill; the telephone receiver would be replaced. 'Come on, my boy, tell me more about Amsterdam.' Then, thinking of paperwork, of formalities, of agendas, of minutes, the orthodox procedures which Clore had increasingly insisted upon, Jack would add, 'Of course, you'll let me have a written report for the board.' I made reports on the meetings we had on the Continent, I made my monthly progress reports, I sent him copies of letters, most of the data I suspect not going any further than the Dorchester office. One ameliorating factor was that, with Jack's expected approval, I had instructed Titmuss Sainer to act as our lawyers on the European contracts rather than Linklaters and Paine, which meant that there was communication of sorts with Sainer in his capacity as lawyer rather than as director of City Centre or as Clore's number two.

Jack, in his patent effort to please, in his continuous anxiety to prove that their relationship was truly effective, made strenuous endeavours to show that he was a capable chairman meriting someone like Charles Clore as his deputy. He kept up a feverish pace, but with the tunnel vision of a lemming, resorting to more transactions and to more press releases. It was an inevitable and damning process of diminishing returns. Cotton was in a classic psychological block, resenting Clore's insistence on orderliness, knowing that fundamentally he was right to insist, yet detesting being shackled, unable to accept any form of constraint. Yet despite the questioning and the brickbats, he wanted above all to impress Clore and craved his approbation. In a room full of people, he was conscious only of Clore's presence and of Clore's reactions. The harder he tried to assert and reassert himself as an equal, the colder, the more abrupt, the more slighting was Clore's response. Those of us who were fond of Cotton could not bear to see him wilting, seemingly punch-drunk like a boxer. But by the evening, bolstered by drink, he would feel less of his anxieties, less of his trepidations;

168

he would feel stronger and more courageous. 'To hell with Charles,' he would say with growing bluster. 'I built up the company. Who does he think he is? He's only my deputy chairman.'

One would have thought that when the two mighty barons joined their land and forces together, they would have concentrated on consolidating their joint holdings, before charging out together at the head of their army to conquer more lands and vanquish other barons. Far from it. Jack Cotton's exceptional zest was infectious and in the early months of their marriage, even Clore was caught by it. Ideas of entrenchment were not considered: Cotton and Clore, the two great tycoons, would conquer the world together. It was astonishing how downright absurd were some of their early acquisitions and forays. It was puzzling to perceive that it was possible for so many normally cool, shrewd heads — not only the two entrepreneurs, but also the lesser cohorts running the subsidiaries — to be caught up in the feverish enthusiasm. In some ways the honeymoon had been more of an orgy. Were sane, sensible, prudent people being intoxicated by the sheer overpowering smell of money filtering out of the Renoirs, the Fantin-Latours, the Chippendale board tables, the fumes strongly fanned by press comment and dinner-party gossip? It was deeply disturbing to see that men of such fame and reputation pitched into this heady atmosphere could lose their sense of proportion in a trice and seem to forget everything they had ever learnt from experience.

It was not surprising, therefore, that someone like Walter Flack should surface onto the exotic Dorchester atmosphere and, in full frontal view of all the protagonists, be able to switch from being one of Jack Cotton's most loyal supporters to being one of his most vehement opponents. Once Flack had mounted the horse of ambition, all caution to the wind, he allowed his ill-saddled personal feelings to pervert his admiration for Cotton and transform it into contempt. Flack's own miserable end was a tragedy of delusion: he not only deluded himself into thinking he was on the same level as Cotton, he also deluded himself into believing that he could actually supplant him.

Flack was the most colourful character of the property scene of the day. He had a faint resemblance to the cheeky chappie, Max Miller, and should have worn a hat and cane and spats with his double-breasted waistcoat. He could tell a story as well as anyone with a natural, almost professional timing. His smile was questioning, almost sly, but a mile wide and he had an infectious

169

gaiety which could dissipate and dispel any rising feelings of irritation or anger. His smile was a knowing cockney smile, a centuries-old Lebanese smile, which had encountered and seen all the vices and sins of the world, all degrees of human failings. He was sometimes so winning it was dangerous to be in his company, safer to write a letter or to negotiate with him on the telephone. Even that provided no immunity from his powerful, wheedling charm. He had served in the war: he had had what is called a good war, in fact, the best as far as he was concerned. He had risen steeply from the lowest rank to the height of sergeant; he was extremely proud of his rank, by far the best, he always claimed, and of having risen from the bottom to what he considered to be the top. He knew how to inspire the troops and how to build up morale; he could repel a whole German battalion on his own. He was possibly the most popular sergeant in the entire British army, loving his men and detesting all officers — except one, the Auk, Field Marshal Sir Claude Auchinleck. The Auk was, in Walter Flack's fervent belief (and many others'), the greatest British general of the Second World War, indisputably superior to any other military leader. Flack had served under Auchinleck; he adored the Field Marshal, he worshipped him. He vowed that when he got out of the army, his aim more than any other would be to do something for the Auk. And he did. It was remarkable. By the mid-fifties, when Flack had become a rich man, Auchinleck was president of his company, and with the pride which can only come from a dream come true, an achievement thoroughly realised, he placed a specially commissioned bust of the Auk on a tall pedestal in the most prominent position in his offices. Passers-by could perceive the Auk, in bronze, very military, very correct, through the bow-fronted windows of Walter Flack's reception room facing on to St James's Street. Flack wanted everyone to see it. I am convinced to this day that this was his sole reason for having offices in St James's in the middle of clubland, surrounded by the most notable social and military enclaves, close to Boodle's and White's and Brooks's and the Carlton. The Auk must have had an unexpected but definite affection for this strange little cockney with his strange little touch of genius.

I am sure, too, that the Auk would have been as surprised as I was to discover that Flack was a man with a deep streak of malice in him.

It was a malice that did not seem to fit him at all; it was like somebody else's overcoat, temporary and alien. Yet when he made up his mind to attack he was instinctively cruel, out to kill not merely to injure. In the end it was himself he destroyed. Flack made up his mind that he was the man to run City Centre and, as Cotton was in the way, he decided to destroy him, and because he believed I was in his way, he tried to destroy me as well. By the strangest of ironies, he was one of Jack's earliest and most sincere admirers and it was because of his devotion to Jack that he became a member of the City Centre family in the first place. Nevertheless Walter Flack, in dramatically changing sides from Cotton to Clore, started the pernicious campaign which eventually forced Cotton to resign from the company he had founded. He decisively cracked the façade that the Cotton-Clore partnership was an effective entity.

Sergeant Flack's property group, Murrayfield, had commenced after the war as a by-product of his estate agency business, started with one or two of his partners without any financial backing other than the inevitable overdraft. His first transactions were trading deals which provided a certain amount of working capital, but his big breakthrough came as a result of a tender offer for the Basildon town centre scheme. The Corporation of this new town had decided that it wanted a well-designed shopping centre and with good sense had also stipulated that the tender attracting superior architecture to enhance the amenities of the new town might be more acceptable than the lowest tender.

The way Flack tackled this venture was as characteristic as anything he ever did. The basis of the tender was that the winner would be granted a ninety-nine year lease at a peppercorn rent rising to an agreed level on completion. The developer would be responsible for procuring the finance and would complete the proposed shopping centre. This was a normal arrangement of the time, the risks were taken by the developer whilst the new town would get the commercial centre it wanted. If the development was a success the profit to the developer would be out of all proportion to the risks as the shops and offices would probably be pre-let before construction was completed. The arithmetic was impressive.*

---

* Say the rent to the town was peppercorn until the project was completed and then £30,000 per year for ninety-nine years. On a multiple of, say, twenty, the value of a site would be £600,000. Let us say that the total cost of the project was £1 million and that the estimated rent receivable was 10% on the total cost of £1.6 million, i.e. the building cost of £1 million plus the notional site value of £600,000, making a rent of £160,000 receivable each year. This £160,000 would net down to £130,000 after payment of the £30,000 ground rent to the town. Assume that the developer has borrowed the £1 million at 7%, providing no equity to the institution, i.e. at £70,000, then the gross surplus to the developer is £60,000 per year. But like the previous example the ebullient arithmetic does not end here because the lease to the Corporation would be a

171

Murrayfield, as a new property company, with its Basildon development, was also a good example of the way a single property development could transform the value of a company, with the stock market in its usual way discounting the value well ahead. The most profitable policy for an entrepreneur like Flack to pursue was to bring his company to the Stock Exchange with a portfolio consisting of several undeveloped and uncompleted projects. Why not, when the stock market was prepared to accept a valuation of the shares on the basis of the projects arising from those empty sites being completed and fully let?

For instance Felix Fenston, studying Jack Cotton's growth, saw these opportunities fairly early on and brought a company he owned called Eron Investments Limited, to the Stock Exchange in April 1959. Its net asset value was a minuscule £26,000, but the market value after quotation based on hope value, i.e. on a fully let, fully developed basis, was £500,000. Yet a few months later, Cotton

straight lease with no rent reviews, the Corporation would always receive £30,000 per year for ninety-nine years whereas the rents paid by the tenants to the developer would have, say, fourteen-year leases as in the previous example. At the end of fourteen years, the gross rent receivable would at least double to £320,000 and if one deducts the constant £30,000 payable to the Corporation, the gross surplus to the developer is £290,000; if one deducts also the £70,000 payable on the loan of a million, he is left with £220,000. It may be easier to understand the example if one looks at it as a sandwich. The bottom slice is the £30,000 payable to the Corporation; the centre slice, the interest payable to the lender of the million pounds, is £70,000, and the top slice is the net revenue representing the profit to the developer. In the early days of the boom, the bottom slice was extremely thin and constant and the top slice which was basically the property developer's profit was very fat indeed and doubling every seven or fourteen or twenty-one years, depending upon the rent reviews. After some years the local authorities woke up, as did the institutions, to the effect that gearing had on revenue. Terms had to change, and local authorities and institutions inevitably demanded a percentage of the total rents actually received. But as long as there was a top slice, the developer was always in clover, the covenants of his tenants were usually much stronger than his own, so his top slice, costing him nothing, was always safe. He could sell this top slice, on a multiple, on a YP of thirteen or fourteen — less than the fifteen or sixteen or more he could receive on a freehold. At a multiple of thirteen the value of his £60,000 of top slice would be £780,000 or £2,860,000 after the first rent review, a very healthy surplus considering that he didn't have a penny of his own money involved. If one adds a nought to the above figures for the larger scheme, one can appreciate why there was a stampede in the early sixties to obtain building leases from local authorities for new town centre schemes. If one multiplies by seven one has a rough idea of value in today's pounds.

purchased Eron from Fenston for over a million. Fenston was nevertheless peeved, because, now no longer hope value, the net assets, in under a year rose to over £3 million (£20 million surplus, in today's pounds).

Walter Flack was rich and generous to all the people around him; he gave shares away in his company very liberally whilst it was still private. Many shared in his largesse, and several of his staff found that, as a result of the flotation of Murrayfield, they had more money than they had ever dreamed of. His friends came from varied backgrounds: he was a great snob, liking above all to be surrounded by people with titles, prestige, status. This was part of his neurosis. His was no lukewarm affection; it was, as in everything in his life, 100% or nothing. He was, for example, fond of having newspaper people around him, not the proprietors, the more natural friends of Felix Fenston, not the journalists who were Jack Cotton's preference, but the editors. Soon after I joined Cotton, Flack invited me to his offices to have what he called a 'tayte a tayte' with several of his friends. 'We'll knock some heads together,' he said. When I arrived at St James's, the elegant bow-fronted window was highly polished and the Auk looked out at the bowler-hatted pedestrians with tranquil authority. Walter awaited me on the first floor, beaming, leaning back against the door leading to his mock Regency office, looking very much the Regency buck himself. So proud of the others there, he was barely able to control himself when making the introductions: Dicken Lumley (now the Earl of Scarbrough), Tony Berry, a budding Conservative politician and a city businessman; Rupert Loewenstein, Prince Loewenstein he underscored, scion of a distinguished Austrian family and a successful stockbroker; and here — Flack visibly expanded, his waistcoat with its large chain straining round his plump middle, his excited voice beginning to sound like a Victorian busker, the compère announcing his star act — and here, he gasped, the Prince of Habsburg. 'You know the Prince of course,' he added finally with a touch of rhetoric and a tinge of social wickedness. Flack was certainly determined to overwhelm me so that I would hotfoot report to Jack and describe Walter's growing social lustre. Surprisingly, the subsequent meeting was at a high and professional level. Cotton had asked me to discuss Continental property with Flack, and this was the first occasion we were able to do so. It was soon apparent to me that when Flack was sober and when Flack talked property seriously, rather than to an audience, he was most impressive.

173

On another occasion Walter asked me to dinner. It was at the Mirabelle, the newly affluent property developers' bistro. We were eight in the party, and one of the guests was the editress of a national magazine, two men were editors of national daily newspapers. Walter's objective was clear. He was telling me that Cotton might be getting a good press, but that when it came to the crunch he, Walter Flack, would beat Cotton at his own newspaper and publicity game. Nor was I surprised to see that the editors genuinely liked Walter, as did his grand social acquaintances. It was after this dinner as Walter's guest that I came to the conclusion that Jack's new buddy was no buddy, but a definite menace. Walter had not yet made any overt moves, these were to emerge later. But he had certainly confided his plans to at least one of his editor friends, because this man turned to me during the dinner and asked with weighty innuendo what I thought of the 'great Cotton', a Walter Flack expression. It was a flicker, but a genuine sign of danger.

When Murrayfield became a public company, Walter Flack set about becoming a public figure. He was all out for prestige. He was going to achieve the same sort of status as Cotton and Clore. His was a typical rags-to-riches story, from roller skates to Rolls Royce, from Wills Tipped to Coronas, all done in a flash. The man from the ranks had made good, from a relatively unknown property agent to a member of the City Centre group, from there, who could tell? — head of City Centre in place of Cotton. The Flack fantasies were taking shape. He was going to match up to the big boys. He was on a par with them. And if he could succeed as he did in Basildon, then of course he could achieve anything.

The members of the Basildon new town Corporation had decided that Walter Flack's scheme was the best designed and the most practical. They checked him out and received disturbing information. High marks for expertise, but low marks for financial standing. The worthy members of the Corporation invited Flack to see them, and he duly arrived in the full panoply and regalia of the property man — Rolls, chauffeur, flower in buttonhole, cigar medium to large, ruddy cheeks, slight hint of winter tan and, of course, total confidence. The Corporation, all worthy citizens, were in the council chambers waiting to receive him. The problem was explained as delicately as possible; his tender was the one that they wished to recommend and to approve, but his financial standing was just not good enough. Was there anything, they asked Flack, which would facilitate their making a recommendation for what they regarded as a superior development scheme? Flack, the true sergeant, the man who rallied in the face of fire, was in no way dismayed or jolted. He got up from his seat at the end of the large council table and started walking up and down the chamber, one hand on his chin, the other in a Napoleonic grip on his embonpoint. He stared at the carpet in deep thought. The committee watched, transfixed, following his movement from one end of the council chamber to the other. Suddenly Flack stopped, looked up and said to the worthy committee, 'I've got the answer.' Dead silence. . . . 'I'll give you my personal guarantee.' This totally unexpected answer, with its overtones of humour and desperation, took some time to make its full impact on the committee members. No suggestion could have been more irrelevant, but to a man, the whole committee supported Flack. Of course the personal guarantee wouldn't quite do, but if Mr Flack could demonstrate that he could obtain the finance, then they, the corporation members, would exercise their discretion to allow him more time before making their decision known. Any person other than Walter Flack would have been thrown out on his neck.

Why was Flack initially drawn to Cotton? The basic answer I believe lies in the immense publicity he enjoyed. Jack had become the king of the developers — the looming figure of Samuel was always in the background — and many of the lesser property lights wanted in one way or another to touch Cotton's hem. Walter was very much one of those junior stars, probably the most talented. But unstable and insecure, he persuaded himself that he also wanted to wear the Emperor's clothes. It was the acquisition of Whitehall Court which had brought him and Jack together. In 1959 Flack saw an opportunity to purchase this wonderfully located building on the Embankment, housing its clubs, aristocrats and diplomats, under one of the prettiest roof lines in London. Walter manoeuvred the board of Whitehall Court into a corner and, in order to clinch the deal, he turned to Jack for the quick million he needed. They went into the deal jointly, but in acquiring Whitehall Court Cotton had also neatly arranged to acquire one-third of the equity of Murrayfield. After the merger, Clore felt that a one-third interest in Murrayfield was anomalous. It ought to be sold, or the other two-thirds ought to be purchased. Flack wanted his company to become a 100% subsidiary, he was an avid seller, subject, of course, to contract. (This term 'subject to contract' is unique to the property world. Every property is sold subject to contract in clear bold print. What it actually means is this: if you are the purchaser making the offer to buy and you subsequently change your mind, you can withdraw unashamedly — but the vendor to whom you have made the offer is bound to go ahead; if he withdraws, he is a villain.) I was assigned to work out and negotiate the preliminary terms directly with Flack. It was going to be a friendly negotiation between willing buyer and willing seller. Cotton also wanted me to discuss the Murrayfield portfolio with Archie Sherman, the idea being that the more contact there was with Clore's man the more it would help bring the Clore subsidiary closer to the parent company. There was a strong element of the political move; Cotton was already in the frame of mind where he had to organise his approaches and sell his proposals to Clore.

In the event Cotton's plan could not have backfired more explosively. Walter, the roly-poly charming ex-sergeant with the Edwardian watch and chain, became the agent who set alight the fuel of the Cotton pyre. But Walter would never and could never have attacked Jack, certainly not with such brazen openness, without encouragement from Charles Clore. By way of one or two of his nudges and shrugs, Clore acted as Flack's Iago, exciting his jealousies and ambitions. When Flack finally achieved his burning ambition and was elected to the main board of City Centre he perceived, to his astonishment, that the great Jack Cotton seemed to wilt at these formal meetings before the stronger character of Clore. Walter, always the commercial climber, rationalised his fantasies. He took what he thought was his main chance to become chief executive, with Jack out of the picture and with Clore as chairman. His first moves were oblique rather than direct, making snide remarks about Jack's penchant for partnerships, about Jack's Dorchester suite, about Jack's apparent lack of grasp in operating the business of the group. During those early months, whenever Flack met me he made the gentle and not so gentle dig against Jack with humour and charm, at the same time always remarking with mocking jocularity that in his view Clore would of course be the better man as chairman.

The clash with Walter Flack, serious and intense, then tawdry and finally desperately sad, was in effect the hub of the combat between Cotton and Clore. Once Walter decided to make Jack his target, subtly encouraged by Clore, there was bound to be a full-scale collision. Without the appearance of Walter Flack, the institutions might have remained on the outer edges, seemingly unaware, officially impervious to any problems, but the dangerous ripples caused by Flack not only brought the institutions unwillingly into the centre where they had to admit cognisance of the conflict, but Clore was also provided with the opportunity to make an assessment that the institutions' initial hesitancy indicated that Cotton could be seriously vulnerable and exposed, if and when the crunch occurred. Before Flack's intervention, there was always an outside chance of mediation, of compromise. Now divorce was a certainty.

In Walter's attempt to unseat Cotton, I played an implacably opposing role. I had settled down on the City Centre motorway and was cruising along in top gear, looking for the disaster that lay ahead and, like others amongst Jack's friends and advisers, trying to work out what course could be taken to avert a collision. All of us, in sporadic fashion, made suggestions to him. But Jack was in his enduring psychological cul-de-sac, still utterly convinced that Clore fundamentally liked him and respected him. He was almost vehemently determined to avoid any final confrontation. As Clore told me years later, it was not a question of whether he liked or disliked Cotton, nor was it a question of Cotton's tremendous talent as a property man. That was beside the point — he regarded Cotton as an appalling executive chairman. Jack's reading of Charles's attitude towards him was tragically wrong from the very beginning.

In his vigorous desire to purchase the remaining two thirds of Flack's Murrayfield, Jack instructed me to assemble and analyse all the available data and he arranged that I should go over the figures in detail with Eric Young, Douglas Tovey and Archie Sherman, after discussing them with Walter. Murrayfield was a difficult company to value; most of the assets comprised development projects, many of which hadn't commenced. Walter of course thought each of his projects was worth millions, and his immediate negotiating posture at our first talk was to value everything he had, on a fully completed and fully let basis. Even if there was only a slim chance of obtaining planning approval for a scheme, he wanted the project given full value. 'But you haven't got planning permission, Walter . . .' I insisted. 'Listen to me, my team is the best property team in the country. You chaps at the Dorchester-*sur-mer*, haven't got a clue. You are not in our league. We know all about getting planning.' It looked to me as if this negotiation was going to go on for years. Walter himself was a first-rate negotiator and, though himself in a hurry to complete, knew that Jack was in a greater hurry. I quietly explained to Walter the principles I would adopt in valuing the shares of the company. He was reluctant to agree, claiming that he was only interested in property and in money which were tangible things and not in figures and balance sheets, which were 'a load of codswallop'. He was however very restive and impatient to join the City Centre board, and after that was formalised he was going to 'teach Jack how to do property deals'. He was also, he declared, going to be my commander; as the proposed chief of Europe he would give me orders. I eventually managed to get him to go over the figures and to agree the principles on how best to value the company. Finally he said it was all right with him. 'I always thought, Charles, you valued companies with a pin — now I see you don't even need a pin.' We laughed. I told him that Jack wanted me to go over the figures with Archie Sherman and Douglas Tovey. He had already been informed by Jack. 'You must watch Clore's lot,' he said, 'they know their business, they'll want the other two thirds of my company for nothing.'

This was revealing, at any rate to me, for in a small way it indicated that Flack knew Clore better than was supposed. Flack had always been considered very much a Cotton man, so that we expected some of the wariness from the Clore camp to be centred on Flack's supposed close friendship with Cotton. What emerged in our talks was that Flack was increasingly more status-minded than Cotton-minded, more concerned with his own personal ambitions than any loyalty to Jack. Walter had made his money; he would make more, not only for himself, but for others. But he now intended to increase his net status rather than his net worth. Visibly he became more conscious of his outward trappings. His Rolls was already one of his symbols, and he was anxious that I should visit another, his yacht, then tethered on the Embankment by Charing Cross. He was patently conscious of Clore's glamour, of Cotton's fame, of the surface appurtenances of wealth, of tycoonery. He desperately wanted to be a big shot and to be considered as one by other big shots. He wanted to get into their league. He wanted to distance himself as far as possible from being a property runner, a commission man, a mere estate agent acting for his clients. During one of our 'tayte a tayte' talks, he once leant over towards me and asked 'What do you think of me?' 'Sober or not?' I questioned. His huge winning smile spread around his cheeky chappie face. 'I'll tell you one thing. I'm not some little runner. I'm a big man now, and I'm going to be far bigger than you and Jack think.' I looked at him. The smile had disappeared; he looked drawn and serious and I realised that this was no idle chatter but a *cri de coeur*, a testament of faith.

He could not wait to get on to the main board. 'I'll show them

178

when I'm on the board . . .' was a frequent litany during the weeks leading to the acquisition of Murrayfield. With so many property stars and near-stars flashing around in the subsidiaries, normal and abnormal tensions and jealousies amongst these ego-ridden colleagues were building up. The sky was turning grey; the atmosphere was uneven, people were nervy. Was money intoxicating judgment? Were prestige and power intoxicating common sense? Or was publicity intoxicating ambitions? There seemed to be shifts and movements larger than any single person. Who was manipulating whom? Who and what were the targets and objectives? Motivations seemed to be increasingly Byzantine.

In May 1961 City Centre acquired, on terms acceptable to all parties, the two thirds of Walter Flack's company which it did not own. Two weeks later Walter Flack was appointed a director of City Centre. He was now the equal of the other directors, he was now joining the ranks of Cotton, Clore, Sainer, Plumridge, Bridge, Folliss, Lindgren, Kerman.

Flack had arrived. From the moment he went on to the City Centre board, Walter Flack showed his true colours. There was not a minute's pause. He was the growling killer set on target and almost overnight he seemed a completely different person; it was an astonishing change of personality. The situation had become ugly.

Meanwhile our European property plans, conceived in the Dorchester suite and hatched and breeding in the banking parlours were progressing well, far better than anyone expected. Hambros and Schroders had held my hand securely in Paris and we had already started having discussions with several major financial groups. We had met a number of property owners and real estate agents and had talks with Flack's own contacts in Paris. Jack's idea was that in France we ought to form a fifty/fifty partnership with a French property group, with City Centre providing the development know-how and some money, and with the French partner providing the properties and local knowledge and most of the money. When Brandford Griffiths introduced me to Banque Union Européenne, I saw that we did not have to go any further for a French partner; in Union Européenne we had found the ideal partner for City Centre. The bank had an excellent reputation and senior management to match. It also had two very attractive features which I knew were right for City Centre and which would especially appeal to Jack Cotton and his institutional colleagues. The first was that the Bank was owned by the Schneider Creuzot Group, one of the largest industrial groups in France, a group with formidable financial resources of its own which would offset any criticisms and doubts from those members of the City Centre board who were dubious about the proposed expansion into France. The second feature was that the Bank controlled a property company, Union Immobilière, quoted on the Paris stock exchange. This had great appeal. A quoted vehicle would provide an immediate and ready value for whatever activities City Centre was embarking upon in France; it was also far easier to finance through a quoted vehicle and to obtain Bank of England consents and approvals; City Centre's investment status in London would also be considerably enhanced by having a partner of the calibre of Banque Union Européenne, with the French and UK groups controlling, between them, a quoted French property company. The proposed deal drew no criticism from Clore. On the contrary he knew a good deal better than anyone. He was in any event familiar with the French scene; he had already met many of the important French entrepreneurs, bankers and industrialists. Indeed, Sears Holdings had owned a large French shoe chain and had a well-known presence in Rue de la Paix with its Mappin & Webb showroom. Hambros and Schroders supported the association enthusiastically. Instead of memoranda and discussions and talks and trips and visits, here was a pragmatic and commercial situation. In the City the general sentiments were warmly disposed, underpinned by the knowledge that because of the advice of Hambros and Schroders the Continental plans were being advanced in an effective and elegant way.

Once we had settled the heads of agreement, the top man of Union Européenne, M. Terrail, also a director of Schneider Creuzot, came over with his colleagues to meet Cotton and other City Centre directors. Cotton brought Flack directly into the talks and it was tentatively discussed (though nothing definite was actually settled) that Flack would represent City Centre on the joint-quoted French company. The French had their doubts about Flack. They frowned at his yacht moored on the Seine, his flamboyance, his insouciance and, worst sin of all, his unreliability on timing. On two previous Paris encounters set up to introduce him to the proposed partners, he had been late the first time and had just not turned up at all the second time. Walter hated flying; so any overseas business trip was a major, sometimes insuperable effort. Brandford Griffiths and I had discouraged the Gallic doubts. Our real concern was not Flack's waywardness, but his loose talk about Cotton and especially his occasional and not so occasional remarks about Cotton's competence as chairman. Any suggestion of a boardroom conflict is horror to a bank, particularly to a French bank.

Our French partners enjoyed meeting Cotton, they enjoyed their time in the Dorchester suite, but they returned to Paris distinctly unhappy about Walter. Confidential talks then ensued, an atmosphere much to the taste and expertise of Brandford Griffiths. Banque Union Européenne brought up alternatives. Could I represent City Centre instead? No, said Jack, it had to be a City Centre main board director. Was there anyone else on the main board? Yes, but Cotton had already decided upon Flack, who after all had been the first UK property man since the war to transact a property deal in Paris. 'Good logic for us French, but that was a single purchase, whereas we at Union Européenne and you at City Centre are now embarking on a positive strategic programme.' There was no shifting by Jack. He had committed himself to Walter; he would not budge. Flack on his part was unperturbed by the questions being raised. As far as he was concerned, he was going to be the leading property man of the Continent, a mere stepping stone to taking over from Jack as managing director of the entire group. Clore for his part, having accepted Flack as a colleague on the main board, responded to him in a more overt friendly fashion. Meanwhile, the murmurs from Walter himself criticising Jack Cotton's competence as chairman became more audible; Big Daddy sitting at the top of his boardroom table remained unconcerned. He was sure Walter would cool down; Walter, bless him, was too easily excitable. It was a temporary situation — difficult, certainly — but temporary.

Jack judged Walter to be an exceedingly talented property man whose undoubted talents would sooner or later be recognised by the French. And, if he were going to be really troublesome, what better ploy than to create this niche for him across the Channel, out of harm's way? What Jack refused to take into account was that Walter had switched his loyalty to Clore after his main board elevation. I pointed out to Jack, in respect of our plans in France, that he would have to take more heed of Walter's reckless talk and indiscretions, because Walter was not only having an unsettling effect on our polite and very intelligent new French partners, but also on our shrewd merchant banking advisers.

As part of the negotiating and working committee implementing the transaction with Union Européenne, we had organised an effective *modus operandi* which would operate the business on an efficient basis and provide each partner with the necessary assurances and safeguards. Some of these devices were inevitable cross-Channel smoke-screening for psychological and national reasons, others were for very practical business reasons. The top board was to meet every three months in Paris or London and the management committee each month in Paris. The chairman of the board would, of course, be French and would be strictly independent, an elder statesman, at the end of his career, a non-executive, perhaps a previous director of Schneider Creuzot, in his sixties and obviously respected in the highest levels of Paris business and political circles. He would be a competent businessman and a good diplomat, a man who would take his responsibilities seriously, not in awe of anyone on either side. This paragon actually existed. He was selected by Schneider and invited with alacrity on both sides to become chairman. The top board would consist of three directors from City Centre — Cotton, Clore and Flack — and three from Union Européenne and the French institutions. The managing director would be a highly respected French real estate man whom Union Européenne had known for many years. The crucial operating activity was of course the management committee, which would be made up of the independent chairman, the managing director and one director each from Union Européenne and from City Centre. This management committee would evaluate proposals and commit the company within a wide authority granted by the board. Walter Flack would of course represent City Centre on the management committee.

In the event, it was this management committee which brought about Walter's downfall, and not by accident, but quite deliberately. I was one of the principal people to cause that downfall. It was done essentially to save the *entente cordiale* and to save Jack; in the event, miserably and painfully, it proved to be of no avail and saved nothing.

Walter was also brought down for another reason. This was because he had literally terrified someone out of her wits — Jack's secretary, Denise Tapper. The first inkling came on the day of Jack's big annual party during Ascot week, Thursday, Ladies' Day. Nadia and I drove over to Marlow, as did all the other guests after the races. We walked around the flowers, watched an occasional boat meandering up the river, sipped champagne and devoured strawberries and cream. We were in a small group of five or six, when Walter came over looking slightly dishevelled, but still dapper in his grey Ascot suit. He had a glass in his hand and it had probably been a fixture for most of the day. Without any ado, not waiting for introductions, he pulled me aside and said, 'Charles, your head is going to roll. I am out to get you and I am out to get Cotton.' He paused to empty his glass. 'You are the *éminence grise* of City Centre. You're dangerous.' He glowered at me; the others took no notice. I recall my priggish reply quite distinctly: 'Walter, you have just said that on your host's champagne.' His voice took on a nasty tone. 'To hell with Cotton and to hell with you.' This was certainly not the Walter I had known when we had first met. 'Your head is going to roll, Charles, and don't you forget it.' He lurched off.

An *éminence grise* during Ascot week: shades of Richelieu indeed. He was out of control, possibly hysterical. How would it end? Next day I warned Jack. He took it quietly, impervious to any threats of danger. Brandford Griffiths and I had a bleak lunch the following week. The negotiations with our proposed Continental partners were going smoothly, almost too smoothly. We feared the Flack time bomb with great foreboding. When was it going to explode in our faces? In the midst of this gloom, at 8.30 that evening I had an extraordinary telephone call at home from a distraught Denise Tapper.

She had been to a cocktail party and had bumped into Walter Flack. Her hostess, a tireless worker for charity to whom Jack, as with many others, had been extremely generous over the years, had invited Miss Tapper to the party. It was not surprising: Jack's secretary was cultured and attractive; she coped effectively with his constant stream of visitors and the phone calls streaming in from all over the world. Everyone was treated by her with natural courtesy, even though there were frequent abrupt interruptions with Jack's irate commands for Tapper to come into his boardroom immediately, to get someone on the phone immediately, to take dictation immediately. Denise Tapper brought a certain order to the Dorchester suite. Even the Clore camp treated her with respect. She was indispensable. And, like many of Jack's personal staff, she worshipped him. On the telephone she was crying uncontrollably. It was difficult to understand what she was saying, but it seemed that at the party Flack had taken her into a corner and had launched into a tirade against Jack. He had told her that Jack was a rotten chairman, that he didn't know what he was doing, that he drank too much, that he would have to resign soon, that Clore thought so too, that the banks and the institutions would stop supporting him, that the City had lost confidence in him. All this was bad enough. Then

183

he started attacking her personally, accusing her of intrigue, and he threatened to speak to his editor friends that very night, to spill the beans specifically pointing to her as the arch-intriguer. It was strong stuff, particularly as Flack knew that an attack of this kind could utterly destroy Miss Tapper. He was showing neither scruples nor courage. He had not once confronted Jack directly: the innuendo, the insults, the threats, were made to others for onward transmission. I did my best to calm her fears by insisting that it was just talk on Flack's part, and that as far as the newspapers were concerned it was empty bluster. I had heard of boardroom conflicts, but I had never heard of an attack on the secretary of a colleague, literally scaring the life out of her.

In the morning I went to the Dorchester. Miss Tapper seemed her usual self. Whether she had spoken to Jack about Walter's outburst I didn't know, but when I saw him and strongly urged that unless he did something immediately, the Flack situation, already dangerous would get out of hand, he nodded without comment. What should be done, I suggested, was to make the management committee meet once a fortnight, instead of once a month, a timetable which the French had originally suggested. Cotton knew as well as I did that a regular meeting once a month was already almost too much for Flack. We knew that he couldn't possibly keep to a regular fortnightly schedule and that inevitably he would have to be replaced as the City Centre representative. In which case both of us, knowing Walter's temperament, were fully aware that he would resign in fury and anger from City Centre. Of course, we also realised that when this happened it would not only deal with the Flack problem, but would safeguard the sensitive banking associations introduced by Hambros and Schroders. We had to demonstrate to our new Continental partners that we were serious. There were others in City Centre who could take over Flack's function without controversy and who would more than satisfy our partners' trepidations.

Cotton was now finally convinced that Flack was dangerous. He made up his mind immediately. Walter would have to go. It was the first time that Jack fully appreciated the dangers inherent in his own position. Walter had given away a lot in his attack on Tapper, particularly the fact that the institutions had been got at. This unnerved Jack; the institutions were his final bulwark, his final support in any conflict with Clore. He now appreciated that they might start questioning his own capability as the top man, they might even start siding with Clore in his criticisms against him. And where would Plum, his closest institutional supporter, stand in any confrontation?

The Tapper incident seemed to restore Jack's decisiveness. He now actively sought the advice of his closest friends. He listened carefully and quietly. They all told him the same thing. His position could not be worse; a boardroom conflict had to be avoided at all costs; it was essential that there was no row; he and Clore had to work together; the alternative was unthinkable. And if it came to a boardroom conflict, the institutions might well be forced to support Clore and vote against him. Jack gave the impression that he was pulling himself together. He was more like his old self. He was in focus. He decided that he would follow more assiduously Clore's oft-repeated wish that he separate the functions of chairman and managing director, and that he ought to find a managing director. He had what looked like a promising further talk with John Buscombe of Shell. He ran his meetings more efficiently. He drank less. It was the old Jack Cotton once again. Or so it seemed.

The proposed French administrative change, as expected, proved to be Walter Flack's final undoing. He turned up for the first management committee meeting and for the third one. He missed the second and the fourth. The French chairman wrote formally to the chairman of City Centre. After that, rigidly maintaining strict protocol, he had a formal meeting with Jack Cotton in London. It was not what the partners had agreed; he was the independent chairman, and it was not only a personal discourtesy to him, it was an indignity to all concerned and an insult to the major shareholders, not counting the public shareholders. One couldn't run the company this way, it was ineffective. It could not go on. Surely someone reliable from City Centre could attend instead of Flack.

Walter's immediate reaction to the posture and criticisms of the French made his own position infinitely worse. He claimed the French were unpleasant partners; and who was this independent chairman anyway to criticise him? He, Walter Flack, had forgotten more about property than the chairman would ever know. He didn't have to go to formal meetings in Paris, he could direct operations from London. Flack hit out indiscriminately, his talk became wild, and even those who supported him in City Centre, openly or otherwise, were forced to voice their disapproval. Walter found himself on his own; very soon hardly any director on the main board was on his side.

The French, proceeding inexorably on protocol, formally asked

185

for a replacement.

To Walter this was an outrage. He was not being treated as a big shot but as a little property runner. It was more than he could or would take from anyone. He phoned Jack and furiously demanded a meeting, demanding also that I should attend. It was ten o'clock in the morning. He came into the boardroom, greeted Jack with a wave of his hand, ignored me and went straight to the walnut drinks cabinet. He poured out half a tumbler of whisky. Jack didn't blink an eyelid. It was a non-meeting and a non-discussion. Walter just looked at Jack and just looked at me and kept on drinking. He was clearly ill. After a while Jack quietly suggested to Walter that he should finish his drink and come back later that day.

Walter Flack resigned from the French property company and Archie Sherman, Clore's own property expert, took his place soon after. On 15 January 1963 Walter Flack resigned from City Centre itself. The next day, two of his friends, loyal to the last — Rupert Loewenstein and Anthony Berry, also resigned from Murrayfield. The *Guardian* commented: 'There have been rumours in the City for several weeks of serious policy disagreement not only between Mr Flack and Mr Cotton but between Mr Cotton and Mr Clore.'

The man had cracked, possibly because of excessive drinking, possibly because he'd made too much money too quickly, or possibly from a general instability. I personally believe the cause of his crack up arose from his insecurity, from his craving for recognition and for prestige. He desperately wanted to get on to equal terms with the big Cs, but in the end the two Cs treated him as if he really were a runner. At Murrayfield he was the chief, revered and loved and respected. If he had retained his own set-up, running it himself with his excellent team, with his own boys, if that had been enough to fulfil him, he would have earned the respect which he wanted so much from the big men, from the Cottons and Clores. But he wanted something more; he no longer wished to be a sergeant in the ranks, he now desperately wanted to be an officer, a general amongst other generals. Though he had admirable abilities as a property developer and dealer, he deluded himself that he was fit for the top executive suites of business where tycoons could fundamentally alter commercial situations by their personal exercise of power. In his own mind he over-promoted himself. He came to believe that he was better than a mere platoon sergeant. That belief cost him his life. It led him to City Centre, to Cotton and to Clore, to the Dorchester suite, and to a misconception which destroyed him.

After he resigned, he wanted nothing whatsoever to do with anyone at City Centre. He loathed all of them, especially Clore. He felt he had been betrayed and vilified, that he had been most shockingly treated. He would sell all his shares on the open market and he would sell them as quickly as possible, instructing his brokers to get on with it and to dump them at any price. He went on a selling spree. The price dropped, almost plummetted to 250p. Then the price stabilised and started moving upwards. He had sold all his shares. Walter Flack, like a meteor in reverse, departed the City Centre scene of action. He had fired the initial shots, he had attacked the chairman leaving him severely wounded and fatally exposed. He left the battlefield a broken, dispirited and tragically bewildered man.

Nearly three months later, on 22 March, Walter Flack was found dead in his bath by his chauffeur. The verdict was accidental death. The great smile had departed for good.

Chapter Eleven

Mr Clore of Park Street, Mayfair

It was wholly characteristic of Mr Clore that his London house and his personal office should be in the same Mayfair street. Economy of words, economy of effort, economy of expenditure — except when entertaining at home — derived from an uncluttered, orderly approach to the routine of life. If there was something obtrusive between A and B then it had to be refined or removed whether that something was a physical entity, a tangible fact, or an irritant problem. Clore intended to reach B in the simplest way possible and nothing and no one must stand in his path. Ruthless simplification was the hallmark of his life and business; no overtones, no undertones, no fibbing, no ploys, no diplomacy — just say it, do it and get it.

An excellent example of his method, working immaculately for decades, was his tie to Mr Kay, 'my personal man' as Clore described him, whose first name I never knew until my mother called him Freddie when he drove her for a while after Clore's death. Kay was Clore's personal chief of staff, and was considered so perfect that even the Duke of Marlborough, the father of the present Duke, was prompted to exclaim to me after one of Clore's shoots that he did not know 'how Charlie could possibly do without Kay'.

He couldn't but that was how he organised it: Kay ran both the London house at 95 Park Street and Stype, the country house at Hungerford. He was not only the major domo, he was Clore's valet, butler, chauffeur, and even his loader when Clore went to friends for shoots in England and on the Continent. No wonder that the fastidious Marlborough, who always knew a good thing when he saw one, respected Clore for having someone like Kay, so perfect, so indispensable, so imperturbable and, of course, so economical.

The routine at 95 Park Street commenced at 7 a.m. exactly each weekday morning when Kay telephoned Clore on the house phone and placed the *Financial Times* outside his bedroom door. Clothes were arranged in the dressing room, and if Clore had a girlfriend staying with him, the perfect Jeeves would cope without any specific instruction. The house itself was large, on four floors with paintings and sculptures and *objets* in every room. At 8.30 a.m. Clore would descend for his breakfast, a simple cup of tea; then he would read *The Times* — the obituaries first — and the *Mail* — the gossip column first. He would depart, wearing a soft trilby with a slight rakish tilt, and would then walk down Park Street, from his house at Number 95 near the Oxford Street end, to his office at Number 22 near the Dorchester end. He would walk back at around 5.30 p.m., read the *Evening Standard*, look at the news on television and then prepare to change for dinner, nearly always in black tie. He would return well after midnight, sometimes alone, more likely *à deux*.

There were some set patterns, so for example, on Tuesdays at 6 p.m. he would have his weekly chat and drinks with Tovey. At the end of the week on Fridays his chef and footman would drive to Stype at midday to prepare for the week-end's entertaining; he would depart, driven of course by Kay,* after tea in time to arrive before dinner. Kay's wife, the head housekeeper with several maids under her, would already be there to help greet the guests arriving at Stype for the weekend.

As we grew more friendly, Nadia and I visited frequently. The two major occasions of the year were Ascot and Christmas; during the rest of the year we would go down once, sometimes twice a month. Each weekend when he was in England, Clore had friends down, and on only one occasion were we the sole guests. Curiously Sainer never stayed. Once or twice he came to dinner after the Newbury races, yet, close as they were in business, Clore kept Sainer somewhat apart from his social life. Though Clore was a difficult if not a mean man, usually morose, abrupt, prickly, he was always an excellent host, and Stype, with its easy informal atmosphere, seemed to soften his more habitual truculence and seemed to bring out in him a sense of stability and contentment which eluded him in London.

He had purchased the Stype estate, covering over 2,500 acres,

---

* On one occasion, driving down the M4, Kay nearly scraped the car — a superbly maintained Rolls — and Clore barked: 'Hey Kay. Take care. This is not just a car you are driving, but £20,000.'

from the first Lord Rootes. He almost bought nearby Ramsbury, but chose Stype instead because he did not want anything too imposing. Lord Rootes subsequently purchased Ramsbury himself and later it was sold to Harry Hyams. During the Christmas stay, punctuated by Clore's birthday on Boxing Day so that he received and expected two presents from his guests, we might visit Hyams at Ramsbury. I once asked Clore why he had not himself chosen Ramsbury; he replied, 'Harry needs it, I don't.'

Stype, with its ten or so bedrooms mostly on one floor, had the feeling of a ranch house, notwithstanding its ornate furniture and paintings. Meals were always superbly served, the cuisine and wine were of a very high order. There were usually a dozen to two dozen people for lunch, the same for dinner, the ladies in long dresses and jewellery, the men in dinner jackets, with Clore eyeing each of us to see who was wearing something from Selfridges or Garrards or Dolcis. If not, why not, was his question to anyone who wasn't. During the day there were walks or reading or looking at the horses in the stud — he was a breeder on a large scale; there was swimming and sauna in the spacious pool house; we could study the orchids in the greenhouses tended by the full-time orchidist, or take a look at the cows in the cow-shed, as Clore described it with grim understatement (the cow-shed actually being one of only two fully automated milking stations in the country and costing over £1 million). On Sunday after tea he returned to London, driven back by Kay, who had managed everything down to the smallest detail, as demanded by the ever-watchful Mr Clore.

On Monday morning he would once again walk down Park Street to his office at Number 22. There, in a slightly gloomy Mayfair mansion, was housed his personal office and his personal office staff. His vast empire was master-minded from what was essentially a rather modest establishment — in typical Clore fashion. Apart from himself there was only Boswell, his personal accountant, a switchboard operator, a shorthand typist, and his very competent secretary Miss Gelman, whose sister had married into the family, so that she in a way provided family comfort and organisation. She made his social and travel arrangements and filtered all his business calls. She was an efficient fixture who organised his business timetable with a matter-of-fact charm and intelligence. A routine had been set up at Number 22 as it had been at Number 95 and at Stype, and it was rigidly adhered to by Miss Gelman. Most of Clore's meetings took place at his office on the first floor. Sears was run by the heads of the subsidiaries from their various operating centres, later centralised to a minimal extent from offices in the Selfridges block. The vast conglomerate was controlled by Clore from Park Street, and its operation was exercised by Sainer from his law office in Serjeant's Inn. And this Sainer did with a talent for organisation which was quite outstanding.

Thus there was order, method, routine all around Mr Clore. He demanded it and got it. Everyone, including Sainer, was afraid of his wrath, worried by his displeasure, anxious about his reactions. His strength of character was awesome. As Jack Cotton himself was soon to discover.

For Clore had decided in his own mind that all Cotton's commitments had to be discussed and approved. Cotton's methods were disorderly and Clore could not abide them. One of his first formal disagreements arose over Cotton's decision to purchase Felix Fenston's Kensington properties. Cotton had agreed to buy without consulting Clore and without a board commitment. Eric Young had been brought in by Cotton to agree the procedure and the details of the acquisition. When Clore learnt about the transaction at their usual Monday morning meeting he was visibly disturbed. Sainer checked with Young whether he, as chief surveyor of the group, had recommended the deal; if he had, it meant in effect that City Centre would have to go ahead even though Clore was against it. Young was put in a difficult position. It was made clear to Cotton that if he made commitments without prior discussion and without prior approval there would be protests. Soon after this incident, and on many occasions thereafter, Cotton complained to Young that Clore was knocking his deals, particularly the joint companies with the pension funds. 'Clore,' he said, 'only understands balance sheets. He doesn't understand property.' 'Then why does he like the Samuel Estate transaction?' Eric asked. 'Because he loves Mayfair, and because he's a snob and likes being in with Lord Bearsted.' This rang true. Clore certainly was a snob and he certainly did like being surrounded by titles, but he liked money even more, and surely, we all thought, he would avoid a permanent row with Cotton because it could only damage the price of their shares. I also tackled Cotton about Clore's tendency to criticise his deals and on one occasion asked, 'What does he feel about our European plans?' 'Don't pretend to be naïve, my boy,' he said. 'You know the answer as well as I do. He is in it for the money.'

I felt relieved, and disturbed. Relieved that Jack was talking in a realistic way about Clore; disturbed because it needed only one false move in Europe for Clore to start knocking that as well. I had hoped that this could be avoided, but it was beginning to look as if it was a forlorn hope.

Our plans to take Cotton and Clore into Europe were proceeding at an efficient pace. Since establishing the set-up in France where Archie Sherman was in charge of the Clore camp instead of Walter Flack, we had fixed our attention upon Belgium, concentrating on the then second largest bank, the Kredietbank.

The connection between Hambros Bank and the Kredietbank of Brussels was old-established. The head of the Kredietbank was M. Collin, about seventy when I first met him, the most respected banker in all of Belgium. M. Collin was an outstanding personage, as was his colleague, M. Brusselmans, the main board director of the Kredietbank who was going to look after us, listen to us and introduce us to his other colleagues. Whilst M. Collin was known throughout Europe and had a great reputation, M. Brusselmans, a senior director of his bank, was barely known outside Brussels. Yet here was a man with the rarest of banking insights, able to discern the crucial weakness of a borrower even when such weakness was not known to the borrower himself.

Of all the Continental bankers whom we saw and did business with, Brusselmans was the first to discern the probability of a serious conflict between Cotton and Clore, and he discussed it with me with a probing tact which was sensitive and sure, and which could not have been improved upon by the most experienced of diplomats. Having assessed the pros and cons he decided that the conflict, when it arose, would not do any harm to the Kredietbank's relationship with Hambros and with Schroders, and so he lent all his support to his endeavours. The purpose, of course, of our initial meetings with the Kredietbank was to acquaint ourselves with the property scene in Belgium. We had several initial meetings with Brusselman and his colleagues, and I came to the rapid conclusion that there was no point in going any further in looking for a possible partner for City Centre. The Kredietbank like Union Européenne, City Centre's partner in Paris, controlled a large property company, in this case owning property right in the centre of Brussels. The bank itself owned numerous other properties throughout Belgium which could present interesting development sites for a possible joint company. I had already recommended to Cotton that it would be more prudent for City Centre to have a bank as its partner in each of the countries in which it embarked on real estate on the Continent and indeed, as I have observed elsewhere, I encouraged the application of this same principle at Intershop. In Paris with Union Européenne this decision was to a large extent fortuitous, but with the Kredietbank it derived from a growing knowledge of how the system worked on the Continent.

The principal reason was that banks were far more entrenched in the financial network than our own UK banks. European banks were capital markets in themselves; they owned and controlled industrial and property companies. Discussions with the Kredietbank progressed rapidly; City Centre would own half of the joint company and the holding company of the Kredietbank, with Belgian institutional associates, would hold the other half; a public quotation would be sought at an early date. Solicitors were instructed, Titmuss Sainer acting for us.

Cotton now became excited, but in a deliberately controlled and cautious manner, like a leopard preparing to pounce. He sensed that something very big indeed was emerging, bigger even than Manhattan. He perceived a significant pattern of business enterprise which could have a profound effect on the growth of City Centre in particular, and on British-owned foreign real estate in general. He could moreover see that what was happening in commercial terms was vitally important in his conflict with Clore. He knew full well that because of Clore's innate cupidity he too would become excited by this unique pattern of partnerships with other banks in each of the countries of Europe.

'Do you have to smoke cigarettes?' I was startled. I was with Cotton in his boardroom going over the preliminary figures of a French property company, I looked up. Buoyant with the work we were doing, he was smiling at me behind his cigar smoke. 'Dear boy,' he said, 'a cigarette is like beer, but a cigar is like claret. When you have really appreciated a cigar you couldn't possibly smoke a cigarette again. Try it. Promise me you will only smoke cigars for the next month. Bless you.' I not only smoked cigars for the next month, but for the next ten years. I became a connoisseur of cigars. Jack's Monte Cristos were not to my taste and I finally selected a lovely small cigar, the Punch Margueretta — a minor claret of great distinction, especially if laid down for more than three years. I did as Jack asked, and carefully cut and lit my Marguerettas, smoking around twenty a day. As I relished the aroma, Jack would give me a baleful look; perhaps he mused that it would have been better if I had stuck to beer. Later my collection of cigars grew into one of the largest in England. I also ordered a 'cabinet', the small cedar-lined cupboard which holds 2,500 cigars, each one rolled at the same time from the same tobacco leaves. As it turned out it was the last 'cabinet' made in Havana. Castro thought it an unnecessary capitalist manifestation and decreed its end. Mine arrived in England four years after it was ordered, and exactly three weeks after I had given up smoking for good. Though Jack would have regretted my decision to stop smoking, he would have chuckled at my timing. After I got to know Clore better, I would occasionally send him a box of Marguerettas. Once I sent him a two-year-old box instead of the three-year cuvées. It gave him a bad cough and soon after that he himself gave up cigars. I claimed that he should be eternally grateful to me, as my over-young extra-strong Marguerettas were the cause. An abrupt grunt in response indicated semi-agreement. Jack would have enjoyed these nuances more than anyone.

The man who shared my first room at Hambros was Maurice Whinney who, like myself, had come into the bank through Sir Charles Hambro. He was ex-Foreign Office and the idea was that Whinney would be a sort of liaison man in London with Hambros' own representatives in Europe. As at that time there were only three representative offices, one in Zurich with Paul Kern and Count Seilern, one in Paris with Brandford Griffiths and one in Milan with John McAffery, Whinney rapidly came to the conclusion that he was not going to be fully stretched. He soon discovered that the representative offices of a merchant bank worked in diverse ways, each different from the other and all of them very different from the way the Foreign Office worked. But there were similarities; he was particularly impressed by the banking intelligence network. Their representatives seemed to know precisely what was going on in their territory: whom to do business with, whom to avoid, what the other banks were doing, what business and people they had turned down, the strength of the economy, the strength of the government of the day.

The bank representatives were in daily touch with '41' by telephone and made frequent visits to London. There seemed to be no regular system nor any formal organisation. For instance, although Kern — the great gnome of Zurich — was in charge of that office, he was not on the board of Hambros Bank, whereas his assistant, Count Seilern, was. In Milan McAffery, another SOE wartime friend of Sir Charles Hambro, was an active insurance broker on his own account, apart from being the bank's representative. In Paris Brandford Griffiths, who ran the office with his delightful assistant Jacques de la Doucette (who was more useful to us for belonging to the Jockey Club than for his celebrated wine), was not at that time a director of the bank, an appointment for which he yearned.

Kern knew every bank in Germany worth knowing and looked after Germany as well as Switzerland; Brandford Griffiths, an expert on France, also looked after Belgium. Whinney himself looked into Spain, but that part of Europe seemed to be McAffery's Catholic province. There appeared, however, to be a free run in Holland. Whinney made one or two trips and insisted that there was extremely good business to be done in banking and in property in Holland. He had been particularly impressed with some of the people he had met at the Netherlands Overseas Bank, and had arranged for one of its bright young men to come over and meet me. He duly arrived: Dr Hans Spruit. For a Foreign Office man, just a few weeks into banking, Maurice Whinney had hit a bull's eye with singular ease. His own diplomatic network was invaluable. In those days the embassies looked down on trade and gave their commercial attachés, normally the grammar school entrants, the back offices. But Whinney had done his homework. The situation in Holland, as he explained, was very similar to England: it was a trading nation and the only Continental country with an effective capital market; pension funds were on the same scale as ours; the property investment market was just beginning to take shape; long-term finance was available. It all looked extremely promising.

By the time we started in the Netherlands, Cotton was in touch with me at least once a day. City Centre Europe was now uppermost in his mind and he was playing his cards very close to his chest. He would insist that on returning to London from the Continent I came directly to the Dorchester from the airport or, if this were not possible, to Marlow over the weekend. He wanted to know every aspect of the golden eggs being laid. His judgment was remarkable — with no direct experience of property investment or finance on the Continent he not only understood every feature, he was also unerring in every decision he took. He had also made up his mind that this was an area of activity where Clore would be completely won over by his resolution and expertise.

The Netherlands Overseas Bank directors themselves, Dr Keuning and Mr Altes, came over to the Dorchester together with Senator de Wilder, the Chairman of the Dutch Mortgage Bank, the proposed partner with the Netherlands Overseas Bank for City Centre. They discussed the possibilities of participation with Jack. Because of the special nature of the Dutch capital market we were able to go one stage further in Holland than in Belgium or France, for by bringing in the mortgage bank, we established a coherent source for 100% of all the finance, long- and short-term, required for any development or acquisition. No wonder Jack was thrilled.

City Centre Europe was now well past the formative stage in France, Belgium and Holland. Walter Flack, sadly, was already forgotten. Once management had been set up and applied effectively in each of the countries we could start looking further afield into Italy and Germany. There was a tremendous amount of work to be done, and Cotton decided that we should batten down and entrench. We kept our fingers crossed that he could surmount his disagreements and arguments with Clore; he was obviously hoping that the grand European design would in some way appease Clore. But what he and I and the merchant banks forgot was that the institutional shareholders in City Centre, though approving the European expansionist schemes, were not inherently enthusiastic. By now, in general terms the institutions of City Centre had accepted the property cult in the UK and indeed in the United States. Europe, however, was something else. The timing for property expansion into Europe from an entrepreneurial point of view was perfect, but for the institutions it was premature, far too much for them to assimilate. Even the Pearl took a parochial, non-international, non-European posture. Wasn't Cotton taking on too much? Was Clore sufficiently rigorous about Cotton's expansionist plans? Plumridge took me aside. He was worried about Europe and to my dismay he added that he thought Clore was also worried; I had not heard him quote him before on any subject. Perhaps City Centre Europe was an albatross not an eagle. I became newly concerned and talked about my anxieties at '41'. It was the first time I voiced any apprehension outside the Dorchester; indeed I became so concerned I asked Peter Folliss to spend a day with me at the bank for his guidance and advice before one of his City Centre board meetings.

Ironically, the structure of City Centre Europe was emerging in a solid fashion. We were formulating a unique and highly effective plan. Most, if not all of the finance would come from our powerful Continental banking partners who would also provide the initial ingredients of a property portfolio. City Centre would provide relatively little money or guarantees, but would of course provide the know-how and would be an equal partner. Cotton was disciplining his excitement like the excellent bridge player he had been in his youth, and he was giving the most careful consideration to the best means of managing a great European plan. Cotton's first thought was that there ought to be a separate European department based in London under the direct control of the City Centre main board. However, as City Centre's European partners were banks and major banks at that, the consensus from Hambros and Schroders — in fact, from the 'committee' of Mallinckrodt, Brandford Griffiths and myself — was that the two merchant banks might themselves consider taking an equity in the City Centre European business, as serious relationships were being forged by the two merchant banks on behalf of City Centre with major Continental partners who were themselves banks. The problem was becoming complex in other respects also. Should Hambros and Schroders take an equity position in a specially formed City Centre European holding company based in London? Or based in Amsterdam? How should City Centre hold its Continental interests? What about exchange control restrictions? How were the tax implications to be sorted out? Eventually it became neatly divided into two separate facets, one real estate and the other finance, and the thinking veered towards a holding company based in Holland owned by City Centre, with the possibility of Hambros and Schroders becoming small equity partners. This holding company would have its own quotation in due course and would own the separate investments in France, Belgium and Holland and other, later, Continental investments. In each country these local interests would have separate stock exchange quotations wherever possible. The banking partner in each country would take up its own shares in each of the separate companies and later, if appropriate, in the Dutch holding company.

Around this time too, sounding-out discussions took place with the Deutsche Bank in Frankfurt. The first encounter lasted all day and questions were fired at us with typical Teutonic thoroughness. (At that time there was great rivalry between the Deutsche Bank headed by Dr Abs, and the Dresdener Bank headed by Dr Zeigler. When Dr Abs, who was known as God in banking circles, was asked what was the difference between him and Dr Zeigler, he replied, 'The entire alphabet.') Dr Abs' colleague who received us in Frankfurt was a charming German called Krebs. He came over and lunched at the Dorchester with Cotton; serious interest was shown in a possible association which to a certain extent derived from the

197

respect Deutsche had for Schroders and for Mallinckrodt.

We also had meetings in Rome, the man in charge a mere Cardinal running the Vatican Bank which controlled Italy's largest property company Generale Immobiliere. This company was later notorious for its association with Sindona, the Sicilian financier who was a friend of Hambros' representative in Italy, John McAffery. (McAffery wanted me to meet Sindona at this time, which on some instinct I refused to do, so McAffery refused to talk to me thereafter.) At the Vatican Bank with its religious overtones we naturally pointed out that the two leading shareholders of City Centre were Jews. The response was delightful. Don't worry, our founder was Jewish too.

As we roamed the Continent, we found the financial and investing institutions eager to acquire British property techniques and know-how. Notwithstanding the great amount of hard work put into our plans, the ease with which we were able at City Centre to establish associations on the Continent only reflected the avid keenness of the Europeans. Our financial and property plans were exceptionally well prepared and the partners chosen were impeccable. City Centre was set to make enormous profits — with virtually no cash investment.

Yet business is people, not money. It is people, rarely events, who destroy the best laid plans, and the two tycoons in City Centre were two people in conflict. All Clore had to do was to see Jack every Friday afternoon for a few moments on his way to Stype. All Jack wanted, literally and emotionally, was a pat on the back from Clore. On humane grounds alone it should have been done by Clore. But if it also meant making hundreds of millions of painless pounds? The cost of a pat on the back? Clore's folly was indescribable.

And if City Centre Europe had gone ahead as planned, the subsequent British property invasion of Europe, a disaster in many respects, would have been established in an entirely different manner. City Centre's policy, superbly stage-managed by Hambros and Schroders, of having associations with leading banks in each country supported by a quoted stock was and is the most effective way of investing in and developing property in Europe. The worst possible method is to be spurred on by English real estate agents obsessed not with their clients' well-being, but with their own fees. The wrong method is for a property company to do a single isolated deal (with or without a local partner); the wrong method is for a UK institution to be persuaded to go on to the Continent hand-in-hand with its equally ignorant UK property partner; the wrong and almost criminally stupid method is to provide UK bank guarantees for overseas developments.

The right way, the Cotton way, is to work closely with the European banks as partners. City Centre did it the right way from the start, and if its plan had succeeded, the Continental property débâcle of the early seventies, which cost British pensioners, insurers and shareholders hundreds of millions of pounds, might well have been avoided. It should be recalled that in that débâcle, losses on the Continent were incurred not by Continental banks, but by UK banks, not by Continental institutions, but by UK institutions, and not by Continental companies, but by UK companies.

By the end of 1962 Clore had reached a decision. Cotton must be stopped from making commitments. Clore started regarding City Centre Europe as an integral part of the Cotton disease, the disease of expansion made for expansion's sake, of transactions made for publicity, of associations made with too much equity given away. Clore set a stony face to Cotton's great positive features; he only saw the negative aspects. Clore, one of the great money-makers of the century who could smell lucre before anyone else, ruined one of his best-ever money-making opportunities because he refused to acknowledge in Cotton what he had perceived before the marriage — that Jack Cotton was himself also one of the great property money-makers of his age.

Too many different transactions were coming up from Cotton without prior consideration and prior financing. Clore now knew that when it came to the crunch he would almost certainly be able to win over the institutions. He calculated, correctly as it turned out, that Plumridge, Jack's most intimate institutional colleague, would move from one side to the other. Walter Flack had already tested the strength of institutional support for Cotton and found it less than 100%. Mr Clore of Park Street, Mayfair, tidy, orderly and methodical, walking every morning from Number 95 at the Oxford Street end to Number 22 at the Dorchester end, had made up his mind. Cotton had already been warned many times. He refused to be curbed. He was incorrigible. The marriage was over. The only possibility now was a divorce. Jack Cotton had to resign.

Chapter Twelve

'I Will Kill Charles with Kindness'

Every Friday afternoon the ritual of the weekend began. The great exodus for Marlow. A flurry of activity in the Dorchester suite. Last-minute phone calls. A hurried meeting with Eric Young or Freddy Lindgren, the chauffeur bustling in and out. A further file to be put in the bulging briefcase. Was Mrs Beaman ready? Tapper, get her on the telephone. Also on a Friday afternoon Charles Clore would leave for Stype. In the early halcyon days of the merger, Charles would sometimes drop into the Dorchester on his way to the country; this was Jack's golden hour during his golden honeymoon. Later, when Charles stopped this habit, Jack would telephone him instead. If it were an amiable call, the weekend started happily, if not, Jack would attempt to pass it off. His weekends at Marlow helped him sustain his sense of proportion, and now, during 1962, when he began to realise the worst of his horrors — that he might well lose out and have to resign — the Marlow weekends would form the bedrock of his sanity. Not that he dropped business until his return to the Dorchester on Sunday evening. Far from it. The phone rang incessantly. Many of his friends lived in the lush Thames Valley, Aubrey Orchard-Lisle was within binocular distance, Desmond Robinson, a property lawyer and brother of the Cambridge philanthropist, lived near Henley, and they entertained each other gregariously over the weekends. It is easy to understand Jack's affection for his Marlow house amongst the multi-coloured tulips with the serene river flowing a step away. Its riverside calm helped to assuage the terrors lapping around him. By Sunday lunch, he would have recovered his strength and rhythm. He became impatient to return to Park Lane, to his suite, to the Sunday evening meetings which had already been arranged. It was back to the conflicts, but he felt strong enough to face them, having convinced himself that Clore would be more amenable.

So, by the time he got back, Jack was more relaxed, several drinks had made him feel better and he was sure then that things would turn out all right. By Monday morning however he was once again unsettled. He would look at his papers in an anxious, desultory way, prepare himself for the Monday morning meeting now held at Park Place and now nearly always disagreeable. He was generally uneasy and it was affecting and sad to see him in this condition. He would occasionally expostulate that he had no intention of leaving his company, that he could still work with Clore, that the institutions would surely never let him down. It was evident that he was ill with worry, a state aided and abetted by his heavy drinking, but he would kill Charles with kindness. Almost until the very end he believed he could do it. Three months before his resignation, I entered Jack's room to find him sobbing by his desk. His faithful Tapper, expecting that I would have good news which would bolster him up a bit, had motioned me in. Jack had just completed a telephone conversation with Clore. His hand was shaking and his wide brow was wet. He turned his back to me to look on to the velvet green of Hyde Park. In a quiet voice, he said, 'You see the effect that man has on me? Why does he behave like this?' I said, 'Because he wants you out.' Cotton turned round, looking at me. 'He won't win, I will win. And I am going to tell you how I shall do it. I shall kill him with kindness.' It was the same old refrain. My reply surprised me more than I think it did Cotton. 'Don't worry about the kindness, Jack, just kill him.'

Cotton was quite serious. He was sure that Charles Clore would be won over by his inexhaustible decency and by his property genius. Charles Clore was not won over. Nor could he ever be won over by kindness. It was a word he hardly understood. Kindness to Clore was a manifestation of weakness; and weakness to Clore was something to be exploited. The Cotton blandishments had no effect on him.

To Jack Cotton and to his friends Charles Clore didn't have a clue about property. Property, Cotton declared to his cronies, was a business for experts which needed flair, experience and specialisation — not diversification, which was his perennial dig at Clore. To succeed in property, he stressed, forcing a deliberate gaze on anyone who seemed to be inattentive, one had to go ahead most times without prior financing. What was needed was property acumen, astuteness and real knowledge of the game. Finance would always look after itself as long as one never compromised on location. Money for property was easy. Sites, projects, transactions came first, he insisted, refilling his glass; money came after. His listeners were aware of his special pleading, aware that being on the defensive he had to bolster up his own confidence to vindicate himself and aware that in exhorting his friends in this fashion they would be his more enthusiastic advocates when they next encountered Clore.

What Cotton ignored was the fact that large public companies cannot in the long run rely only on the temperamental horsepower of just one man. He ignored the fact that Clore, and any sensible institution, would be fully justified in wanting budgets and in wanting a firm financial policy. On his own, before the merger, his style and pattern were recognisable. But he ignored the fact that there had been such a quantum jump in size by City Centre that the new scale of operations demanded a continuous detailed communication with the banks and institutions not only in the UK but also in the US and on the Continent. These banks and institutions would now have to impose an indirect but constant surveillance, for too much money was involved. They could, moreover, under no circumstances have their confidence in management dented or jeopardised. Having backed management, management had to perform. The kernel of their support was their confidence in that management, something quite intangible, something which could easily be destroyed by a conflict, particularly one at board level. Any loss of confidence and their backing could disappear altogether. Any rumble in the press, any gossip in the City, and they would start asking awkward questions. Their backing therefore was double-edged; one edge could easily cut to the quick a long-standing friendship and support. They would, in any conflict, have a single allegiance — to themselves. They would look inward, take counsel and then act quite dispassionately.

Cotton ignored the fact that any doubts from the institutions would not only be raised against him but also against Clore who would of necessity, apart from his own personal doubts, seek to get them on his side. In any boardroom conflict the two institutional directors of City Centre, George Bridge of the Legal and General and Edward Plumridge of the Pearl, would be especially vulnerable. Cotton chose to ignore their delicate exposure, chose not to see their point of view. This was his blind spot and it cost him his chairmanship, his career and, in my opinion, also his life. All the danger signals had been there since Flack, but Cotton was opaque. Look, he would say, at my Pan-Am, look at my Big Top, look at my French operation.

He sought a haven in his long-standing sanctuary, the press. Here he had always felt comfortable and at ease. The adulation was still there but ominously the criticism had begun. In early 1962 Charles Villiers happened to be with Jack at the Dorchester and found himself in the midst of an informal press conference. One of the reporters asked Jack, 'Where are you going to wave your magic wand next, Mr Cotton?' Villiers realised immediately that this effect on Cotton's ego could only be disastrous. 'The trouble with some of the great entrepreneurs', he observed to me, 'was that they had dreams of glory which were way ahead of their managerial and financial capacities.' Jack Cotton had his dreams of glory because many of his dreams had already come true. His head was turned, his heels had left the earth. He became emotionally and intellectually incapable of admitting that he had any serious faults or that his lack of managerial capacity could be a serious defect. How could there be any question of defects when he was considered the world's leading property developer? Since the Pan-Am project, when the first symptoms of megalomania had appeared, he had become progressively worse. In July 1962 a major profile about Cotton appeared in the *Sunday Times*. He was described as 'the undisputed top property man in Europe' and, in comparing Sir Isaac Wolfson, the founder of Great Universal Stores, and Charles Clore with Jack Cotton, the author stated that 'perhaps Cotton is the greatest intuitive operator of the trio'. Jack preened himself; this was music to his ears. But these were the very melodies which increased his fantasies and provoked his critics.

He once said, in response to these critics and as an attempt to endorse his personal way of conducting business and rebut Clore's opposition, that 'The Americans want complete security before they will start a building. They want the tenants all tied up. I prefer to rely on my judgment, and if there is no tenant on the doorstep, I still go ahead and build.' Years later, Clore told me that when he read this he shuddered. The authentic Cotton element of bravado was only too evident. What he was really saying was that if I, Jack Cotton, the greatest and best, say that I'm building, then prospective tenants will queue a mile for the honour of getting me as their landlord.

Earlier during the honeymoon period, the City editor of the *Evening Standard*, William Davis, had written, 'Finance, I am sure, will not bother Cotton and Clore unduly. At the moment they are getting all the money they could wish for.' Now the same writer, less than a year later in the midsummer of 1962, was writing, 'Is Cotton

203

taking on too much? How can one man, aged fifty-eight years, handle so many deals? In the City and no doubt elsewhere many people are beginning to wonder.' As soon as this piece appeared I pointed out to Jack that if one of his longest-standing admirers in the press was asking questions of this nature he should take full stock. Jack shrugged it off, but it must have hurt because he had a particular respect for Davis's views.

The banks, the pension funds, the insurance companies could not afford to shrug it off. Their representatives were accountable, and they were worried men. Cotton's friends were, if anything, even more worried. Freddie Lindgren, not in the best of health, remonstrated with Jack. He must slow down, he must do less. Peter Folliss remonstrated with Jack. Clore was a piranha; he would bite Jack's head off: 'for goodness' sake, Jack, appoint a chief executive and do it quickly.' Isadore Kerman remonstrated with Jack. He had particular knowledge of Clore's contempt for Jack's inability to curb himself. Of all Jack's friends Kerman was the most respected by Clore. They were on speaking terms; there was a dialogue between them. Kerman warned Jack that there would be an ugly fight ahead. Jack heard what he had to say, but took no notice.

During 1962 the conflict became more and more common knowledge. Flack's loose talk to all and sundry had taken hold, pervading not only the property world but well outside it, in industry and in financial circles. Jack, meanwhile, was as usual sustaining himself by doing just what Clore most deplored, embarking on new transactions. None of these transactions, Jack insisted, could be achieved by anyone else. When Erwin Wolfson died in June of that year, Jack was visibly upset. He visited New York more frequently, taking more direct interest in the progress of the Pan-Am building. He felt more comfortable in New York, less harassed. During the summer and autumn he was to a certain extent diverted by his son Gordon's romantic entanglements and by his son Jeremy's marriage. But there was one transaction which he was sure would end all carping and criticism, which would be a true peak of his achievement: the association he was forging with 'that great British company run by great British gentlemen', the Cunard Shipping Company.

In October 1962 there was the astonishing announcement that Cunard and City Centre had 'started discussions that had reached an advanced stage' for the joint development of most of the Cunard properties not only in the UK but also abroad. The first approach had come from a Merseyside shipbuilding associate of Cunard's.

Would Jack Cotton like to see Sir John Brocklebank, the chairman of the Cunard Shipping Line? Cotton said he would be very happy to. Actually he was ecstatic. He couldn't wait to tell Clore. Cunard was one of the most prestigious names in the world. Partners with Cunard. This would make everyone sit up; even Harold Samuel would have to admit his envy. As for his critics, they would have to eat their words. Why should he change his ways? He would have to be accepted as he was. Cunard had come to him because he was the best.

Clore *was* impressed. But imbued with the native East End Jewish scepticism which was as much a part of him as his mild cockney accent, he questioned Cunard's motive. Clore always worked on the 'club rule' which, paraphrasing Groucho Marx, simply said that there must be something wrong with any club that wants you as a member. Clore sniffed problems at Cunard. Were they more severe than the stock market seemed to be aware? Shipping was in the doldrums. In February 1962 Clore had had to deny to the press that he was bidding for Cunard. He said, 'I am not interested in taking over the Cunard line. There are some people who are buying Cunard shares, but they are playing around with a great institution.' Was the exclusive Cunard club now so badly off that it had to seek City Centre as a member? Of course they had wonderful freehold properties. Perhaps a good deal or even a bargain was in the offing. An association with Cunard certainly had to be examined carefully, but as far as Clore was concerned it had to be commercial or else.

Jack did not get the message. He was after prestige, and once again his obdurate refusal to act on advice was his undoing. The Cunard transaction was one which he should have pursued and concluded on entirely pragmatic, commercial grounds alone. The idea was for Cunard to form a joint company owned 50/50 with City Centre, which would have the Cunard properties transferred to it at an agreed valuation, with Eric Young as the group surveyor acting for City Centre and Donald Taylor of Weatherall Green and Smith acting for Cunard. The transaction was similar to that involving the Samuel Estates. But whereas the Samuel family was prepared to be paid by way of City Centre shares, which made financial sense, Cunard wanted cash, thus endorsing Clore's assessment of Cunard's real needs and proving his 'club rule'. A cash payment by a development company for mainly investment properties was untenable. It could only be justified if there were a major discount in value in order to allow it to be financed; shares did not require financing, they could simply be issued to Cunard as they had been issued previously to the Samuel family. The investment yield on the Cunard properties would probably be at 6%. But in order to make it pay for City Centre on a cash deal, those same properties would have had to be valued on a 7.5% basis — an excessive discount. The agreement reached with Cunard was that the deal would come into effect as soon as Young settled the valuation with Taylor. Young delayed agreeing the valuation, fully aware that the minute he did so, City Centre was committed. He was in a dilemma. If he agreed the valuation, City Centre would be committed and all hell would break loose. If he did not agree the valuation, he would have to oppose the transaction formally in his report to the City Centre board and would find himself in formal opposition to Jack Cotton. Clore was of course fully aware of Young's dilemma.

By Christmas 1962, Jack was generally ill at ease. He was sleeping badly at night and during the day got tired more quickly. Eric Young had not seen him as depressed as this before and discerned in him a new, defeatist strain. Each evening Jack was drinking more heavily and although his fabulous memory had still not forsaken him, his speech was more and more slurred. Young found him distracted too, lacking in concentration even when discussing the Cunard association.

With the arrival of 1963 Jack hoped for a significantly better year. He was looking far more now to Europe for his salvation. He would get rid of Flack as soon as possible, and with Archie Sherman in Flack's place the ripple effect would be stemmed: Sherman would have a calming effect on everyone — the French partners, the financial advisers, the institutions, and the City Centre main board directors.

1963 started badly and it never recovered. Flack resigned in January and the *Times* report remarked that there had been dissension in City Centre for some time. In February Jack gave a long, rambling interview to the *Sunday Telegraph* which lacked grip and clarity; some of us had the impression that he was not sober at the time. In early March the Pan-Am had its official opening and this buoyed him up. Although it was more Juan Trippe's day than anyone else's, proper homage was paid to the deceased Erwin Wolfson, the speeches reflecting genuine respect for this proud, combative but well-mannered Manhattan developer, the indomitable originator of the great building. Jack had a brief respite in Nassau before returning to London. Walter Flack died in the second week of that month, and some of us who were saddened by this were also smitten with a feeling of guilt.

Back in London Jack at once felt harassed. Everyone wanted to see him. All he wanted to do was go down to Marlow for the weekend. On his first Friday afternoon, Eric Young collared him just as he was leaving. 'What's happening?' 'I'm going straight down to Marlow.' 'You can't possibly go to Marlow until we have solved the Cunard deal. Charles has called me a bloody fool and he won't agree the deal. I have delayed the valuation for months and I cannot delay any longer.' Cotton lost his temper and slammed his fist on the boardroom table. Eric Young, the self-effacing ex-Coal Board surveyor, was having his first ever row with his chairman. He knew he must not budge. 'Jack, I am very sorry. You know the deal is wrong. You know that once I agree the valuation, the group is committed.' Cotton stared at Young and said, 'I hate your bloody guts because I know you're right. All right. I will tell them at Cunard I cannot possibly go on.' 'That is the only way,' said Eric.

So ended the Cunard transaction, Jack's last attempt to rehabilitate himself, his last attempt to form a joint company, his last attempt to 'show them' that Jack Cotton was the brightest and the best, that Jack Cotton was more than worthy of having Charles Clore as his deputy chairman, that Jack Cotton was going to kill Clore with kindness. His deputy chairman was forcing him to climb down, and what made it particularly galling was that it had had to happen through his own man — the decent, correct professional, Eric Young.

But far worse was to come when he had his first meeting after his return with Edward Plumridge, 'dear Plum' of the Pearl Assurance, his great friend and institutional supporter and the Pearl main board director in charge of its investment policy. How were the men at the Pearl regarding the dissension at City Centre? And what had been going on behind the gothic walls of that oligarchic institution?

207

Chapter Thirteen

The Fall of Big Daddy

The man could weave a great spell. No wonder he was called Big Daddy. It was a lot more than charm: Jack Cotton's decency was rock solid, his brain sparkled with ideas and wit, and he had a talent for friendship which endeared him to people who had known him for ten minutes or ten years. Until he developed his streak of megalomania, stirred up by his debilitating love affair with the press, his personality, his emotions and his abilities were in easy harmony, creating a remarkable impression on everyone who met him. This happened time and time again: with the lofty academics from Brasenose, with the volatile bureaucrats of New York, with the bigwigs of the City establishment, with nervous and not so nervous journalists, and of course with the powerful institutional managers, both the retiring and the not so retiring.

One of the most retiring and one of the most powerful was George Bridge. The actuary and later general manager of the Legal and General; the prime innovator of the rent review for which feat alone he ought to go down in City history; the chief architect of his own institution's great success in property; the quiet, thinking, prudent institutional man: George Bridge on Jack Cotton's board listened carefully to the City Centre atmospherics, trying his best to see if peace could be achieved. He was immune to Cotton's charisma, but not immune to Cotton's ability. He had welcomed the merger with Clore, because Clore implied restraint. Perhaps Cotton's exuberant mishandling of the Monico development, in which the Legal and General had a 50% stake, could have been avoided. He had also welcomed the merger because it brought the Prudential Assurance into the City Centre group, the Prudential being Clore's largest property loan-holders.

In the institutional league table, the Prudential had always stood out because of its size and because of its exclusivity. The authoritative

Prudential lent weight to even as august an institution as the Legal and General. Whatever the Prudential's view, it was an ever-present factor in the minds of the managers of other institutions. It was certainly a factor in the minds of George Bridge and Edward Plumridge. Bridge could be relied upon to support Cotton as long as there was no serious problem. But the Prudential would react immediately to any concern about Cotton expressed by Clore, and if the Pru became anxious, that would be a serious problem. There was continuous pressure from the Clore camp, not only to Bridge but also to Plumridge that as Jack was still making commitments, not curbing himself at all, he had to go. Bridge was aware that there was already a serious problem. In any conflict between Cotton and Clore, Bridge knew that his institution would not go beyond the point where support for Cotton would be considered controversial, which, in institutional terms, meant where the conflict had become public knowledge, had been mentioned in the press, had not been kept behind closed doors.

Which investment manager said what to whom and where and when is never known. Whispered conversations took place, positions were taken, pressures built up. The power of this firming-up of the institutional consensus is awesome, for when the collective view is declared, it is as good as acted upon, being immutable and non-negotiable.

The heavy armour of the institutions was taking its position. At this juncture to avoid further controversy, it would close ranks and would look to the one of its kind most intimately involved, to make its collective view known. In this case it was the Pearl Assurance. The Pearl however was not only involved financially; two of its top men, indeed the two most important, Kitchen the Pearl's chairman and Plumridge the Pearl's investment director were involved personally with the main protagonist. This, if anything, hardened the 'view' of the Pru and the Legal & General against Cotton.

The Pearl was in a most sensitive position and it was this personal aspect which for a while obscured the issue. Kitchen and Plumridge were two of Jack Cotton's closest friends. In strict City terms it was an extraordinary anomaly and at the Pearl itself it had fundamental consequences because the growing differences between Kitchen and Plumridge over Jack Cotton almost shook that institution to its rafters.

The personal support of an institutional manager for an entrepreneur can mean millions to his net worth. Jack Cotton always had his finger on this financial pulse and was of course very pleased to meet Plumridge soon after he came down to London from Birmingham. Theirs was an instant friendship, with Plumridge an ardent fan from the very beginning. The friendship flourished as Jack became richer and more renowned and as Plumridge became more important at the Pearl, where his early forays into property were bearing a rich harvest. Plumridge was elected a director of Jack Cotton's company with the express approval of his own Pearl board. Then there arose the oddest of situations because both the top men at the Pearl became devotees of Jack Cotton: soon after Plumridge's appointment to the City Centre board Kitchen got to know Cotton, and a genuine friendship sprang up between them too. Kitchen, the shrewd, high-living insurance magnate, fell head over heels for the equally shrewd and high-living property magnate. They enjoyed each other's company enormously and spent many convivial evenings together; Kitchen having the ability to polish off a bottle of whisky and remain cold sober, his famous drinking companion hardly able to drink a single scotch without it going straight to his head.

Naturally Plum was put out. He had been there first. He was junior to Kitchen at the Pearl which in any event he resented because he felt he was cleverer, and now it would seem he was going to be junior to Kitchen at City Centre. This spurred him to get to the most inner part of Jack's life, to be as useful to him as possible, to become totally essential to his operation, to make himself indispensable. He became a crony, he became the unpaid unofficial finance director of Jack's company, and he became a constant visitor to the Dorchester Hotel. He was under Big Daddy's spell. Probably no such relationship of this kind had existed before, that is between a full-time employee of an insurance company and the founder chairman and major shareholder of a commercial company in which that insurance company had an important stake. The principle of impartiality had not been broken; it had never existed. But if that chairman became a problem, what then? It would be an impossible position for all parties concerned, particularly the institution. Which is exactly what happened.

Jack imagined that his new institutional associates, the ICI pension fund, the Unilever pension fund, the Imperial Tobacco pension fund would have a bearing on his institutional relationships. They didn't. The big three were the Prudential, the Legal and General and the Pearl. The Prudential Jack realised would go for Clore; the Legal and General would be strictly impartial. With the Pearl there was

210

absolutely no doubt at all. They would back him up to the hilt. Their unswerving support would sway the others, and he would win the day. Plumridge and Kitchen would never let him down.

Plumridge sounded out his colleagues at the Pearl. One of the key people was Freddie Garner, later chairman of the Pearl. Plumridge would frequently discuss his worries and anxieties about Cotton with him, and the other colleagues. These talks would take place in their various rooms in the Pearl headquarters, a huge mausoleum-type building, sand-coloured with a Gothic façade, looking discreetly out onto Holborn, its impressive church-like fenestration denoting strength and long-term confidence. These top managers were derived from the hard-working, straightforward professional classes, sensible, cautious, stolid. It was as closed a set-up as it is today: there were and are no outside directors at the Pearl. It was vital for Plumridge that his colleagues like Garner were given all the details and provided with all the information about his anxieties regarding Jack Cotton, so that the overall top executive management consensus could emerge.

Confronted with the most horrible situation he had ever encountered, Plumridge, as he told me later, felt in a terrible state, unable either to sleep or to concentrate on any other matters. It was, he said, the worst period of his life. His ordeal was agonising. He realised that Jack Cotton would have no doubt that Plumridge would back him through thick and thin. He also knew that Kitchen supported Jack unequivocally and was prepared to stick his neck out.

He sounded out the other institutions. He reached the conclusion that if he, like Kitchen, supported Cotton, it would plunge the City into one of the nastiest scandals ever. Not only would the Pearl be the odd institution out, but the scandal, bad enough as a boardroom fight, would be incalculably worse if it developed into a messy shareholders' battle. If this happened, not only would the shares plummet, but the scars and wounds would remain for years.

But Plumridge was emotionally involved. Jack was not only someone for whom he had the greatest respect and admiration but a man too for whom he felt deep affection. At this period he was also concerned, like other of Jack's friends, about Jack's physical and mental state. He knew that his eventual decision had to be based on unemotional grounds, and that the only grounds were what was best for the shareholders, what was best for the institutions, what was best for the Pearl, what was best for the City — in that order. Cotton's predicament had to come after all that. Personal loyalty did

211

not seem to be relevant; but Kitchen stood fair and square behind Jack. The Pearl consensus looked as if it were going the wrong way. Kitchen was livid and the simmering tension of ambition and animosity between him and Plumridge boiled over. It had been bound to happen sooner or later. Plumridge not only wanted to oust Kitchen from Jack's side, he also wanted Kitchen's job. Though Jack had managed the separate and dual friendships with the two men over the years with consummate skill, the complicated structural levels were bound to collapse under real stress.

Plumridge finally came down on the side of Clore. This was also the decision of his top colleagues. Despite being chairman, Kitchen could not get his way. The decision once made, Plumridge had his job cut out. He had to inform Cotton. Once informed, Cotton was finished.

At the most crucial moment of his career, Jack heard directly from Plumridge that the Pearl was going to back Clore. He was stunned. Plumridge, he said, was a Judas. This damning *cri de coeur* from the man he had revered more than any other, reverberated in Plumridge's mind until the end of his days.

Clore, now sure of Jack's defeat, decided that the best person to persuade him that he should go quietly was Isadore Kerman, Jack's school friend and trustee. Clore and Sainer spoke to Kerman. Without any institutional support Jack was thoroughly exposed; he had lost out. As far as he was concerned, Plumridge had pulled the rug. He would never forgive Plumridge. But whilst he knew he had been defeated he still refused to resign. Finally Clore told Kerman to tell Jack that if he did not resign 'we will have to throw him out'.

Now at his nadir, Jack's fondest allies, the press, also started asking questions. On 5 May 1963 the *Daily Mirror* came out with a large headline. 'Will Cotton and Clore part?' It stated that 'rumours of a serious boardroom rift between property tycoon Jack Cotton and Charles Clore surged through the City. The talks suggest that they will soon be parting company.' Jack was in New York. Questioned from there about reports of his strained relations with Clore he said, 'I know nothing about it. There are always differences about things like personalities and so on.' The *Daily Telegraph* on the same day said that relations had become so strained that 'some way of easing them has become imperative. Failure to see eye to eye on important policy decisions has led to a series of informal discussions to seek ways of resolving their differences'.

Jack's constitution could not withstand the strain. He had been warned for months to take things easy. He had his first heart attack, a relatively mild one, on the aeroplane: he found he could not sit down. On 16 May Jack had a bout of pneumonia. The pressure was finally taking its toll. He had been looking forward to attending the opening of the Cotton Terraces at the London Zoo, to be graced by the presence of Prince Philip. His eldest son Derek had to represent him and Prince Philip referred to 'a tycoon-sized donation from Mr Jack Cotton'. On the same day Charles Clore abandoned the smoke and boardroom battles of London to visit his farms at Hungerford. He wore brogues but was otherwise in City attire.

Jack had a second heart attack. Mr de Bakey, the renowned heart surgeon of Houston, was called in. On 17 June, Jack, at Marlow, was trying hard to recover. The phones rang incessantly at the Dorchester. Miss Tapper said he was now up and about, but still weak. On the same day Charles was shooting pheasant, woodcock and snipe and he commented that there were no mallard or duck. The gamekeeper told him that was because there was no water. Clore replied, 'Then make some lakes.' Soon after the bulldozers went to work.

The end was near. Isadore Kerman pleaded with Jack: the board would go with Clore; if Jack did not resign as chairman there would be a battle royal; Jack was bound to lose; it was better to face facts. But Jack dug in; he refused to budge. He hated being a loser. Eventually, after listening again to his persuasive, understanding old friend he accepted the inevitable and he told Kerman that he would resign. He wrote his decision on a piece of blue personal notepaper and gave it to Kerman.

But he was going to go in his own way. He was not going to go to London for any formal board meeting. They had to come to him. For the formal termination, for the final *coup de grâce*, they would have to come to Marlow.

Chapter Fourteen

Resignation at Marlow

Charles Clore, Leonard Sainer, George Bridge and Eddie Footring went to Marlow in Sainer's Rolls. Kerman was already there when they arrived. So was Turner the secretary. Freddie Lindgren arrived with John Mayo from the company's solicitors. Plumridge was absent. Folliss did not have the heart to attend. It was the most unusual board meeting held by City Centre. It was like a scene from a Fellini film. Driving through the summer hush of a quiet weekday away from the hurly-burly of London to the soft green Thames valley, the directors and functionaries of City Centre Properties Limited were attending a board meeting to be held in the dining-room of the property magnate's country mansion. There was only one item on the agenda: the resignation of the chairman.

Jack's colleagues arrived, sad, sombre and cheerless for this chilling formal severance. Jack was restless and ill at ease but courteous and dignified. Outwardly he seemed the same, but the soup-plate black eyes held no expression. The meeting commenced immediately. Jack Cotton ceased to be chairman of his own company. His colleagues shuffled out. There was some desultory conversation. They departed. The swans on the Thames barely gave them a glance. Inside the house, it was a dark elegy.

The announcement from the company on 3 July 1963, stated that as a result of medical advice he had to give up business activities for at least six months. 'In these circumstances, he had relinquished the chair but would still remain a director.' At the next AGM it was proposed that he be appointed president. George Bridge was appointed the new chairman. Most people assumed that Charles Clore would take the chair. But he declined. He said, 'I am very sorry, I will not take Jack's place.' Perhaps a part of him had been killed off with kindness.

Chapter Fifteen

Exit the Bow Tie

Why does the shadow mimic the substance with such cruelty? The next days Jack looked the same, he wore the same well-pressed suit, the white shirt was as spotless, the bow tie was as neat as ever. The purposeful walk seemed the same. It was his eyes that gave him away: without lustre, without expression. Then one knew everything was different, and this was when some of his friends started crying.

He stayed at Marlow. He would rest there a while, then he would return to the Dorchester for a few days before going to Nassau to recuperate. He would try to sleep. He had to keep away from the telephone, he had to try not to think. If he harped on things his hand would shake and he would want a drink. He must stop drinking, he mustn't see people, he mustn't think about it.

Very slowly he began feeling his old self again. To hell with Clore and City Centre. He would start again. He saw his friends. The Cunard directors said they still wanted him to stay with their property company. They at least recognised his worth and were acting like gentlemen, unlike his former colleagues.

On 24 September he went to his first outside engagement since his illness, an American Chamber of Commerce lunch at the Savoy. He ate carefully, keeping to fish and cheese. Reporters besieged him. 'Will you now resign as a director, Mr Cotton?' 'Resign?' he replied with a semblance of his former energy. 'Of course I'm not resigning. As you know my illness was serious. But I'm a lot better now. I'll be back in full harness by the end of the year.' The reporters warmly wished him the best of luck.

On 17 October Jack sailed to New York on the Cunard's pride, the *Queen Elizabeth*. He planned to spend a few days in New York with 'dear Peetah' and to return on the *Queen Mary*. On the evening before he left, Eric Young had a drink with him at the Dorchester. Well-meaning and well-mannered as always, Eric said to Jack: 'I'm terribly sorry. I hope you have a good holiday. At least you got something out of the Cunard deal. You will get the best treatment of anyone on the *Queen*.' Jack seemed subdued and sad. 'Eric, I have made a lot of mistakes in my life. I made one big mistake: I sold out my company.' As Young recalled, Jack then looked up at him with a wan smile. 'And Eric, I didn't wear the trousers.' Next morning he sailed for New York.

Plumridge was thoroughly mortified. He felt like a pariah. Jack had left for New York, refusing to speak to him. Many in Jack's entourage also treated him as a traitor, myself included, and would not have any contact with Plumridge until years later, despite his repeated attempts to justify himself. He sent a cable of good wishes to Jack on the *Queen Elizabeth*. Cotton's cabled reply, succinct and to the point, stated that he had never thought Plumridge could ever be so disloyal. It was this reply which struck Plumridge with permanent remorse. Ten years later, when he and I were back on terms, remarkably good terms as it turned out, Plumridge, still at the Pearl and still under Kitchen's chairmanship, still suffering deep remorse, would sometimes ask, 'What else could I have done? The Pearl had to vote against Jack.' Or 'The other institutions forced me.' On one occasion after we had just concluded a fairly exciting transaction, he glowed and said, 'It's like old times,' then, gripping my arm: 'I loved Jack but what else could I do?'

Whilst Jack Cotton was sailing back from New York on the *Queen Mary*, constantly inveighing against Plum, City Centre announced on 29 October that it would not meet its 40 per cent dividend forecast. George Bridge in his new role as chairman stated that the company was undercapitalised and there was a need to consolidate.

On 31 October Charles Clore was one of seven British Friesian breeders in south-east England who were teaming up to make bulls available by artificial insemination.

The same week the *Sunday Times* wrote that anyone who had invested £100 in Jack Cotton's company at the earliest possible moment when it was quoted on the Stock Exchange would have had an investment worth £200,000 — if they had sold just before the merger with Clore.

Jack was treated royally on both *Queens*. He adored recognition and he felt somewhat better. Soon after his return he was invited to have lunch with Isaac Wolfson. It was during the Jewish festival season and Wolfson, being very observant, would be at home in

Portland Place after the synagogue service. He would forgive Jack for his non-attendance at the service. Jack after all was a great giver to charity and that was one of the most admirable and blessed of Jewish traits.

Felix Fenston's comment that one can be a seller without realising it, which he made after he saw Jack about the Royal Garden site and subsequently sold him his entire company, Eron Investments, was to apply to Jack himself with far more poignancy in respect of his puzzling invitation from Sir Isaac Wolfson. Jack went to lunch and returned totally bewildered, even disorientated, having tentatively agreed to sell Wolfson his family trust's entire shareholding in City Centre. 'Isaac wants to buy my share in City Centre. How did he know? I didn't know I wanted to sell. I didn't know until he mentioned it.' This was Jack's expostulation to me immediately after his return from Portland Place. I had arranged to have tea with him. It was a pale autumn afternoon and Rembrandt's wise old man was calmly gazing at Jack, who looked quite blank. He had resigned as chairman of his company, but until that day he had not realised that he was a seller of his shares. On 19 November, it was announced that the trustees of the Cotton family settlements had sold their shares in City Centre for £8 million. It was said that Jack's personal holding was not involved.

The next day, at the Annual General Meeting, Jack was appointed president of City Centre, proposed by George Bridge and seconded by Charles Clore. Jack did not attend the meeting. Press reports also stated that the Cotton settlement's shares would be purchased by Sir Isaac Wolfson and by a consortium headed by Hill Samuel, put together by its chairman Kenneth Keith. It also stated that Wolfson and Keith would be joining the board of City Centre.

Early in December Jack was awarded the Zoological Society Gold Medal, its highest award and given only five times since 1826. Jack donated a further sum for an aviary to be designed by Lord Snowdon and Cedric Price. On 10 December, Jack sailed to the Bahamas under doctor's orders to stay at his house there for two or three months. His doctor stated that he was still seriously ill and needed a good long rest. This was his last trip. He would not return to England alive.

Jack tried to relax, but he did not try to stop drinking. Christmas and New Year came and went. The Iliffe house was pink and white and cream, beautifully proportioned with a spacious garden and a private beach. The luminous sand lay between the garden and the turquoise sea. This was the open heath, where nightly Jack cried out in agony.

During the day he talked with his family and with Denise Tapper who came to visit. He was pleased to see other friends, especially Aubrey and Bunty Orchard-Lisle. He spoke to Peter Folliss every day on the telephone. He called Eric Young from time to time, also Geoffrey Kitchen, his Birmingham and London intimates. He spoke to Lindgren and to his sons and daughter.

On 1 January 1964, Cotton's 61st birthday, Eddie Footring was appointed managing director of City Centre. The new orderly procedure was a weekly meeting with his new chairman, George Bridge, at his office at the headquarters of the Legal and General.

Two weeks later I had lunch with Clore at Claridge's. He had phoned me at Hambros Bank one morning, saying, 'It's time to get together.' It was a surprising, perhaps pivotal, lunch. As soon as we sat down, not wasting a minute, he asked, 'Why can't we be friends?' I said I didn't see how we could. What he had done to Jack on business grounds was one thing, but on human grounds he had behaved deplorably, not even phoning him once to enquire about his health. Clore looked at me levelly and said, 'You're right. I won't phone. I will visit him in Nassau.' This was, I believe, the precise beginning of my friendship with Clore. In his thoroughly incisive way he had accepted, without further ado, what he knew was necessary. His previous lack of gentility was not at issue. He had not thought of paying his respects to Jack; it had now been brought to his attention. He knew he was in the wrong and he was going to rectify the situation. Though still lacking in humanity, his reaction was simple, direct and honest. He had decided to make amends and he made the arrangements.

Within a fortnight of that seminal lunch we met again, at Claridge's. This time I was host and this time he broke to me the news of his purchase into M. Samuel. On 13 February it was announced that he owned over 14% of the equity of that exquisite family bank; one of the fruits of his friendship with Lord Melchett.

In February I was Jack's guest. I flew from New York to Nassau. The house was filled with children and grandchildren. I stayed at the nearby hotel. Jack insisted on showing me my room. On the terrace he pointed out the spectacular view of the sea, the pure sandy beach was ringed with palm trees. He put his arm round my shoulder. 'Don't worry my boy, everything is all right.' His voice shook with emotion.

For several days we swam and sunbathed and lunched and dined. He seemed stronger and occasionally his voice would sound firm as it used to, with that familiar trenchant timbre. But he was drinking heavily, and whenever one looked him in the eye, one only saw a dull opaque expression. I told him all about my encounter with Clore and that he had promised to come and visit him. He stared at me. 'Charles, blast him, all right.'

On 23 February, Jack resigned as a director of City Centre. He said from the Bahamas, 'So long as I am not carrying out any executive duties I wouldn't wish to have any responsibility for decisions the board might make.' And he added, 'I am one hundred per cent better and extremely happy. I hope to have a lot of life about me yet.'

Early in the evening, on Saturday 21 March 1964 he died. His heart finally gave up. There was a raging thunderstorm and the phones were unclear. His daughter Jill, and Gordon his middle son, were with him. Gordon couldn't get through to his brothers. He phoned Alex Kaye. Could he help? Certainly. Kaye phoned Derek Cotton in Birmingham. Jill returned on the plane bearing Jack's coffin. It arrived at London Airport on a bleak Tuesday morning. A van arrived from Birmingham to take Jack to his final resting place.

I went to the funeral by train with Harry Sporborg. The burial ground teemed with dark-clad Lowry-like figures. Most were friends from London. Everyone that afternoon felt a sense of loss and I am certain that all who knew Jack Cotton still feel that same sense of loss twenty years later.

Chapter Sixteen

Exit the Black Tie

City Centre without Jack Cotton was not a ship without a captain, but a ship with too many admirals. The chairman, George Bridge, was an insurance man, the deputy chairman, Charles Clore, was an industrialist, Sir Isaac Wolfson was a retailer and Kenneth Keith was a merchant banker. Each of them could easily have led a fleet, but none of them was available to run a ship. The guiding spirit, the visionary, the craftsman who really understood his trade, the helmsman was missing. Eddie Footring, a competent trustworthy property lawyer, was a competent and trustworthy managing director. He would be able to keep the ship tidy, but as to its direction, there was no one on the main board of City Centre Properties who could or would provide it. The biggest financial problem arising from Plumridge's now notorious convertible issue, was how to service that loan. The second biggest problem was the narrow equity base of the group. 'If only it had not been a convertible issue but an ordinary rights issue,' Eric Young observed to me. 'If only,' I replied in return. In the year after Jack's death, Footring's job was more that of a liquidator. Properties were sold in order to service and pay for debt. Some of these properties were like the properties in the CLRP portfolio, too gorgeous ever to be sold. But sold they were, including some of the choicest items in the original Clore portfolio. Clore's original rationale in merging with Cotton, was that Cotton was an outstanding property man of great expertise, and that the price was marvellous. Where was this property expertise now? And as to the marvellous price, it had dropped like a stone. If only, some of his cohorts observed, he had merged his own property company with Sears, his industrial conglomerate . . . . . if only.

Jack's sprawling, untidy empire was made less untidy. As it was cut up, losing a limb here and a limb there, having already lost its driving force, it was now losing its *raison d'être*. Around the boardroom table was ranged a most impressive array of brains, money and power. The big shots had taken over.

Cotton's City Centre was now as Clore wanted it. A tidy and orderly machine. But the machine was going backwards not forwards. If only there had been another way of handling Cotton . . . . . if only. Footring's later remark, terse and lapidary, is as apt as any other made at this time: 'I personally don't think the merger should have taken place. But once it did, it was a tragedy it didn't work.'

In June there was provisional probate on Jack's estate, and many specific legacies were directed, including a distribution among '. . . persons who have rendered any service or kindness to me during my lifetime, or been close friends of mine, the executors consider I would buy some memento.' Thoughtful and considerate to the last.

On 29 June, Charles Clore's daughter Vivien, now eighteen, had a coming-out dance at the Savoy for 300 guests. The River Room was redesigned as a pink Forest of Arden.

Three months later, on 30 September, Jack Cotton's Thames lawn, with its acres of tulips, the Georgian style riverside house with many of its principal rooms panelled in pine, was sold at auction. His daughter Jill said, 'It is a sad day. My father lived there for nineteen years.'

During that summer, Charles was in Deauville attending the Sales in a natty white suit with two-tone shoes. He bought Mont Blanc II, which was said to be the only pure white thoroughbred in the world.

In the autumn of 1964, on 19 October, City Centre announced that its dividend had been cut. The cause it stated, was high interest rates and delays in completing certain of the developments.

Ten days later Charles Clore took a large party of friends to the opening of a postgraduate students' centre at the Weizmann Institute near Jerusalem which he had donated. They travelled in a specially enlarged First Class section of the plane, and the party included Marcus Sieff and Prince Radziwill.

In 1965, in April, Charles and Francine threw a 21st birthday party at Annabel's for Alan Clore. There was no present from his father because Charles wanted to wait for the results of his son's Finals at Oxford.

In October Charles Clore embarked on one of his most important acquisitions, the large Lewis's department store group, whose jewel was of course Selfridges. At that time it was the biggest stores bid ever made. In an interview during the bid Clore said he was 'just a little man with ordinary tastes and ordinary ideas. I have no power. The editor of a provincial newspaper has more power than I have.' On 22 November, after a fierce battle, he won what was his most gratifying prize: Selfridges. Next year in March 1966 he appointed Sainer's sister Winifred his personal assistant at Selfridges. In May he won the Oaks, his first classic. The horse, Valoris, was ridden by Lester Piggott. In June, on the Monday preceding Ascot, he gave a ball at the Hilton. There were gilded cages for peacocks and doves, raised terraces with pink arches and white balustrades. We were served *foie gras* flown from France, trout poached in champagne, and chicken with truffles and mushrooms.

In July Clore wrote a perceptive article in the *Spectator* calling for incentives to increase productivity and a sales tax on all essential goods. I asked Clore whether Sainer had written the article for him, it had the smack of Sainer's thinking and brain. 'What a question,' he replied smugly. Nearly a year later, in 1967, he wrote another piece for the journal. This article was also well thought out. The budget 'was most disappointing because incentives were needed by way of reduced taxation.' I didn't bother to ask him who had written it. I was convinced it was Sainer.

In May there was an interesting piece in the *Observer* by its business editor: 'Ironically, Clore's master company, Sears, now seems to be approaching the position that could once have excited Clore himself as a potential take-over proposition.' The return on capital, 25 per cent in 1960, had dropped to less than 10 per cent.

In March 1968 Clore closed the Furness shipyard. It had cost £8.5 million in the previous five years, despite £5 million spent on modernising. Also in March, Alan Clore left England to become a tax exile. Alan had asked me for advice and I had told him firmly that he would only be able to get on to his own feet if he got away from his father. I told Charles the same thing. 'Alan is a late starter,' I said, 'and he's better off away from you.' Clore's reply was: 'Don't talk nonsense.'

In April the *Sunday Times* forecast that Charles Clore would be taking over the City Centre chair from George Bridge later in the year. For four years Eddie Footring had been retrenching the finances and the portfolio, diligently seeing Bridge every week and equally diligently reporting progress at each tidy monthly board meeting.

Charles Clore's brother David, who had joined Hill Samuel when it had acquired Investment Registry, retired. 'I will be taking things easy now,' he said. 'I am the lazy brother. Charles can't retire — he's got too many shareholders to look after.'

Charles Clore was not interested in retiring, though the fire may have somewhat dimmed. On 25 August 1968 the *Sunday Times* forecast proved accurate: five years after Jack Cotton resigned as chairman, Charles Clore was appointed chairman of City Centre in place of George Bridge.

A month later, on 20 September 1968, Charles Clore, whose chairman's seat was barely warm, agreed a bid with Harold Samuel. Land Securities now owned City Centre Properties Ltd. One of the first things Samuel did was to sell City Centre's interest in the Pan-Am building. The buyer was the airline itself.

In June 1969, Charles Clore's daughter married a stockbroker. I had never taken to Vivien although she stayed with us one summer at our villa in Ischia. He refused to attend her wedding. Years later Charles asked me: 'You like Alan, but you don't care for Vivien, why not?' 'She's obsessed with money.' 'What's wrong with that? So am I,' said Charles.

Early in 1970 Clore became a major benefactor to London University, donating a sum to initiate the Institute for Advanced Legal Studies. In October Sears bought out the minority shareholders of the British Shoe Corporation.

In February 1971, Nadia and I chartered Lawrence Rockefeller's yacht *Sea Star* for a cruise in the Grenadines. Charles Clore came along too, bad sailor as he was. We boarded *Sea Star* at Mustique, an island paradise conceived by Colin Tennant in which I had taken a large financial stake. Oliver Messel was designing and building a holiday house for us there made up of several pavilions, 'for Nadia,' he urged, 'for my favourite ballerina, how can you refuse to commission me?' I couldn't. The house was half-way up: Clore said let it stay that way. We gave dinner on board for Princess Margaret for whom Nadia and indeed everyone in the Royal Ballet has a great admiration and affection. Islands of tranquillity, we bathed in the milky sea — Bequia, St Lucia, Palm, Antigua, Guadeloupe. Clore was in seventh heaven. He said he had never enjoyed a holiday as much. Later for Easter, Nadia and I were his guests in Israel, staying in his enormous apartment overlooking the lovely campus of the Weizmann Institute. There I bought a painting, a mysterious red horse by Israel's foremost artist Rubin, and asked that it be housed in the Clore building in the Institute. Charles was delighted, and graceful too when he told me he liked my mother's paintings.

'Perhaps she will give me one. Rubin gives nothing away.'

By 1971 Clore and I were seeing each other two or three times a week. He took a great interest in my activities at Spey Investments. He was rather proud of it in some peculiar way. When my own problems started in spring 1971 with the pension funds who were minority shareholders in Spey, he contributed valuable advice. When it came to the point where I required legal advice, he suggested Sainer. By that time Eddie Footring had joined Sainer's firm, having left City Centre after its acquisition by Samuel. Between them they handled my side of the dispute.

In June 1971, at last, he received his knighthood. He was tremendously bucked. No longer Mr Clore, he was Sir Charles. A great honour, and about time, he mumbled.

In the early seventies, in the run-up to the financial crisis, he marked time, and survived considerably better than I did, for in 1974 in that crisis I lost a fortune. In December of the same year Clore had his 70th birthday party at, of all places, the Dorchester Hotel. There were hundreds of guests.

In 1975 Nadia and I left England to live in Paris. I saw my French banker friends and also those in Zurich and Amsterdam. I visited Houston three or four times, studying the real estate scene, and I almost decided to work from there. I got involved with the Habitat Stores Group, helping to arrange the financing which led to their great expansion, and I created a considerable surplus on my original shareholding into which I brought Alan Clore as my partner. It was one of his first business ventures on his own account.

It seemed to run in the family. First Alan, then Vivien, now Charles. He too was going to become a tax exile. By the time he came around to first mentioning it to me in early 1976 in Paris, it seemed that a lot of preparatory work had already been done. My immediate reaction was that he had made a terrible blunder and I urged him to reconsider: an international business man and social lion in many capitals he certainly may have been, but he only truly felt at home in England. His forebears may have only recently come from Russia but he was an Englishman through and through. He may have given vast sums to Israel, visiting that country frequently, with passion and sincere fervour — Israel was a home for the Jews. But his home was still England. He loved his life, the weekly routine, the regular morning walk from one end of Park Street to the other, the regular return in the evenings. It was well-patterned and satisfying. During the day he attended to his business, followed by his dinners or dates at night. And after Annabel's opened he liked to end his late evenings there, sometimes driven home by my chauffeur which gave him minor pleasure because it avoided a taxi fare. He loved his regular weekends at Stype, with its sumptuous entertaining, and above all he enjoyed his shooting, hoping vainly that he could show his friends each year that he was an improving shot. He was now giving it all up. For what? I asked. He replied in one laconic word: tax. 'You of all people,' I said. 'You've got so much money, what difference can it make? You love England too much. You're going to be too miserable for words.' 'I'm okay,' he insisted. 'Lots of friends in France, lots of pretty girls here who might prefer an old Englishman with a bob or two.' We smiled. 'You and Nadia are in Paris, I will see Edmond. I will travel a lot,' then twinkling, 'New York, Israel, Acapulco, you name it.' He wasn't convincing, although we knew from Janet Milford Haven that our being in Paris had been a definite factor in his mind.

The die had been cast. The plans had been made and were being implemented stage by stage. It never for a moment occurred to me that he would envisage resigning as chairman of Sears merely because of his tax plans.

Eating, drinking, living and working hard, usually until the small hours, he was now concerned with and spoke openly, about his health. For a man who never referred to his personal problems or possessions, the fact that he was giving gratuitous information of this nature was a worrying sign. For some while he had a mild sugar problem, then he mentioned to me that he required a major operation. He was very secretive and merely said it was abdominal, some blockage. Nothing was said but most of us feared it was cancer. He went into the London Clinic on 4 July 1976 and came home weak but confident. Whatever it was, the operation appeared to have been a success.

On his trips to Paris he stayed at the Plaza Athénée, the Ritz having become too dreary for him. He started idly looking for an apartment in Paris. He didn't want anything grand and said he wasn't going to spend more than £1 million. This seemed reasonable to him. He didn't want to compete with Edmond. I said it would be cheaper and more reasonable to stay at the Plaza, Charles Forte might even give him a discount. You're right, he said; and thereafter, whenever he was in Paris, he stayed at the Plaza and declared that he got a special price. You've got to be careful, he stressed, what with the awful exchange rate. One day he, Alan and I lunched

225

at Maxim's. Each of us thought one of the others was host. It was droll, in the end I caved in and paid. There was a look of satisfaction from father to son. But during these months Charles was tense. He loathed being away from Stype and away from London.

One evening in Paris we arranged to meet in the bar at the Plaza before going out to dinner. Nadia was in London and Charles had just flown in that day. Casually he told me that because he was becoming a tax exile and also because of the 70-year rule, he was going to retire as chairman of Sears. I took off with a sudden outburst of fury. 'There is absolutely no reason for you to resign,' I said, 'merely because you're going non-resident. It's absurd. I think you are being bloody stupid.' He too blew up.

I didn't recover my composure until hours later. We went off to the Grand Véfour for dinner. We talked calmly about Isaac Wolfson, still chairman of Great Universal Stores and well into his seventies, and I pursued my argument that Charles could easily have set the same rules for himself at Sears. The 70-year-rule was nonsense for founding forces of the calibre of Isaac and Charles. We talked of a well known peer of the realm, a good friend of ours who was doing his 'year' and had no intention of giving up the chairmanship of his large public company. The two examples were unassailable. But Charles was too far down the road. We went to Régine's to join friends and chatted and danced until well past three in the morning. I dropped him at the Plaza. Next day when we lunched together neither of us made any reference to the row we had. At lunch he was more interested in a girl sitting behind me until I had to tell him, for goodness' sake, either listen to what I'm saying or go and join her.

On 6 December 1976 it was announced that Charles Clore would retire as chairman of Sears and that the new chairman would be Leonard Sainer.

Soon after this Clore had more health problems, with his prostate gland this time, and he went into the Wellington Nursing Home in St John's Wood for an operation. It was a success and he was relatively chirpy. When I went to visit him I could see only Arabs swarming all over the place. 'Aren't you scared?' I asked. 'Only of the doctors,' he replied. He spent much of his time in Paris, and travelling. In 1978 Nadia and I decided to move to Monaco. Charles had already decided to do the same. He purchased a fabulous three-storey apartment with enormous terraces and with its own swimming pool, directly opposite the Casino and a two-minute walk from the Hôtel de Paris.

1979 was an unhappy year. Charles was due to have a further

operation in July at the London Clinic. For the first time, he appeared anxious and nervy. One afternoon in St Jean Cap Ferrat, we were accosted by a gipsy. 'Don't run away,' she screamed, 'you'll live to be a hundred.' Charles beamed, slapped my shoulder. 'You heard what she said.' During the months before the operation he insisted on seeking me out more and more. Our row in the Plaza had induced new confidences. We had two forms of dialogue. One was his incessant deprecation of me: he was terribly disappointed, why hadn't I done better? I had a brain but why was I so stupid? He admired me in some ways but why didn't I grow up and fulfil myself? On and on he went. He had my best interests at heart, he said, but why didn't I pull myself together? Listening to all this, I did not demur. He was right as usual. He understood possibly better than I did that I was still in some sort of daze over the collapse of Spey Investments. We still never talked about it.

The other form of dialogue between us during these months was a constant harking back to the past, a sort of extended troubled reminiscence. Mostly about his old and departed friends: Felix Fenston, Stash Radziwill, Gene Vamos, Louis Rawlings, Harry Massey, Max Rose, Vladimir Rachewsky; also about his early life, his family, especially his brother David, his business, his charities, reminiscences too about Jack Cotton and about City Centre.

Charles entered the London Clinic on Sunday 1 July 1979. On the Friday before, he wanted to go to Annabel's with Janet Milford Haven, Nadia and myself. On countless occasions the four of us had been out together in London, and also in Paris and in New York. I felt in my bones that this was going to be the last time. Perhaps Charles did too. The four of us dined there at our usual table. Louis and Michael could not have been more solicitous: 'Sir Charles' was one of their favourites. Charles was host at this last supper, whereas on all the previous occasions it had invariably been me. Janet and I insisted on caviar and Dom Perignon Rosé. Charles became testy, but I said it was a tease because I insisted on paying the bill. Charles immediately ordered another bottle of Dom Perignon.

On Sunday at 4.00 p.m. after lunch he waited in his bedroom at Claridge's for his perfect Jeeves, Kay, to drive him to the London Clinic in Upper Wimpole Street. There were tears on his cheeks and he told Kay, 'I don't think I will come out.' For weeks he put up a terrific fight. It seemed he was going to pull through. Early on Thursday morning, 26 July he asked his nurse for his morning newspaper, and before she could reach him, he died.

Chapter Seventeen

Epilogue

On Thursday 4 February 1982 I gave a lunch at the Ritz for Freddie Lindgren who had come over to London from Majorca. He thought it would be nice to see some of Jack's old friends. He sat on my right, Isadore Kerman was on my left, sitting next to him was Louis Freedman, and next to him Edward Erdman, then Douglas Tovey, a place for Eric Young and then Aubrey Orchard-Lisle. We waited for Eric until past 1.30 p.m. and we thought he was probably held up by the train strike. There had been no message. The previous Monday he had said he was looking forward to coming, though he sounded frail on the telephone. After lunch we learnt that Eric had died the day before.

Life goes on. Leonard Sainer is chairman of Sears Holdings — Aubrey Orchard-Lisle is the senior consultant partner to Healey & Baker — George Ross Goobey is chairman of a property company — Jocelyn Hambro has retired as chairman of Hambros' parent company — Harry Sporborg is still advising Lord Fitzwilliam — Charles Villiers is deputy chairman of British Steel — Louis Freedman is a steward of the Jockey Club — Douglas Tovey lives on his estate in Nettlebed — Lord Zuckerman is no longer the Government's distinguished scientific adviser, and has retired as the Secretary to the London Zoo — Isadore Kerman is still senior partner in his law firm — Freddie Lindgren lives in happy retirement in Majorca — Gary Arnott is still happiest using the most sophisticated computer techniques — Oliver Marriott is the chairman of a large quoted property company — Archie Sherman lives contentedly in Israel — Eddie Footring has just retired from Titmuss Sainer — Max Rayne is chairman of London Merchant Securities and of the National Theatre — Bill Zeckendorf Jr is a successful real estate developer in Manhattan — Alan Clore, the late starter, over a year ago mounted a $300 million bid for a Houston energy company.

Edward Plumridge died in May 1975. During his last years he was blessed with an extremely happy second marriage.

Harold Samuel was knighted in 1963 and was created Lord Samuel of Wych Cross in 1972. Still trim, his crinkly hair turning white, a little more portly, he has hardly changed in the twenty odd years I have known him. Harold Samuel, the chairman of Land Securities: the most majestic property investment company in the world, which has a market value five times greater than the market value of the Pearl Assurance, three times greater than the Legal and General, and about equal with the Prudential Assurance itself; Land Securities which acquired CLRP with its gorgeous portfolio of property jewels in 1968; Land Securities with its portfolio of properties worth over £2,000 million, with its hundreds of subsidiary companies, amongst them City Centre Properties Limited with all of its own countless subsidiaries including Felix Fenston's Eron Investments, Walter Flack's Murrayfield Estates, Charles Clore's City & Central and Jack Cotton's Monico site in London and his Big Top in Birmingham. When will the spinning stop?

Index

233

operational set-up, 82-3, 85-88; to organise team, 87; different property policies, 88-9; secrecy of major decisions, 90; bid for CLRP, 97-99, 101-2, 104, 105-7; methods, 102; annual Ascot party, 102-3; heavy drinking, 103, 206; discourtesy to Clore at Pan-Am lunch, 107-8, 112, 167; friends and aides, 115-119; multiplicity of meetings, 119-20; City Centre's capital and borrowing base, 120-22; and the pension funds, 129; Joint Companies, 130-2; European property market, 141, 142, 145-9, 173-4, 179-82, 186-186-93, 195-7; and Intershop, 148, 151; and Samuel Properties, 154-55; car parks, 156, 157; and Brasenose College property, 160-3; his methods anger Clore, 167; attempts to please Clore, 167-8; Walter Flack, 169, 171, 174-87; misreads Clore's attitude, 177; and Clore's criticisms, 191; Clore wants him out, 199, 201; 'killing Clore with kindness', 201, 207; megalomania, 203; common knowledge of conflict, 204; unsuccessful Cunard transaction, 201, 207; *Sunday Telegraph* interview, 206; his fall, 208-13; and Plumridge, 117, 209-12, 216; heart attacks, 212-3; and the London Zoo, 213, 217; resignation as City Centre chairman, 6, 76, 213, 214; elected president, 214, 217; voyage to New York, 215-6; City Centre settlement shares sold, 217; in Nassau, 217-9; death, 85, 112, 219; funeral, 219

Cotton, Jerry, Jack's son, 29, 90, 204

Cotton, Jill, Jack's daughter, 29, 219, 221; wedding, 35

Cotton, Marjorie, Jack's wife, 29

Cowan, Sydney, 154

Cricklewood Skating Rink, 47

Crickmay, John, 38, 58-60

Cunard, shipping company, 50n., 215; City Centre's unsuccessful transactions with, 204-7

Curtiss chain of shoe shops, 52

Daily Express, 35, 52

Daily Mail, 189

Daily Mirror, 212

Daily Telegraph, 212

Danilova, Alexandra, 97

Davis, William, on Cotton and Clore, 203-4

De Bakey, heart surgeon of Houston, 213

Dellal, Jack ('Black Jack') and Dellal company, 154-5

Derry & Toms, 50

Deutsche Bank, Frankfurt, 197-8

Dolcis shoes, 52, 190

Dolin, Anton, 97

Dorchester Hotel, 94, 136, 155; 162, 224; Cotton's suite, 26, 64, 86, 90, 93, 100, 102-3, 106, 146, 155, 162, 163, 200

Dorland House, Lower Regent Street, 33

Doucette, Jacques de la, 195

Dresdener Bank, 197

Duncan, Sir Val, 87

Dunlop House, St. James's, 36

Dutch Mineworkers pension fund, 73

Dutch Mortgage Bank, 195

East, Barry, 23, 58

Edgeson, Stanley, and Edgeson family, 34

Edinburgh, Duke of, 213

EEC, 141

Electricity Council pension fund, 30n

Ellis, Frederick, 52

EMI, 87

Empress State Building, Earl's Court, 37

Erdman, Edward, 30n., 228

Eron Investment, 20, 39, 172-3, 231; sold to Cotton, 173, 217

Esdaile, Alfred, 47

Europarks Ltd., 159
European League for Economic
  Co-operation, 141
European property market, 141-51,
  179-83, 191-2
(D.H.) Evans, 50
Evening Standard, 53, 189, 203
Express Dairy Group, 37

Fantin-Latour paintings, Cotton's,
  103, 152, 162, 169
Fenston, Felix, 23, 36-7, 58, 66,
  117-8, 132, 159, 172-3, 227, 229;
  and Cotton, 20, 26, 39; Eron
  Investments, 20, 39, 172-3, 217;
  and Hyams, 117-8; Kensington
  estates bought by Cotton, 191
Financial Times, 8, 9, 14, 32, 189;
  growth, 11
Finney, David, 105 and n., 119-22;
  and City Centre capital and
  borrowing base, 120-2
Finney Ross, auditors to City Centre,
  105
Fitzwilliam, Earl, 105, 228
Flack, Walter, 39, 102-4, 113, 117,
  141, 146, 148, 169-71, 173-87;
  support of Cotton, 169, 175;
  and Auchinleck, 170, 173; streak
  of malice, 170; aims to run City
  Centre, 171; and Clore, 171, 174,
  176-8, 184-87; Basildon town
  centre, 171, 174-5; and
  European property market, 174;
  Whitehall Court, 175; turns
  against Cotton, 176-9; director of
  City Centre, 179; and Union
  Européenne, 180; French concern
  about him, 180-1; on joint board
  and management committee, 181,
  182; outburst at Ascot party,
  182-3; frightens Denise Tapper,
  182-5; the French request his
  replacement, 185-6; resignation,
  186-7, 192, 206, 187, 206
Folliss, Peter, 75-7, 89, 108,
  109 and n., 136, 137, 140, 145,
  158, 159, 196, 214, 218;
  Hambro's man in New York, 65;

and the Pan-Am building, 75, 76,
  111-2; and Cotton, 76, 77; and
  Clore, 76; on the Clore-Cotton
  merger, 91-2; on Cotton's future,
  133-4; director of City Centre,
  179; remonstrates with Cotton,
  204; sacked by Jocelyn Hambro,
  77; death, 76, 77
Fonteyn, Dame Margot, 136
Footring, Eddie, 88, 93, 214, 221,
  224, 228; and City & Central, 54,
  88; and the Clore-Cotton merger,
  82; managing director of City
  Centre, 88, 218, 220, 223
Forte, Sir Charles, 225
Frankland, Joyce, leaves Kensington
  property to Brasenose (1586), 160
Fraser, Sir Hugh, 49-51
Fraser, Lady, 50
Fraser, Lionel, 105
Freedman, Louis, 36, 116, 228;
  and Ravenseft, 23
Freeman Hardy & Willis, 47, 51
Freeman, Norman, 126, 128
Furness shipyard, closed by
  Clore, 222

Garner, Freddie, 211
Garrards, 54, 190
Gayler, Eric, 148
Gelman, Miss, Clore's secretary, 190
Gelsey, William de, 154
General Motors, 71; new building
  on Savoy Plaza site, 134
Generale Immobiliere, Italian
  property company, 198
Germany, City Centre operations
  in, 196-8
Glamford Estates, 26
Golden Cross Hotel, Strand, 36
Goldsmith, Jimmy (Sir
  James), 54, 84
Gordon, Charles, early career, 7;
  Cambridge University, 7; joins
  Investors' Chronicle, 8; analysis
  of property companies, 15, 21-3;
  property editor, 21, 63, 64;
  meetings with Cotton, 39, 64-5;
  and the Cotton-Clore merger,

228; and Cotton, 30-2, 34, 116;
and Healey & Baker, 30, 31, 48;
home at Marlow, 32, 200; and
Montague Burton, 49; the Clore-
Cotton merger, 80, 81; and CLRP,
101

241